To Suzie —
A UW colleague!
Margery

Excited to Learn

Suzie

Hodges

Tukwila School District

Excited to Learn

Motivation and
Culturally Responsive Teaching

Margery B. Ginsberg

CORWIN
A SAGE Company

FOR INFORMATION:

Corwin
A SAGE Company
2455 Teller Road
Thousand Oaks, California 91320
(800) 233-9936
www.corwin.com

SAGE Publications Ltd.
1 Oliver's Yard
55 City Road
London EC1Y 1SP
United Kingdom

SAGE Publications India Pvt. Ltd.
B 1/I 1 Mohan Cooperative Industrial Area
Mathura Road, New Delhi 110 044
India

SAGE Publications Asia-Pacific Pte. Ltd.
3 Church Street
#10-04 Samsung Hub
Singapore 049483

Acquisitions Editor: Dan Alpert
Associate Editor: Kimberly Greenberg
Editorial Assistant: Cesar Reyes
Project Editor: Veronica Stapleton Hooper
Copy Editor: Sarah J. Duffy
Typesetter: C&M Digitals (P) Ltd.
Proofreader: Dennis W. Webb
Indexer: Sheila Bodell
Cover Designer: Leonardo March
Marketing Manager: Stephanie Trkay

Printed in the United States of America

A catalog record of this book is available from the Library of Congress.

ISBN: 978-1-4522-5953-6

This book is printed on acid-free paper.

15 16 17 18 19 10 9 8 7 6 5 4 3 2 1

Contents

Preface

This book responds to the question: How can primary and secondary educators consistently support student motivation across diverse student groups? It provides strategies and tools that teachers can adapt to different content areas and grade levels.

Although there is widespread agreement among researchers and teachers that motivation is positively related to educational achievement, the task of supporting student motivation in diverse classrooms is a highly nuanced endeavor. Who we are culturally and how we interact with learning experiences is an intriguing intersection of language, values, beliefs, behaviors, and personal history that is continually evolving. The ideas, principles, and models proposed in this text respect this understanding and offer useful ways to encourage student motivation to learn across cultural groups.

At the heart of this book is the Motivational Framework for Culturally Responsive Teaching. The motivational framework is a guide and a tool offering motivational strategies for teachers to make instructional plans as well as to carry them out with activities that evoke the motivation of a broad range of students. This framework has been generative for nearly two decades and has been used to develop new ideas and directions for lessons, units of study, and ongoing school improvement. Its four essential conditions—establishing inclusion, developing attitude, enhancing meaning, and engendering competence—align with recent research findings on how to create optimal learning environments to promote student engagement (Shernoff, 2013).

In primary and secondary schools that have used the framework to plan and improve teaching, it has consistently contributed to impressive learning outcomes. It has also influenced school climate. Teacher, family, and student surveys and qualitative research indicate that the motivational framework assists schools in becoming more positive and supportive of students, teachers, and the broader community (Chopra, 2014; Thompson, 2010). This is especially important at a time when public education is struggling against the threat of privatization and teacher turnover in both charter schools and regular public schools is at an all-time high. A 2014 report from the Alliance for Excellent Education indicates that roughly half a million U.S. teachers move or leave the profession each year; that's a turnover rate of about 20%, compared to 9% in 2009 (Haynes, 2014).

Schools have more students than ever before whose perceptions and ways of making meaning vary from one another and from their teacher. With rising inequality in the United States, the implications for primary and secondary education are significant. Education is a human right. It is also the foundation of healthy communities where capable, creative, and productive problem solvers collaborate on complex social, environmental, and technological challenges. In a society with such pressing challenges, we must have pedagogical alternatives that disconnect teaching and learning from the rewards-and-sanctions mentality which undermines substantive learning and produces winners and losers.

Although I realize the education profession shoulders responsibilities for which all of society is responsible, it is my intention to offer ideas for teaching that are worthy of the commitment of school staff to intrinsic motivation as the foundation for culturally responsive and academically rich learning. A sustained focus on motivation and culturally responsive teaching is a horizon necessary for any view in which education contributes to resolving the complex social and economic problems facing us today.

AUDIENCE

Primary and secondary school teachers, administrative leaders, instructional coaches, professional learning specialists, and college of education faculty are primary audiences for this book. However, many of the ideas can be adapted to build the instructional repertoires of community college instructors as well. In recent years, important partnerships between high school and college faculty have emerged to create seamless academic mobility for students. This book can support this crucial work so that educators at all levels of a system can align and advance instructional knowledge based on principles of intrinsic motivation.

Finally, this book will be useful to the staff of before- and after-school programs, tutors, counselors, and other student services personnel. The motivational framework is easily adapted to different contexts. Advisors, counselors, and social workers can use the motivational framework to create a counseling environment in which students feel included, positive, engaged, and able to succeed.

CONTEXT

The enterprise of instruction as a primary influence on student learning operates within the shifting context of local, state, national, and global politics. While teachers, administrative leaders, and other school staff have an enormous influence on student learning, we work within a larger policy environment and continuously negotiate competing commitments. Nonetheless, the instructional approaches in this book are pragmatic, are clearly delineated, and offer up-to-date applications of research to enrich teaching and learning.

OVERVIEW OF THE CONTENTS

The ideas in this book are presented in either a narrative or an outline format. The narrative format allows a fuller description of theory or concepts. The outline format provides a way to share specific activities, and these activities take the form of Topic, Purpose, Time, Materials, and Process. Because of the time constraints teachers face, I wanted to provide adequate specificity for teachers to take ideas and run with them.

Chapter 1, "Culture and Motivation to Learn," provides an overview of the intersection between motivation, learning, and culture. A primary concern is that what theorists, teachers, and community members felt once worked for classroom teaching and student learning is now inadequate. The chapter provides a rationale for intrinsic motivation as the foundation for teaching and learning and advocates for teachers to view instructional planning as motivational planning. This includes understanding students' lives, perspectives, and interests, and using this information to help students (1) feel a sense of belonging, (2) see themselves as decision makers who are challenged by and engaged in relevant learning experiences, and (3) achieve success in ways that students value and are of value to others. Chapter 1 also examines why students' responses to learning activities reflect their cultural backgrounds and why social scientists today regard intellectual processes as inherently cultural. Finally, this chapter provides an opportunity for readers to examine their own cultural values and compare these values to those that tend to dominate in the United States.

The primary focus of Chapter 2, "Critical Features of a Motivating and Culturally Responsive Classroom," is intrinsically motivating instruction in culturally responsive classrooms. It explores the Motivational Framework for Culturally Responsive Teaching as an instructional model that responds to the question: How can teachers support the intrinsic motivation of learners within and across cultural groups? You will see that the motivational framework supports rather than supplants teachers' knowledge. It interacts with teachers' content knowledge and knowledge of students. To provide examples of how lessons that are planned with the framework might look in primary, middle, and high school, Chapter 2 offers three different scenarios in three different subject areas. It also provides a planning tool based on the motivational framework as well as a graphic organizer to help teachers align motivational strategies for individual lessons or unit development. For professional learning specialists or school improvement teams that want to introduce the framework to others, Chapter 2 includes a sample process that builds on what teachers are already doing. In addition, this book's Epilogue provides a process for an introductory book study.

Chapters 3–6 define, illustrate, and provide instructional strategies for the motivational conditions. Each of these chapters is devoted to one of the four conditions: "Establishing Inclusion" (Chapter 3), "Developing a Positive Attitude" (Chapter 4), "Enhancing Meaning" (Chapter 5), and "Engendering Competence" (Chapter 6). These chapters describe how each motivational condition embodies two related criteria, following this order: respect and connectedness for (establishing) inclusion, volition and relevance for (developing a positive) attitude, challenge and engagement for (enhancing) meaning, and authenticity and effectiveness for (engendering) competence. While the verbs that are part of each motivational condition are important because they contain an action, abbreviations and acronyms can help readers remember the conditions. An acronym educators find helpful is I AM Competent! I is for Inclusion, A is for Attitude, M is for Meaning, and C is for Competence.

Due to my own background and professional experience, examples in Chapters 3–6 are often from the social sciences. However, whenever possible, I illustrate pedagogical strategies that teachers from other disciplines have used. While not exhaustive, teachers and other professionals who work in schools will see that most of the strategies in this book connect to a broad range of disciplines and can be used with many different content standards. For easy reference, the strategies that are included in each of the four chapters on the motivational framework are listed at the end of each chapter.

Chapter 3, "Establishing Inclusion," helps teachers create a safe and respectful learning environment where students are connected to one another and to the teacher. An undergirding assumption of this chapter is that a supportive learning community depends as much on a teacher's capacity to promote cooperative interactions as it does on instructional effectiveness for individual learners. The practices in this chapter take the form of presentations about students' lives and interests (see the section on opportunities for multidimensional sharing), small-group work structured to promote equitable participation and learning, and "historians" or note-takers who post their notes on a webpage so that students have a way to compare and contrast their recollections. This chapter also provides detailed information and tools for cooperative and collaborative learning.

Chapter 4, "Developing a Positive Attitude," focuses on choice and relevance. Developing a positive attitude is a motivational condition that is frequently overlooked by educators. At the end of the day, how we teach has the most enduring impact on students' attitudes. If we expect students to have a positive attitude toward learning, our instructional practices must take into account students' perspectives, interests, and strengths. Strategies in this chapter include setting goals with students, building on the strengths of English language learners, helping students understand and attribute success to effort, and using multiple intelligences to learn.

Chapter 5, "Enhancing Meaning," provides activities that challenge and engage students for in-depth learning. Activities include metaphors and stories, case study methods, simulation, games, thought-provoking questions, guided reciprocal questioning, and an extensive section on problem-based and project-based learning.

Chapter 6, "Engendering Competence," focuses on assessment practices that motivate success. The entire enterprise of assessment challenges teachers for many reasons, one of which is the time that valid, reliable, and motivating assessment requires. This chapter reviews research and provides guidance on feedback, grades, and avoiding cultural bias. It also provides concrete strategies for authentic performance tasks, self-assessment, closure activities, journals, and rubrics. It concludes with tools for teachers to use to assess the motivational impact of instruction from the perspective of students or colleagues.

The Epilogue speaks to the importance of building on students' strengths and provides a set of guidelines for implementing the ideas in the book. Because collaboration and professional learning are vitally important to successful experimentation, it also introduces the next volume of this two-book series and provides an outline for a brief book study with school staff. In the Appendix you will find tools to consider and adapt. I want to encourage you to elaborate on these resources in whatever way you believe can help students thrive.

Ultimately this book seeks to provide a coherent integration of research and teaching strategies that can help teachers vitalize students' natural curiosity and academic potential. Without a deliberate approach to motivational planning, our attempts at creating schools where students are excited to learn can become a process of trial and error that lacks cohesion and continuity. This book provides a framework that has well-coordinated sets of motivational strategies for a range of learners. Having the courage to challenge ourselves as cultural beings and skillful professionals is essential. All students, from all backgrounds and prior academic experiences, can learn in a motivating way. This book provides a realistic approach for that goal.

Acknowledgments

This book is the result of a lifetime of learning with friends, colleagues, and students. These people shared resources and perspectives. They also tried out ideas in their own contexts and helped me consider new possibilities. All of this has been grounded in a shared set of values about the significance of public education in a world where learning with and from others is one of the most important and hopeful things we do.

In this regard, I am grateful to my friends and colleagues who teach and lead in public schools and systems of schools: Kimberly (Armstrong) Hedrick, Ailene Baxter, Catherine Brown, Jocelyn Co, Anthony Craig, Meredith Cronk, Rachel Johnson, Megan Kelley-Petersen, Zoe McGuire Manzo, Shaun Martin, Laurie Morrison, Paul Robb, Princess Shareef, Mollie Smith, Sahnica Washington, Julia Zigarelli, and Sonny Zinn.

I am also grateful to my friends and colleagues who work outside of schools and school districts to help the ideas of students and on-the-ground educators thrive. Special thanks to Amy Berk Anderson, Nancy Beadie, Helen Beattie, Cristine Chopra, Carol Coe, Camille Farrington, Mike Knapp, Brad Portin, Paul Robb, Cathy Thompson, Anita Villarreal, Spencer Welch, and colleagues in the Urban Education Leadership Program and the Center for Urban Education Leadership at the University of Illinois–Chicago. When Kathy Kimball recently retired from leadership preparation at the University of Washington, she left behind a lifetime of opening doors for others. I was proud to be her colleague and even more so to become her friend. Over the years, Suzanne Benally, a champion of human rights and indigenous languages, has been a trusted confidant and a dear friend. She inspires this work.

I also want to thank Dan Alpert, senior acquisitions editor at Corwin. Dan helped me conceptualize this book. He combines his respect for educators and commitment to serving historically underserved students with kind and pragmatic wisdom. Dan is also extremely patient. Thank you, also, to the entire Corwin team: Kimberly Greenberg, Cesar Reyes, Veronica Stapleton Hooper, Leonardo March, and copy editor Sarah Duffy.

It was my good fortune to work with Sarah on this book as well as a prior Corwin book, *Transformative Professional Learning: A System to Enhance Teacher and Student Motivation* (2011). Sarah is kind, skillful, and perceptive. In addition, she keeps things rolling!

Matthew Aaron Ginsberg-Jaeckle and Daniel Mark Ginsberg-Jaeckle are my sons. They do serious social justice work and have the affection of people in their communities and beyond.

And finally, I am deeply grateful to Raymond Wlodkowski, my partner in life and learning, for his ideas, sense of adventure, and careful reading of this book.

About the Author

 Most recently, **Margery B. Ginsberg** was Distinguished Professor and lead faculty for the online MA in adult and professional learning at Edgewood College, in Madison, Wisconsin. Prior to her move to Chicago, Margery was an associate professor at the University of Washington-Seattle, where she taught aspiring school and district leaders and served as lead faculty for an educational leadership doctoral program. She was also a founding partner of the Center for Action, Inquiry, and Motivation (www.aimcenterseattle.org), which was located at Cleveland High School in Seattle, hosted most of the courses she taught, and became a professional learning center for the region.

Early in her career Margery taught in high-poverty urban and rural communities, including the Menominee and Southern Ute Reservations, eventually serving as a U.S. Department of Education Title I technical assistance provider to state education agencies and coordinator of migrant education in a nine-state region. As a consultant, she works nationally and internationally to support systems of education, schools, and teachers in developing innovative programs that support student motivation, persistence, and graduation.

In 1995, with Dr. Raymond Wlodkowski, Margery introduced the Motivational Framework for Culturally Responsive Teaching, which has been the foundation for several comprehensive school reform demonstration designs, including one of two high schools to receive the 1999–2000 U.S. Department of Education's Model National Professional Development Award. While Margery served as a consultant at Cleveland High in Seattle, the school was honored with a Washington State School of Distinction Award for increasing its graduation rate by over 30%. For her work with schools, Margery was recently honored with the 2013 American Educational Research Association's Relating Research to Practice Award in the category of professional service.

Her most recent books are *Transformative Professional Learning* (Corwin, 2011), *Teaching Intensive and Accelerated Courses* (Jossey-Bass, 2010), and *Diversity and Motivation: Culturally Responsive Teaching* (Jossey-Bass, 2009), which won the 2010 Cyril O. Houle Award for Outstanding Literature in Adult Education.

Margery's work provides the foundational material for two video series, "Motivation: The Key to Teaching and Learning" (Association for Supervision and Curriculum Development) and "Motivation for All Students" (School Improvement Network). She has a PhD in bilingual/multicultural/social foundations of education from the University of Colorado-Boulder.

She currently lives in Chicago, Illinois, and can be reached at margeryginsberg@gmail.com.

1 Culture and Motivation to Learn

None of us are to be found in sets of tasks or lists of attributes; we can be known only in the unfolding of our unique stories within the context of everyday events.

—Vivian Gussin Paley

Within the last decade, there has been a profound change in the context of most of P–12 education—the transition from a national industrial society to a global digital information society. Computer literacy, social media, and the Internet are woven into the fabric of most children's lives by the third grade (Barone & Wright, 2008). Nonetheless, culture and motivation remain integrally bound in how students learn, and characteristics, ranging from race to social class, indelibly influence educational engagement.

This chapter introduces the essential role of *intrinsic* motivation in the success of students from similar and diverse backgrounds. It explains why motivation and culture are inseparable, linking these concepts to teachers' primary spheres of influence—student-teacher relationships and instructional repertoires. Because feelings of safety inside *and* outside of classrooms are foundational to academic motivation, this chapter provides context for how government policy and personal values impact students' motivation to learn, especially in relation to students of color, low-income students, students who are recent immigrants, students with biological disabilities, and students who are lesbian, gay, bisexual, or transgender (LGBT). This chapter also establishes the theories and research to support the teaching methods throughout the rest of this book.

MOTIVATION IS ESSENTIAL TO LEARNING

Motivation is the energy that human beings direct toward achieving a goal. Across all ethnic and cultural groups, the primary sources of motivation reside in *all* of us. When we can see that what we are learning makes sense and is important according to our values and perspectives, our motivation emerges. Like a cork rising through water, intrinsic motivation surfaces in an environment (Ginsberg & Wlodkowski, 2000) where students learn because the learning experience is valued and rewarding, resulting in their academic engagement and success.

As a crucial feature of rigorous learning, intrinsic motivation is validated across disciplines such as cross-cultural studies (Csikszentmihalyi & Csikszentmihalyi, 1988), education (Elliot & Dweck, 2005; Vansteenkiste, Lens, & Deci, 2006), bilingual education (Cummins, 2003), adult education (Wlodkowski, 2008), and work and sports (Frederick-Recascino, 2002). Given that teachers' knowledge and skill make a larger difference for student learning than any other single factor (Darling-Hammond & Lieberman, 2012), instructional interactions need to be *motivationally significant* as well as content rich (Cochran-Smith, Davis, & Fries, 2004).

Everyday reasoning, as well as research, indicates that motivated students surpass unmotivated students in learning and performance. But what motivates students to learn—students who are younger and older; low, medium, and high income; ethnically similar and diverse; first-generation college students and students with an educational legacy in their family; lesbian, gay, bisexual, transgender, and straight; biologically agile and differently able; monolingual, bilingual, and multilingual; male, female, and those whose gender identity is mixed; from families with undocumented members and from indigenous communities? The setting students are in, the respect they receive from people around them, and their ability to trust their own thinking and experiences influence their concentration, imagination, effort, and willingness to persist in spite of challenges. People who feel unsafe, unconnected, and disrespected are often unmotivated to learn (Tatum, 2003). Such a conclusion does not explain all of the issues and barriers related to how students continue to learn, but without a doubt, day-to-day, face-to-face feelings affect whether students stay in school and whether they are willing to direct their energy toward learning.

There are many assumptions about motivation because it is something that can be neither directly observed nor precisely measured. Although there has been some neuro-scientific progress, motivation research with students tends to focus on their emotions, behavior, words, and stories for indications of interest, effort, perseverance, and completion. While much of this information provides valuable clues for teaching, it remains difficult to understand the intentions of others. Misconceptions abound on matters of will and purpose, especially when culture, ethnicity, language, life experience, and orientation toward learning markedly vary among students and between students and educators.

THE CULTURE AND MOTIVATION CONNECTION

Culture is the deeply learned confluence of language, values, beliefs, and behaviors that pervade every aspect of a person's life, and it is continually undergoing changes (Geertz, 1973). Culture is dynamic and changing. It is not an isolated, mechanical aspect of life that can be used to directly explain phenomena in the classroom or that can be learned as a series of facts, physical elements, or exotic characteristics (Ovando, Collier, & Combs, 2003). This means that the study of culture is not an experimental science in search of a *law* but an interpretive one in search of *meaning* (Geertz, 1973). It implies that there are few hard and fast rules about the ways in which diverse human groups learn and work together. Even within a supposedly unitary majority culture, there is significant variation (Gay, 2010). With few exceptions, the variation and distinction within cultural groups transcend a single set of cultural norms even when a common bond of history, political oppression, religion, or language creates a strong sense of peoplehood (Banks, 2006). A consequence of failing to understand this is stereotyping.

Stereotyping is rooted in our assumptions about the "average characteristics" of a group. We then impose those assumptions on all individuals from the group. In fact, some of the characteristics commonly associated with European Americans—for example, Christianity, individualism, and social conservatism—have become so pervasive that these traits have become a form of taken-for-granted national "commonsense" (Blum, 2005). Stereotypes and other biases that reside within learning environments become agents of historic patterns of marginalization.

Human beings are socialized in one or more cultural communities with values and beliefs that are transmitted through stories, song, spiritual beliefs, interactions with family and friends, world events, and political orientations. The ways in which educators teach and students learn is mediated by such cultural influences. No learning situation is culturally neutral. Generally, if we teach as we were taught in P–12 and higher education, we sanction individual performance, prefer "reasoned" argumentation, advocate impersonal objectivity, and condone sports-like competition for testing and grading procedures. Further, when we accept our own cultural norms as universal, when students disengage we may see deficit rather than difference. One common example occurs in classrooms where teachers rely heavily on the Socratic seminar, one of several instructional methods that, in the absence of adequate student preparation, tend to favor those for whom assertive public discourse is part of everyday life. Should a teacher perceive this form of active participation as evidence of being smart, entire groups of students who view modesty and deference to others as a form of respect may find themselves at risk of failure.

Since culture is inextricably connected to personal motivation, a "seek first to understand" orientation toward students is wise. This wisdom can be found in many ethnic and faith communities and it is particularly relevant in classrooms today. Yet to understand other people, to avoid stereotypes based on a narrow set of assumed group characteristics, and to be open to the meaning that is created through authentic interactions requires educators to personally apply such wisdom. A later section of this chapter, "Personal Appreciation for the Concept of Culture," offers ways to accomplish this quest.

CHANGES IN THE CULTURAL LANDSCAPE

Classrooms in the United States today differ markedly from 40 years ago, when many of today's educators were still in school. In 1970 more than 60% of the nation's 9.7 million immigrants originated in Europe, 19% in Central and South America, 9% in Asia, and 10% in other parts of the world. By 2000 the number of immigrants from European countries totaled 15% (U.S. Census Bureau, 2007). The wave of immigration absorbed by the United States during the 1990s was the largest in 70 years, and today at least one out of every four people in the United States speaks a language other than English at home (Suárez-Orozco, Darbes, Dias, & Sutin, 2011). In California, one in three school districts has a student population with 75% of students considered to be "long-term English learners" (Olson, 2010). Although schools are becoming increasingly aware of ways to support the development of content knowledge while students are in the process of learning English, we seldom address the impact of immigration policy on children and youth, a relevant motivational issue.

IMMIGRANT YOUTH

Immigrant youth, including children born to immigrant parents, represent approximately one-third of all children in the United States (Passel, 2011). Between 2005 and 2050, it is projected that the U.S. population will expand by 48%, with immigrants expected to make up 82% of that growth (U.S. Census Bureau, 2007). Changes have already resulted in a new and dynamic

U.S. landscape, one in which many members of immigrant communities have moved beyond port-of-entry cities to suburban metropolitan areas and rural communities (Hernandez, Denton, & McCartney, 2007). With such changes, the consideration of schools as monocultural environments with rigid educational norms seems increasingly out of touch.

THE IMPACT OF GOVERNMENT POLICIES AND SOCIAL BIAS ON MOTIVATION

A particularly troubling aspect of immigration's effect on education is the plight of the children of undocumented workers. Although issues related to undocumented workers and families exceed the focus of this book, it is important to note that approximately one-third of the estimated 37 million immigrants in the United States are unauthorized, and nearly two-thirds (64%) of the children living with unauthorized family members are U.S. citizens (Passel & Taylor, 2010). In 2011, 397,000 individuals were deported and more than 46,000 of these individuals were mothers and fathers of U.S. citizen children (Wessler, 2011). Fear of deportation is not restricted to a few states or a few ethnicities. In addition to Latinos, relatively large proportions of recent immigrants from Asia and Africa are unauthorized, and all unauthorized groups are vulnerable to long periods of parent-child separation and consequent social-emotional problems (Tienda & Haskins, 2011).

The threat of a family member's deportation is one of several policy-related influences on students' lives that affect academic motivation. A number of factors related to race, ethnicity, and income, such as discrimination, segregation, and political scapegoating, affect large numbers of learners and put academic motivation in competition with priorities such as health care, secure housing, and—for older youth—employment (Crosnoe & Turley, 2011). Although educators make a difference in the lives of students, such political decisions and social outcomes influence students' motivation and may undermine even the most inspired educators' pedagogical innovations.

VALUES AND POLITICS ARE INESCAPABLE

History is replete with examples of the ways in which racism persists over time, often in virulent forms (Lipsitz, 2006; Marabel, 2002). The legacy of the United States includes the appropriation of Native American land, the enslavement of African peoples, and the exploitation of Japanese, Chinese, Filipino, and Latino labor. White power and privilege are maintained through law, politics, property ownership, economic rights, and immigration, as well as organizational policy and social structures (Foner & Frederickson, 2004; Katznelson, 2005). Whether or not educators acknowledge the pervasive impact of political decisions on their work, politics is inherent in the teacher-student relationship (authoritarian or democratic), the readings chosen for a course of study (those left in and those left out), and course content (a shared decision or the teacher's prerogative). (Giroux, 1992)

Values and politics also reside in the discourse of learning (which questions get asked and answered and how deeply they are probed), the imposition of standardized tests, grading and tracking policies, and the physical conditions of classrooms and buildings, which send messages to learners and teachers about their worth and place in society (Shor, 1993). Political/social values can be found in attitudes toward nonstandard English as they are reflected in the curriculum and in the way schools are unequally funded depending on the economic class of students served.

Education is political because it is one place where individuals and society are constructed. Human beings and society are developed in one direction or another through education, and the learning process cannot avoid being political (Shor, 1993, p. 28). A pedagogy that consciously integrates an ethical perspective begins not with test scores but with questions. What kinds of citizens do we hope to create through education? Are they educated citizens who can earn a living family wage? Are they citizens who experience joy in learning throughout their lives? Are they citizens who are effective advocates for social justice and active civic participants? Are they citizens who are prepared to contribute to a fair global economy? What kind of society do we want, and how can we teach in ways that reconcile conflicting values and expectations (Lipsitz, 2006)?

THE IMPACT OF EDUCATIONAL OUTCOMES THROUGHOUT LIFE

Although high school graduation rates have steadily improved in the United States, students from low-income families continue to perform significantly lower on assessments of literacy and mathematics achievement *before they start kindergarten.* These differences tend to persist as students progress through school and raise considerable equity concerns (Lee & Burkham, 2002). Nearly half of African Americans have a high school diploma or less. In contrast, more than seven in ten Asian Americans ages 25 to 64 and more than six in ten European Americans have completed some college (EPE Research Center, 2007). In the 21st century, with wage stagnation and economic policies that contribute to low wages among people without college degrees or certificates, a college degree has become more important than ever before.

A college graduate in the United States earns on average $23,441 more per year than a high school graduate and $31,595 more than a high school dropout. And while only 7% of 24-year-olds from low-income families had earned a 4-year college degree in 1999–2000, 52% of students from high-income families had completed a postsecondary degree (Olson, 2007). From 2000 to 2012, the full-time employment rate for young adults (26- to 30-year-olds) with less than a BA declined substantially to 53% for those with only a high school diploma, compared to 70% for those with a BA. Not only is making learning more accessible and motivating at every level of education a matter of equity, it has significant pragmatic value (Carnevale, Hanson, & Gulish, 2013).

While educators may agree with the U.S. Department of Education's commitment to making the diminishment of the achievement gap between groups of children the "new civil right" (Ballasy, 2011), the educational requirements for successful economic integration are higher now than in the past, when basic literacy and numeracy often provided entry to secure jobs that paid a family wage (Erisman & Looney, 2007).

Higher standards and the limited preparation of teachers and administrative leaders for working in diverse communities have contributed to another significant motivational and ethical concern—the disproportionately high number of low-income students of color who are referred for remedial support and intervention. Race and ability have been woven into a perverse justice narrative that racializes disability and suggests that low-performing or nonconforming students are "the problem" (Artiles, Bal, & King-Thorius, 2010).

The idea of "fixing" nonconforming students is associated with popular ideology in the United States about individualism, and it is kept in place with metaphors such as pulling oneself up by one's bootstraps. Although individuals are responsible players in their academic success, the failure of schools to support historically marginalized students in this effort is exacerbated by an accountability movement that encourages teachers to spend inordinate amounts of time on test-taking skills and tests, often at the expense of one of the most fundamental influences on student motivation—teacher-student relations that enable teachers and students to know each other as human beings.

THE IMPACT OF CULTURAL DOMINATION ON THE RIGHT TO LEARN

The right to learn has been a struggle for over 5,000 years (Du Bois, 1949), with similar and different challenges for each generation. In the United States many educators are two generations removed from legally sanctioned educational segregation. Yet despite efforts to integrate schools through policies such as busing, the formative experiences of many educators have been in relatively homogeneous school programs, schools, or communities. Given that 87% of educators are from Anglo American homes, many teachers and school leaders grew up unaware of or unprepared to critically examine our dominant or higher status environments. For heterosexual European American educators whose families immigrated to the United States several generations ago, it is not a stretch to think of personal attitudes and norms as universally valued and preferred.

As mentioned earlier, a dominant group can so successfully project its way of seeing social reality that its view is accepted as common sense, as part of the natural order, even by those who are disempowered or marginalized by it (Freire & Macedo, 1987). We may not imagine that we hold negative assumptions or stereotypes toward people with different sets of values or beliefs. In fact, for some, it may feel like heresy to acknowledge that Anglo Americans and dominant Western norms enjoy a position of privilege and power in this country's educational system that has diminished other norms as valuable as cooperation and interdependence (Stephens, Townsend, Markus, & Phillips, 2012). The roots of dominant perspectives may be from an earlier time, yet their currency is maintained through policies and practices that perpetuate powerful ideas about "normality" (K. Baker, 2011).

Although culture is taught, it is generally conveyed in ways that are indirect or a part of everyday life (Anzaldúa, 1987; Young, 1990). This is one of the reasons that it is difficult for most of us to describe ourselves in culturally explicit terms. The times we are likely to experience uniqueness as cultural beings occur when we are in the presence of people who appear different from ourselves. As an example, a person from a family and community that is emotionally demonstrative and sees this as a sign of open communication may embarrass or concern a person whose upbringing intertwines restraint with virtue. When we meet others whose family or community norms vary from our own, it is akin to holding up a mirror, provoking questions we might not otherwise think to ask. While contrasts can spark a search for interpersonal understanding, there can be strong ideological underpinnings that can interfere with these interactions.

Many educators are aware that what may seem empowering on one level inhibits communication on another. This dualism is evident when we stress the importance of kindness while ignoring all but the most blatant acts of bigotry. Organizational cultures that promote honest, direct, and respectful discussions of race and identity are essential to overcoming the disconnect that occurs when superficial relationships become more important than the deeper meanings of difference (Tatum, 2003).

THE SCHOOL EXPERIENCES OF LESBIAN, GAY, BISEXUAL, AND TRANSGENDER YOUTH

This understanding applies, as well, to sexual orientation and the school experiences of LGBT youth. In the 21st century, many educators remain unaware of the hostile conditions and the implications of hostile conditions that many LGBT youth struggle against on a daily basis. A national survey of over 1,700 sexual minority adolescents conducted by the Gay, Lesbian, and Straight Education Network found that about 75% of self-identified LGBT adolescents reported hearing antigay remarks "often" or "frequently" at school. Most survey respondents reported that they had been harassed or threatened and nearly one in three students had been physically attacked (Kosciw & Diaz, 2006). Further, U.S. high school students who report same-sex attractions and/or same-sex sexual experiences are at least twice as likely as other youth to report having attempted suicide (Russell & Joyner, 2001).

While difficult discussions about discrimination and hostility benefit from relevant data that expose the consequences of oppression on LGBT youth, the despair from data can overshadow the strength within LGBT communities. In recent years families of LGBT youth have won significant lawsuits against school systems that discriminate or fail to create a safe environment. Further, LGBT youth and their allies are working with schools and school districts to create influential anti-bullying policies and programs, including Gay Straight Alliances. Significant work lies ahead. The relationship between harassment and lower school attendance, lower grade point average, and lower educational aspirations is clear (Kosciw & Diaz, 2006).

From a motivational perspective, historically dominant students suffer as well as students whose emotional well-being is directly impacted by micro-aggressions such as regular verbal and nonverbal put-downs. The energy it takes to block things out when injustice is evident is the same energy that students need to focus on academic goals. The antidote is well-informed and open conversations about significant societal problems that are played out in schools. This can positively impact motivation and learning across student groups because when students are able to collectively confront tough issues, they are able to feel more energized for learning (Tatum, 2003).

For more extensive research on the experiences of LGBT youth, see *The Health of Lesbian, Gay, Bisexual, and Transgender People* (Institute of Medicine, 2011). There are also several websites and books that provide perspective and activities to help educators work with students to examine and confront inequalities based on race, gender, class, age, language, sexual orientation, physical/mental ability, and religion. Two valuable sourcebooks for facilitating social justice conversations are *Teaching for Diversity and Social*

Justice (Adams, Bell, & Griffin, 2007) and *Open Minds to Equality* (Shneidewind & Davidson, 2006). Also, *Rethinking Schools Magazine* is a highly motivating and academically rigorous resource for teaching about equity and social justice.

MOTIVATIONALLY EFFECTIVE CLASSROOMS

The previous sections introduced the importance of motivation as a cultural, ethical, and instructional concern. Later chapters introduce pragmatic approaches to working with motivation as the central goal in culturally diverse classrooms. Here, we'll explore the qualities of motivationally effective classrooms and return to some of the underlying reasons for such a focus. We will spotlight differences between intrinsic and extrinsic motivation.

Although vulnerable to distraction, motivation is innate and educators are a critical influence on how it generates learning. While we do not technically "motivate students," because students have innate motivation, we can nonetheless influence, encourage, and inspire students to direct their motivation toward important academic goals. Educators often notice that the same students who respond apathetically in one class energetically challenge themselves in another class or with peers in the hallway (Ginsberg, 2011). Realities of this sort help us know that students are motivated even when they are not motivated to academically engage with a particular subject or teacher. Nonetheless, the challenge of teaching large numbers of students with limited time and dwindling fiscal resources can lead educators to believe that student motivation is well beyond their influence.

Fortunately, experience and research provide an attainable image of motivating classrooms. Those environments occur when conditions, structures, and activities respond to the motivational needs of diverse groups of students so that every student (1) feels respected by and connected to others, (2) understands the relevance of her or his learning experiences, (3) experiences challenges that are within reach, and (4) is able to authentically identify academic growth in personally and socially valued ways (Brophy, 2004; Csikszentmihalyi, 1997; Deci & Ryan, 1991). These essential instructional attributes are within our reach as educators.

Another formidable reality is that enthusiastic teaching begets motivated learning (Cruickshank et al., 1980). As educators, one of our most important responsibilities is to stay motivated ourselves—to advocate for the conditions for our own learning that we seek to create for students and to experience a sense of deep purpose in our own learning that prevails against shifting policy agendas, fiscal constraints, and daily challenges.

The purpose of this book is to demonstrate how we can accomplish this state of engaged purpose as individual teachers and partner with other educators, families, and students to enhance learning.

CONTRASTS BETWEEN INTRINSIC AND EXTRINSIC MOTIVATION

Although intrinsic and extrinsic motivation may work together, there are tensions between these two different types of motivation. Extrinsic motivators are frequently used in education, especially in high-poverty schools. A popular metaphor for extrinsic motivation is the "carrot and the stick." This orientation is based on an assumption that human behavior is primarily driven by the opportunity to receive a reward or avoid a sanction. An example of this is when we complete an assignment for a grade (reward) or correct an error because a grade will be lowered (sanction). This way of thinking contrasts with an intrinsic orientation to motivation whereby we learn because the learning experience is rewarding in and of itself. The learning process elicits emotions such as interest, concentration, satisfaction, knowing, worth, esteem, appreciation, and vitality.

To be extrinsic, rewards and punishments are not a part of the actual learning experience. For example, it is possible to keep students focused on a short-term task by offering a reward such as earning pizza for reading. Further, students understand the significance of grades for reasons of recognition, credentialing, and promotion. Classrooms are generally silent when students are taking quizzes, which are scored and graded. Motivationally, however, this approach to teaching can negatively influence academic outcomes and future attitudes toward learning. In this way motivation is analogous to other forms of energy use and their consequences. Energy sources such as solar, nuclear, and fossil fuels "work," but they all have different by-products. For example, burning coal produces more pollutants than using solar energy. A by-product of overreliance on extrinsic motivators is superficial learning. A common example is cramming for a test for the purpose of avoiding a bad grade. Many of us can recall the ephemeral nature of last-minute learning. Information learned in this manner fades quickly. Therefore as educators, if we advocate for substantive learning yet rely on instructional rewards that encourage students to take the most expedient route to accomplish a goal (getting a passing grade), we are undermining deeper learning.

Given that the importance of extrinsic rewards such as grades and grade point averages increases as students advance in school, and given the disproportionate number of historically underserved students who drop out of school each day, it is legitimate to question whether extrinsic motivation systems are genuinely effective for students across racial, ethnic, and cultural groups. Cross-cultural and interdisciplinary research underscores this concern (Ginsberg & Wlodkowski, 2009). Evidence suggests that with an intrinsic orientation to learning, students

- engage in learning in the absence of, or in spite of, rewards or threats;
- lose their sense of time because it seems to quickly pass;
- experience a loss of self-consciousness;
- initiate learning without being coerced or forced;
- maximize their energy, concentration, and effort;
- value learning outcomes;
- ask probing or substantive questions;
- feel capable, creative, and joyful; and
- develop the habit of learning for learning's sake.

With an extrinsic orientation to learning, students

- participate in learning primarily for the promise of extrinsic rewards;
- adopt a cursory approach to accomplishing a goal (as in cramming for a test);
- notice that time passes slowly;
- become easily distracted;
- begin learning experiences reluctantly;
- struggle with low energy, effort, and concentration;
- adopt an indifferent stance toward learning outcomes (except for their value in attaining adequate grades, academic credit, or other extrinsic rewards);
- ask questions that are superficial or off task; and
- approach tasks with limited creativity and joy.

A conservative estimate is that extrinsic rewards, such as grades, promotion, and money, are ineffective for at least a third of students in our schools (Wlodkowski, 2008). Teachers have been threatening students with poor grades, lower test scores, and ultimate failure for over a century and students are still flunking, dropping out, and withdrawing from school with little remorse (Farrington, 2014). Using only extrinsic incentives to inspire learning is a form of educational engineering that implicitly views students as inferior, inert, and in need of motivation. Such an orientation dims our awareness of learners' own determination and promotes their dependency.

It is part of human nature to be social, curious, active; to initiate thought and behavior; to make meaning from experience; and to strive to be effective at what we value. However, the most favorable conditions for learning vary among people. To engage learners requires educators to be aware of the various ways students make sense of the world and interpret their learning environment. Students who find reading, writing, calculating, and expanding their stores of knowledge interesting and satisfying are likely to be lifelong learners (Merriam, Caffarella, & Baumgartner, 2007). The tendency to find such processes worthwhile is considered to be the trait of motivation to learn: a propensity for learning that develops and endures over time (Brophy, 2004). The way we teach can make learning a compelling means to a better future.

Intrinsic Motivation and Culturally Responsive Teaching

Teacher respect for cultural diversity influences students' motivation to learn (Ladson-Billings, 1994; Merriam et al., 2007). By virtue of our physiology and the ways in which we are socialized, we are compelled to pay attention to things that matter to us (Ahissar et al., 1992). What is culturally and emotionally significant to a person evokes intrinsic motivation (Csikszentmihalyi, 1997). Theories of intrinsic motivation recognize and include the influence of culture on learning.

EMOTIONS ARE SOCIALIZED THROUGH CULTURE

While people have common needs and experiences, we also have culturally different values and perspectives. Our emotions are socialized through culture. For example, one person working at a very challenging task feels joy and continues. Another person, who has been socialized within another set of cultural norms, begins to feel frustrated at the same task and does not persevere. And yet another person feels frustrated at this task as well but continues with increased determination. What elicits that joy, frustration, or determination may differ across ethnic and cultural groups because of differences in definitions of novelty, hazard, opportunity, and gratification, and in accepted, appropriate responses to these perceptions (Kitayama & Markus, 1994). To a significant extent the response that a person has to a learning experience varies according to the activity itself and his or her cultural background. To effectively teach *all* students requires culturally responsive teaching (Gay, 2010; Morrison, Robbins, & Rose, 2008).

While the internal logic as to why students do something may not coincide with that of the teacher, it is nonetheless present. To be consistently effective, a teacher has to accommodate that perspective. Possessing such awareness can be particularly challenging to educators, especially when students and/or their families have had experiences of cultural invalidation that their teachers have not experienced or examined. For example, if a low-income student has repeatedly heard educators discuss the consequences of poverty in ways that stereotype or diminish her community, she may detach from learning experiences that are oriented toward making other people appear unhealthy or misguided. Receiving a good grade becomes a lower priority than maintaining her integrity as a community member. Should her teachers rely on unquestioned assumptions about how the meanings of effort and reward combine as a driving force in student learning, they may be misled by what they perceive as insufficient effort in this student's academic behavior.

Scholarship on the possible disconnect between student effort and striving for achievement includes stereotype threat (Cole, Matheson, & Anisman, 2007; Steele & Aronson, 1995), self-theories (Dweck & Molden, 2005), and the history of marginalized peoples (Fordham & Ogbu, 1986). Although it is reasonable to assume that a host of influences account for persistent gaps in academic performance among student groups, these studies spotlight the ineffectiveness of high grades or test scores as a primary motivational influence on learning.

For many students the connection between increasing their effort and receiving an extrinsic reward is neither obvious nor desirable as their main reason for learning. When extrinsic rewards fail to motivate students, they may be described as lacking ambition, initiative, or self-direction. Teachers are more likely to fall back on blameful attributions and deficit thinking when they lack awareness of the ways in which students are motivated by personal definitions of respect, meaning, and success. For these students, such reasoning may be an invitation to further disconnect from learning.

It is reasonable to propose that as long as educational systems continue to connect motivation to learn to extrinsic rewards and punishments, students whose histories, beliefs, and values differ from the norms of school will in large part be excluded from academic engagement and success (Hebel, 2007; Yosso, 2005). Being aware of and responsive to students and ourselves as cultural beings is an essential aspect of equitable instruction.

THE LANGUAGE OF DIVERSITY

Since Chapters 2–7 stress pragmatic approaches to enhancing motivation among diverse student groups, there is a need to discuss the implications of the language in this book. For the two terms that appear throughout this book—*diversity* and *culturally responsive teaching*—there are various interpretations. For example, *diversity* is a word whose meanings are dependent on the context in which it is being understood. An anthropological approach to diversity would provide a comparative view of human groups within the context of all human groups. A political approach would analyze issues of power and class. Applied to a learning situation and the purpose of this book, diversity conveys a need to respect similarities and differences among human beings and to move beyond simply developing personal sensitivity to active and effective responsiveness. This may require constructive action on our part to change ideas and attitudes that perpetuate the exclusion of underserved groups of students and to find new ways to challenge their motivation to learn.

In addition to the various academic connotations of the word *diversity,* some view its general use as platitudinal or euphemistic. Although this book uses the words *diversity, cultural diversity,* and *cultural pluralism* interchangeably, there is the perspective that language associated with cultural differences must acknowledge issues of racism, discrimination, and the experience of exclusion. This argument implicates *diversity* when the word is used as a way to dilute or skirt critical issues by implicitly representing all forms of difference—including individual differences and heterogeneity—within personal identities (Adams et al., 2007; Nieto, 2004). The point here is to acknowledge that each of us has beliefs and understandings that guide and challenge our work within a pluralistic society.

Although the term *diversity* appears throughout this book, the book advocates for social justice education that includes an understanding that social inequality is structured and maintained in ways that protect privileged interests. The term *privilege,* another common term in this book, means unearned access to resources and social power, often because of social group membership.

With respect to *culturally responsive teaching,* this book offers a macrocultural instructional framework known as the Motivational Framework for Culturally Responsive Teaching (Ginsberg & Wlodkowski, 2000). The motivational framework, which is introduced in Chapter 2, is built on principles and structures that are meaningful across cultures, especially with students from families and communities that have not historically experienced success in formal education. Rather than comparing and contrasting groups of people from a microcultural perspective—one that, for example, identifies a specific ethnic group and prescribes approaches to teaching according to assumed characteristics and orientations—the motivational framework emerges from literature on and experience with creating a more equitable pluralistic framework that elicits the intrinsic motivation of learners. A fundamental belief is that a macrocultural framework can provide instructional guidance without reducing dynamic groups of people to sets of stereotypical characteristics. The chapters in this book provide multiple concrete approaches from which teachers may choose in order to more consistently support the diverse perspectives and values that students bring to the classroom. This does not, of course, preclude the need for ongoing examination of one's own socialization, cultural identity, and related practices.

PERSONAL APPRECIATION FOR THE CONCEPT OF CULTURE

This chapter has introduced the idea that underlying educational equity is the understanding that the most favorable conditions for learning vary among people even though all people are naturally curious and want to make meaning of their experiences. Teachers who engage students in learning are aware of differences in how students make sense of their world and how they interpret the learning environment. This chapter has also drawn attention to the prejudicial nature of generalizing about entire groups of people and the need to seek understanding through relationships with students, families, and communities.

Another source of understanding springs from examining how myths and stereotypes are shaped and used to maintain power and privilege. Even in teacher education programs where prospective teachers are exposed to a multicultural curriculum, students can distance themselves from historical and social realities (Au, 2009). The awareness of how people are socialized to accept inequalities makes it possible to expose and disrupt narratives that maintain unequal rules, practices, and power in classrooms and communities. In this way, learning about cultural diversity does not simply mean understanding different beliefs, customs, and orientations that operate in the classroom. It includes understanding how our own values and biases have been shaped and how to provide meaningful opportunities for learning that are not simply the repackaging or disguising of dominant perspectives. These ideas are illuminated in the work of scholars such as Lawrence-Lightfoot (1983), Irvine (1991), and Cochran-Smith (2004).

Several approaches can help personalize the concept of culture. First, it is useful to examine why the term *culture* seems evasive to many people and to examine what we know about it as a concept and as an educational opportunity. As mentioned earlier, culture is taught, but it is often taught in ways that are implicit and conveyed unsystematically (Schein, 2004). This is one of the reasons why it is difficult for anyone to describe in explicit terms who they are culturally. Our own beliefs, values, and usual patterns of interaction most often work subconsciously. Contrast and dissonance make it possible to uncover the rich variation within and between cultural groups.

The most obvious cultural characteristics that people observe are physical. Ethnicity, race, gender, and physical ability are often the antecedents to recognizing possible differences in experiences, beliefs, values, and expectations. Physical characteristics, of course, provide a cursory sense of who a person is. One's families, jobs, organizational ties, and lifestyles draw on a repertoire of behaviors, obstructing a clear view of who someone might be culturally. Similarly, unique personal histories, political beliefs, and psychological traits interact dramatically to distinguish us from other members of our own cultural groups. It is, at best, inaccurate to second-guess a person's cultural identity when the sole criteria are observable characteristics and behaviors.

This is one of the primary reasons why there are no fixed scripts for teaching in a culturally diverse classroom. In most classrooms it is easy for a teacher to misconstrue the motivation as well as the capabilities of students who vary in the ways they speak or remain silent (Delpit, 1988), ask for or boldly display knowledge (Heath, 1983), prefer to work as individuals or as members of groups (Ladson-Billings, 1994), and connect information in different ways. Misconceptions can lead to dangerous assumptions about linguistic or intellectual limitations, underpreparedness, lack of initiative, or arrogance.

Educators, as well as learners, have beliefs and values regarding teaching. These are culturally transmitted through narratives shaped by economics, history, religion, mythology, politics, and family and media communication. As mentioned earlier, the ways in which we experience a learning situation are mediated by such narratives. No learning situation is culturally neutral.

DOMINANT CULTURAL THEMES AND BELIEF SYSTEMS

Unless we as educators understand our own culturally mediated values and biases, we may be misguided in believing that we are encouraging divergent points of view and providing meaningful opportunities for learning to occur when we are in fact repackaging or disguising past dogmas. It is entirely possible to believe in the need for change and therefore learn new languages and techniques, and yet overlay new ideas with old biases and frames of reference. It is possible to diminish the potential and the needs of others at our most subconscious levels and in our most implicit ways without any awareness that we are doing so. Mindfulness of who we are and what we believe culturally can help us examine the ways in which we may be unknowingly placing our good intentions within a dominant and unyielding framework—in spite of the appearance of openness and receptivity to enhancing motivation to learn among all students.

One of the most useful places to begin the exploration of who we are culturally and the relevance of that identity is to ask what values we hold that are consistent with the dominant culture. This question allows us to be cognizant not only of our dominant-culture values but also of the distinctions we hold as members of other groups in society. This is particularly important for fourth-, fifth-, and sixth-generation Americans of European descent. For many descendants of European Americans, one's family's country or countries of origin can be only marginally useful in understanding who we are now as cultural people in the United States. The desire and ability to assimilate, as well as affiliations with numerous other groups (religious, socioeconomic, regional, and so forth), can create confusion about the cultural origins of personal beliefs and values. Furthermore, culture is a dynamic and changing concept for each of us, regardless of the country of our geographical origin. Our cultural identities are constantly evolving or changing, and consequently values, customs, and orientations are fluid. Because we as educators exert a powerful influence over classroom norms, it is important to make explicit those values that are most often implicit and profoundly affect students in our classrooms.

EXAMINING OUR VALUES

One way to gain insight into the elusive concept of culture is to consider the research of sociologist Robin M. Williams Jr. (1970). Several decades ago Williams identified cultural themes that tend to be enduring reflections of dominant values, which in the United States have been northern European. These themes may or may not be operative in a classroom, but because belief systems influence teaching practices, the selected themes, condensed by Locke (1992), may provide a useful source for our reflection on prevailing cultural and political norms in a classroom. In the list that follows, each theme is accompanied by at least one alternative perspective. The alternative examples are meant to invite a consideration or possibly a conversation about counter-beliefs and values that students and teachers may bring to a learning environment:

1. **Achievement and success:** People emphasize rags-to-riches in stories.

   Alternatives: Personal generosity is the highest human value; conspicuous consumption represents greed and self-interest; rags-to-riches is rooted in cultural mythology that overlooks the social, political, and economic forces that favor certain groups over others. Thus, achievement has at least as much to do with privilege as with personal desire and effort.

2. **Activity and work:** People see this country as a land of busy people who stress disciplined, productive activity as a worthy end in itself.

   Alternatives: People believe that caring about and taking time for others is more important than "being busy"; discipline can take many forms and should be equated with respect, moral action, and social conscience; a means-ends orientation has been the justification for such things as cultural genocide and environmental disaster; sustenance is a higher value than productivity.

3. **Humanitarian mores:** People spontaneously come to the aid of others and hold traditional sympathy for the underdog.

   Alternatives: Human beings are selective about whom they will help; for some, personal gain takes precedence over kindness and generosity; for others, human emotion is to be avoided because it makes them feel vulnerable and inept.

4. **Moral orientation:** People judge life events and situations in terms of right and wrong.

   Alternatives: People feel there is no objective right or wrong and that such a perspective tends to favor and protect the most privileged members of society; finding meaning in life events and situations is more important than judging.

5. **Efficiency and practicality:** People emphasize the practical value of getting things done.

   Alternatives: People believe that process is just as important as product and that it makes the strongest statement about what an individual values; living and working in a manner that values equity and fairness is both practical and just.

6. **Progress:** People hold the optimistic view that things will get better.

   Alternatives: People believe that the idea of progress assumes human beings can and should control nature and life circumstances; instead, we ought to acknowledge, respect, and care for that which we have been given, that which is greater than ourselves, and that which is, like life, cyclical. (Interestingly, many languages in the Americas and around the world do not include a word for *progress*.)

7. **Material comfort:** People emphasize the good life. Conspicuous consumption is sanctioned.

   Alternatives: People believe that a good life is defined by sharing and giving things away. The idea that life will be good if one owns many possessions leads to insatiable behavior and greed as well as environmental devastation.

8. **Freedom:** People believe in freedom with an intensity others might reserve for religion.

   Alternatives: People believe that freedom without justice is dangerous; limiting freedom is necessary for equality; accepting the limitations of personal freedom is a sign of respect for others.

9. **Individual personality:** People believe that every individual should be independent, responsible, and self-respecting; the group should not take precedent over the individual.

   Alternatives: People believe that sharing and humility are higher values than ownership and self-promotion; self-respect is inseparable from respect for others, community, and that which is greater than oneself. Individualism can promote aggression and competition in ways that undermine the confidence, self-respect, and human rights of others; independence denies the social, cultural, racial, and economic realities that favor members of certain groups over others.

10. **Science and secular rationality:** People have esteem for the sciences as a means of asserting mastery over the environment.

    Alternatives: People believe the earth is a sacred gift to be revered and protected. The notion of scientific objectivity is based on the mistaken presumption that human beings are capable of value-neutral beliefs and behaviors.

11. **Nationalism-patriotism:** People believe in a strong sense of loyalty to that which is deemed "American."

    Alternatives: People believe that, functionally, "American" has meant conformity to Anglo European values, behaviors, and appearances; the way in which the word *American* is commonly used to describe a single country on the continent of the Americas is presumptuous and arrogant; "American" needs to be redefined in the spirit of pluralism and with respect for other global identities.

12. **Democracy:** People believe that every person should have a voice in the political destiny of their country.

    Alternatives: People believe that democracy is an illusion that perpetuates the domination of society's most privileged members; people must have the means and capacity to use their voices—this requires access to multiple perspectives on issues and confidence that speaking up will not jeopardize one's economic and personal security.

13. **Racism and related group superiority**: People believe that racism represents a value conflict in the culture of the United States because

it emphasizes differential evaluation of racial, religious, and ethnic groups. They argue for a color-blind ideology based on the assumption that social and economic advantage in contemporary life is the consequence of merit and hard work.

Alternatives: People believe that racism combines prejudice with power and is personal, institutional, and cultural. It has been used for over 400 years as a way to secure the psychological, educational, and material dominance of a select group. Without acknowledgment of its existence, it is impossible for members of a society to examine the implications of advantage and power and develop practices that level the playing field.

When we clarify our own cultural values and biases, we are better able to consider how they might subtly but profoundly influence the degree to which learners in our classrooms feel included, respected, at ease, and generally motivated to learn. The range of considerations found in Williams's cultural themes assist us with developing questions to ask ourselves about our own assumptions when we construct reflective questions to enhance a learning experience. A few examples, subject to age-appropriateness, follow:

- Are your classroom norms clear, so that if they are different from what students are used to at home or in their communities, or if students are at the beginning stages of learning English, they are able to understand and negotiate expectations? It may be important to model behavior, provide visible examples of expectations, and elicit information about clarity of communication through student polls or written responses. A common norm teachers in the United States typically share is for students to raise their hand when they have questions. Some students, however, are embarrassed about publically identifying what they do not understand. The anonymity of writing or conferencing with peers and then sharing information with a teacher can facilitate communication. In addition, some teachers use a "fist-to-five" approach to checking for clarity. If students raise all five fingers on a hand, it means they understand what they have learned so well that they could teach it to someone else. Four fingers mean they understand it but would be cautious about teaching it. Three fingers mean they have a good start but are confused about some things. Two fingers mean they don't get it. One finger means they are struggling not to give up.
- One additional consideration is clarity about time. For students from communities where time is not a commodity that can be spent, wasted, or managed, time may be experienced more in relation to natural patterns. For such students, expectations about punctuality require definition and modeling.

- Have you examined the values embedded in your discipline that may confuse or disturb some students? Ask questions that encourage students to represent alternative perspectives, construct panels that can discuss key issues from diverse perspectives, and help students organize their discussion groups in ways that encourage collaborative dialogue and knowledge sharing.

- Are the examples you use to illustrate key points meaningful to and respectful of students? Give one example from your experience and then ask students to create their own examples to illustrate different viewpoints, providing an opportunity for group discussion. Acknowledge the experiences of people from different backgrounds, and be aware of nonverbal language and voice. Seeking feedback through regular anonymous surveys can be instructive.

- Do you have creative and effective ways to learn about your students' lives and interests? In recent years, Gonzalez, Moll, and Amanti (2005), Zigarelli, Nilsen, Moore, and Ginsberg (2014), and other research-practitioners have brought attention to the value of a *funds of knowledge* approach to teaching and learning. Funds of knowledge are cultural experiences and strengths that are revealed through informal interactions with families and students, such as visiting a student's home or eating lunch each week with students. When educators are in the role of learner and listener, a family's stories and experiences along with insights into students' values, feelings, language, identity, and academic strengths can stimulate insight into new ways to engage students in learning. For many educators, this translates into ideas for a more culturally relevant curriculum.

- Other ways to learn about students include a photo board, creative opportunities for self-expression, occasional potluck meals, regularly scheduled discussion topics about local and global problems, acknowledgment of birthdays and cultural holidays, open sharing about oneself, a beverage urn at the back of the classroom as a site for informal discussion, and other similar opportunities.

- Many teachers also use "door passes" or "exit tickets," which are simply 3×5 cards or electronic postings on which students write a response to a question the teacher has asked. Students use their response as their ticket to leave when class is over. When teachers collect these at the door, this has the added benefit of allowing educators to make contact with each student. Here are a few examples of questions for older students: What is one connection that I was able to make between what we learned today and a personal interest or goal? What is one question I wish I had asked today but didn't think of it at the time? If I were teaching this topic, I would want to be sure to include. . . .

- In addition, teachers might create a display to which students submit photos or original reminders about themes that vary from month to month. For example, an experience I had that I will always remember, one of the most beautiful places I've been, something that still surprises me. Teachers might work with students to generate the themes and ask for volunteers to design and manage the display. Instead of buying posters, teachers might ask students to make their own on different topics, such as "words of wisdom" or "wisdom from my ancestors" to post on the wall for inspiration. The section on inclusion in Chapter 3 provides additional ideas. Although most teachers have several ways to become more familiar with the lives and interests of students, the goal is to make a regular point of doing so in ways that include every student.

- Are you aware of nonverbal communication from a multicultural and cross-cultural perspective? For many students socialized within the dominant culture of the United States, physical proximity has little effect on emotional safety or academic effectiveness. Similarly, a well-modulated voice signals authority and knowledge. But these characteristics vary considerably across cultures (Gudykunst & Kim, 1992; Remland, 2000), and a well-modulated voice, for example, is not necessarily one that is approachable or invites thinking. Although research on communication tends to be painted with a fairly broad brush, attention to voice, proximity, and other kinetic characteristics can determine who gets the floor, whose perspective is respected, and who enjoys learning (Andersen & Wang, 2006; Goldin-Meadow, 2003).

In general, a good place to begin deepening cultural awareness is to consider our own repertoire of behaviors in relation to whom we are teaching (Enns & Sinacore, 2004). A small focus group of diverse students can contribute to a more nuanced understanding of significant cultural differences among students.

Peggy McIntosh (1989) has written:

As a white person I had been taught about racism as something which puts others at a disadvantage, but had been taught not to see one of its corollary aspects, white privilege, which puts me at an advantage. . . . I was taught to see racism only in individual acts of meanness, not in invisible systems conferring dominance on my group. (p. 10)

Many of us, regardless of racial, ethnic, linguistic, sexual, or gender affiliations, have been socialized to think of the United States as a just society. It is difficult to imagine that each of us is responsible for everyday actions that can undermine other peoples' motivation with consequences that parallel overt and intentional acts of bigotry. Though history and the broader policy environment bear significant responsibility for social inequality, learning about who we are culturally, as individuals, community members, and educators, can create a consciousness that is satisfying and empowering in ways we may have never dreamed.

SUMMARY

This chapter provided background on the relationship between motivation, learning, and culture, and it gave readers the opportunity to examine some of their own cultural values. It also offered a rationale for intrinsic motivation as the foundation for teaching and learning, emphasizing that instructional planning should be motivational planning. The following chapter, titled "Critical Features of a Motivating and Culturally Responsive Classroom," explores the question: How can teachers support the intrinsic motivation of learners within and across cultural groups? It provides a planning tool based on the motivational framework and a graphic organizer to help teachers align motivational strategies for individual lessons or unit development.

2 Critical Features of a Motivating and Culturally Responsive Classroom

Against boredom, even the gods themselves struggle in vain.

—Frederick Nietzsche

Chapter 1 provided background on intrinsic motivation as a concept and in relation to the social conditions that influence the lives and motivation of youth. Because the motivation of teachers is vulnerable to depletion and diminishment as well, the second volume of this series explores ways to create schools where teachers are valued and energized as professionals who continuously examine and improve their practice. In *The Culture of School and the Problem of Change*, Yale University psychologist Seymour Sarason (1982) noted:

> One of the unverbalized assumptions undergirding the organization and thrust of our schools is that the conditions that make schools interesting places for children can be created and sustained by teachers for whom these conditions exist only minimally, at best. (quoted in Meier, 1995, p. 123)

The primary focus of this chapter is intrinsically motivating instruction in culturally responsive classrooms. Readers will explore the *motivational framework for culturally responsive teaching,* which is a synthesis of interdisciplinary research that responds to the question: How can we as teachers consistently support the intrinsic motivation of learners within and across cultural groups? This book's fundamental assertion is that instructional plans need to be motivational plans. Among the myriad approaches to instructional improvement, such as improving content-specific pedagogy, integrating the arts, maximizing the potential of technology, supporting academic language development among English language learners, and ensuring inclusive practices to create learning environments where students thrive, intrinsic motivation provides a theoretical umbrella to organize teaching and learning (Chopra, 2014).

This chapter also shows how the motivational framework supports rather than supplants teachers' knowledge. As a planning and reflection tool, it effectively interacts with teachers' nuanced understanding of their content areas, students, and community. The scenarios in this chapter exemplify how the motivational framework and teacher knowledge combine to create motivationally vital learning experiences. Included in this chapter's exhibits is a motivational framework that can be used as a planning tool as well as a model for organizing motivational strategies that have been adapted for individual lessons or unit design.

FOUR CONDITIONS OF THE MOTIVATIONAL FRAMEWORK FOR CULTURALLY RESPONSIVE TEACHING

As shown in Figure 2.1, the motivational framework represents four essential motivational conditions: establishing inclusion, developing a positive attitude, enhancing meaning, and engendering competence. These conditions act individually and in concert to enhance students' intrinsic motivation to learn.

Each condition of the framework has two criteria, which ask teachers to consider the condition's existence in the learning environment from the students' perspective. A guiding question is provided for each motivational condition.

1. *Establishing Inclusion* (motivational criteria: respect and connectedness)

   How will we create a learning environment in which students and teachers feel *respected* by and *connected* to one another?

2. *Developing a Positive Attitude* (motivational criteria: choice and personal relevance)

   How will we create a favorable disposition among students toward learning through personal cultural *relevance* and student *choice?*

3. *Enhancing Meaning* (motivational criteria: challenge and engagement)

   How will we create *engaging* and *challenging* learning experiences that include students' perspectives and connections to civic responsibility?

4. *Engendering Competence* (motivational criteria: authenticity and effectiveness)

   How will we create a shared understanding that students have *effectively* and *authentically* learned something they value?

Figure 2.1 The Motivational Framework With Questions

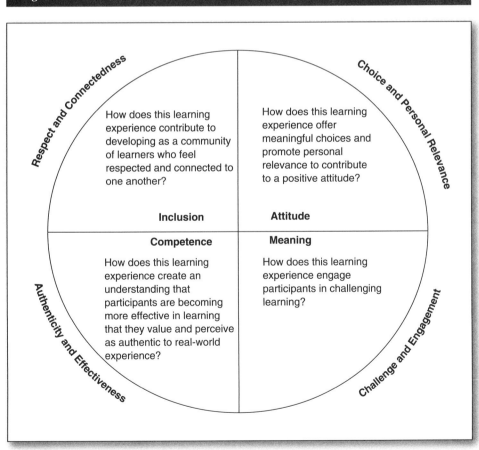

Source: Ginsberg & Wlodkowski (2000).

A mnemonic device that is helpful for remembering the framework is *I AM Competent* (I: Inclusion; A: Attitude; M: Meaning; C: Competence).

Establishing Inclusion refers to principles and practices that contribute to a learning environment in which students and teachers feel respected by and connected to one another. It is the core of genuine empowerment and agency. As human beings we seldom accept high levels of personal challenge unless there is a sense of emotional safety and an awareness that our perspectives matter. Learners are most likely to grapple with uncertainty and dissent in the learning environments that protect the worth and expression of each person's true self. For this to occur there need to be norms and practices that contribute to mutual support and unity among learners. Examples of this include communication agreements and norms for collaborative learning that promotes the contributions of all group members. These and other strategies for establishing inclusion can be found in Chapter 3.

Developing a Positive Attitude refers to principles and practices that create a favorable disposition to learning through teaching and learning that is personally and culturally relevant and attuned to students' control over how and what they will learn. This means that learning is contextualized within students' experiences and interests. It also means that students participate in decisions that include their perspectives on strengths, needs, values, and what matters to them. Conventional wisdom among attorneys is that jurors tend to make up their minds within the first 10 minutes of a trial, after which time it may be more difficult to influence their opinions. Students often have a parallel response to a learning environment. Teachers need to set up a positive response to a lesson from the very start.

Who among us embraces learning when information and necessary skills exclude personal experiences and strengths? Examples of strategies for this motivational condition include goal setting and practices that help students access and build on prior knowledge. One example of this is KUD, developed by Carol Tomlinson (Strickland, 2007), which is a three-column chart for students to differentiate their learning. The K stands for *know,* the U stands for *understand,* and the D stands for *do.* Students draw a line from each know and do statement to the corresponding understand statement. If a know or do statement does not relate to any understand statements, students either eliminate it or add an understand statement that gives it meaning and content. These and other strategies for developing a positive attitude can be found in Chapter 4.

Enhancing Meaning refers to challenging and engaging learning. With a focus on substantive learning, this condition calls for intellectual rigor through deep thinking, critical inquiry, and artistic expression. Examples of strategies for this motivational condition are inquiry-oriented projects, creative problem solving, and exploration of concepts through the arts. These and other strategies for enhancing meaning can be found in Chapter 5.

Engendering Competence refers to principles and practices that help students understand they have learned something effectively in ways that they value and that can authentically contribute to the broader community. This condition also supports continuous improvement through formative and summative feedback that builds on students' strengths and grading policies that encourage rather than coerce learning. Examples of strategies for this motivational condition include rubrics for transparent expectations, demonstrations of knowledge connected to students' frames of reference and communities, self-assessment, and informative, nonpunitive grading practices. These and other strategies for engendering competence can be found in Chapter 6.

The four motivational conditions work together to support intrinsic motivation among diverse student groups. This kind of pedagogical alignment activates the intrinsic motivation that all students possess. Motivating and culturally responsive educators realize that no one teaching strategy or motivational condition will consistently engage all learners, nor will a repertoire of random strategies. For example, a classroom with an exhilarating feeling of emotional safety (motivational condition: establishing inclusion) but lacking serious academic challenge (motivational condition: enhancing meaning) may seem calm and conflict-free initially but is vulnerable to boredom and declining student engagement. Instructional strategies coordinated according to the motivational conditions create an architecture for energetic learning.

Although the chapters that follow provide sets of teaching strategies for each motivational condition, motivational planning should not be reduced to a checklist of "best practices." Motivational teaching is a nuanced endeavor with strategies carried out with individual students in mind. For example, a student who is not accustomed to setting personal goals (strategy) will most likely thrive with a different form of support such as following a learning model (another strategy) than a student who is comfortable with autonomous thinking.

As an instructional language, the Motivational Framework for Culturally Responsive Teaching serves as an orienting tool for planning and making sense of learning experiences. Although research suggests a relationship between the motivational framework and positive learning outcomes (Barnes, 2012; Wlodkowski, 2008; Wlodkowski, Mauldin, & Gahn, 2001), its value as a pedagogical compass for instructional planning has been affirmed by the work of practicing educators across the United States and in Japan, Germany, Singapore, India, Thailand, and Hong Kong. The essentials of the motivational framework are that it

(1) respects diversity; (2) engages the motivation of a broad range of students; (3) creates a safe, inclusive, and respectful learning environment; (4) derives teaching practices from across disciplines and cultures; and (5) promotes equitable learning. While respectful of different cultures, the framework enables the construction of a common culture within the learning environment that all learners can accept.

The motivational framework systemically represents the four motivational conditions of establishing inclusion, developing a positive attitude, enhancing meaning, and engendering competence. These conditions act individually and in concert to provide a congruent set of instructional considerations to enhance intrinsic motivation to learn.

As has been true from the start of public education in the United States, the dominant metaphor is "carrot and stick" (reward and punish), based on a belief that students' academic and social behavior requires "management" (Anyon, 1980). In such an environment, it is not uncommon for students to be punished (low grades, or no recess) for learning behavior that may well be connected to ineffective instruction. Although students share responsibility for their academic and social interactions, respect, relevance, challenge, and fair assessment practices are the highly influential domains of teachers. Across cultural groups, *all* students are motivated, though some may not be motivated to learn what a teacher has planned. In such instances, their motivation may be in another direction, aligned with a different perspective, or part of another set of values, but in any circumstance learners are not inert.

PLANNING AND TEACHING WITH THE MOTIVATIONAL FRAMEWORK

A straightforward way to use the motivational framework for lesson design is to transpose its four motivational conditions into questions. These questions were introduced in Figure 2.1. Exhibit 2.1 provides a sequential approach to planning. The italicized words in the questions are the two criteria that need to be influential, from the student's perspective, for the condition to be present in the learning environment. Ideally all four motivational conditions interact throughout a lesson.

The following scenarios show an elementary, middle, and high school example of the motivational framework in practice. The different ways in which these teaching examples are displayed are intentional so that readers can consider different approaches to communicating about a lesson with the motivational framework.

Exhibit 2.1	The Four Conditions of the Motivational Framework for Culturally Responsive Teaching

Establishing Inclusion: How do we create or affirm a learning environment in which students feel *respected* by and *connected* to one another and to the teacher? (Best to plan for the beginning of the lesson.)

Developing a Positive Attitude: How do we create or affirm a favorable disposition toward learning through *personal/cultural relevance* and *choice?* (Best to plan for the beginning of the lesson.)

Enhancing Meaning: How do we create *challenging* learning experiences that promote deep *engagement?* (Best to plan throughout the lesson.)

Engendering Competence: How do we create or affirm an understanding that students have *effectively* learned something they value and perceive to be *authentic* to their real world? (Best to plan for, when possible, throughout the lesson, and, in general, at the end of the lesson; clear criteria for success should be understood and agreed to at the start of the lesson.)

A PRIMARY SCHOOL EXAMPLE OF THE MOTIVATIONAL FRAMEWORK

Imagine that third-grade students are about to read a text with challenging words. In this scenario the teacher, Suzanne Benally, wants students to probe and remember three to five new relevant words.

Establishing Inclusion (criteria: respect and connectedness)

Step 1: Ms. Benally says, "When I was young, every week we had to memorize 10 new words that the teacher gave us. We couldn't even choose them! We wrote the words 10 times to learn how to spell them, looked up their definitions in a big hardcover dictionary, and used them in 10 different sentences to show that we knew how to use these words. I didn't understand why the words we learned were important. Unfortunately, although I knew I had to learn these words, I found myself getting bored during these lessons."

Developing a Positive Attitude (criteria: choice and personal relevance)

Step 2: Ms. Benally continues, "In this lesson, we are going to notice words together that are new or confusing. Since we are learning about different communities that surround our school by collecting a few ingredients from each part of our city to make a meal for our families, today we will look for new words in the book *How to Make an Apple Pie and See the World,* by Marjorie Priceman (1994). In this book, the main character goes all around the world to find ingredients for an apple pie.

"Although each of you will read this book with a partner in a little while, I want to first introduce it to you by inviting you to read along with me on the first page. Follow along on the wall where I am pointing the document camera so that you can see the words as we read. As we read, let's see if we can find a new word together. There might even be one on the very first page! Okay now. Read out loud with me. When you come to a new word, hum quietly." Ms. Benally uses a pointer to help students focus on each word.

Together the class reads, "Making an apple pie is really very easy. First, get all the ingredients [students hum] at the market. Mix them well, bake and serve." Because many students did a quiet hum when the pointer was on the word *ingredient.* Ms. Benally pauses and asks, "Did you find a new word just now?"

Enhancing Meaning (criteria: challenge and engagement)

Step 3: Pointing to the word *ingredient,* Ms. Benally shows how she would break it into parts to say it, what it means (a part of a mixture), and how to use it. One of the ways she shows students the word's meaning is by pretending to look for ingredients to stir together in a bowl. She then finds a real egg and as she breaks it into a real bowl, she says, "Eggs are good ingredients for making cookies. What is another good ingredient for making cookies?" Next, she asks students to close their eyes and imagine that they are going to collect ingredients for an apple pie: "What ingredient would you look for?" She asks students to draw that ingredient on their lapboards and then write the following sentence, filling in the blank: "My ingredient for an apple pie is _____."

Engendering Competence (criteria: authenticity and effectiveness)

Step 4: Ms. Benally asks students to turn to an elbow partner to explain the new word in their own words. She also tells them she wants each student to be able to teach someone whom they live with about this important word. She wonders out loud, "How will you do that?"

Step 5: Students read with a partner to find two more new words.

Step 6: Just before students exit the room for lunch, Ms. Benally asks them to send her a "tweet" (on a sticky note) that says, "I will teach the word *ingredient* to _____ (name of the person).

After lunch, she will pair students with a partner and ask them to continue reading to enjoy the story and find two new words. In math, students will classify and make a bar chart that shows to whom, as an entire class, they will teach their new word(s).

A MIDDLE SCHOOL CLASSROOM EXAMPLE OF THE MOTIVATIONAL FRAMEWORK

The following learning experience at a large, urban middle school exemplifies another way to use the motivational framework to compose an instructional plan. Although the ideas are organized by separate, specific motivational conditions for this scenario as well as the elementary classroom example, in actual practice these conditions are interdependent.

Goals of the Lesson ("The Blame Cycle")

The goals of this lesson are to help middle school students examine the concept of blame, how it works, and what people can do to control the tendency to blame; to develop higher order thinking skills through a reframing exercise that helps students rethink a problem in a more positive way; and to diminish the tendency to blame.

Establishing Inclusion (criteria: respect and connectedness)

How does this learning experience contribute to developing as a community of learners who feel respected by and connected to one another and to the teacher?

The teacher, Devon Lee, shares a personal story about blame and asks students to do a quick-write based on a time they felt unfairly blamed for something. Students share their examples with a partner.

Developing a Positive Attitude (criteria: choice and personal relevance)

How does this learning experience offer meaningful choices and promote personal relevance for all students in terms of what is learned and how it is learned?

Mr. Lee has written the learning targets and an agenda on the board to invite students into a lesson that provides several opportunities to make their own decisions. After the quick-write exercise, he provides an overview of blame to develop relevance by helping students see that throughout the world all people tend to attribute bad things that occur to forces outside of themselves. For example, on one end of the spectrum students might hear "It was a bad day" or "It wasn't in the stars." On the other end of the spectrum students might hear, "It's her fault" or "He's a . . ." (fill in the blank with an all-too-common label). In pairs, students think about why blame is a tempting default position. For example, it lets people off the hook, gives people a sense of control, and provides a simple solution to complex problems. Next, with a partner, the teacher asks students to think of reasons why blame is a problem. Then he demonstrates a model of the blame cycle using a volunteer's personal experience. Afterward, students map personal blame cycles. Exhibit 2.2 provides a sample blame cycle based on a misunderstanding between a teacher and a student.

Exhibit 2.2 The Blame Cycle

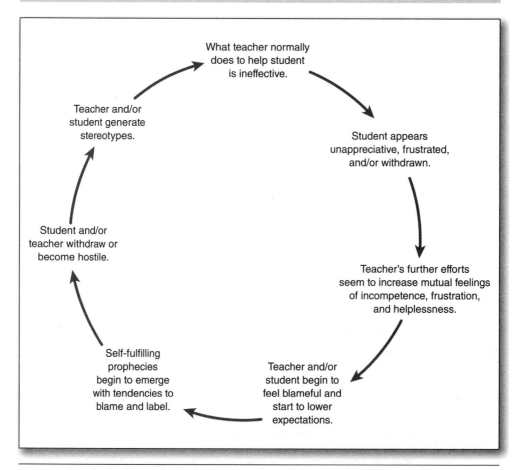

Source: Wlodkowski & Ginsberg (1995).

Enhancing Meaning (criteria: challenge and engagement)

How do we create challenging learning experiences that promote deep engagement?

Next, Mr. Lee tells the class that he will use the volunteer's "blame cycle map" to show how it is possible to interrupt the tendency to blame through a process called *reframing*. To begin this process, he asks students to write a note to themselves about every positive reason that the protagonist might have had for his or her actions. He provides an example:

A student might say that a positive response is "to get even." However, Mr. Lee shows students that another way to say this in a positive way is to say that the protagonist "has a sense of justice." After generating a list of positive explanations for the protagonist's behavior, he asks the student volunteer to select one of the class's positive reframes to work with. It should be something the student can honestly believe about the other person.

Next, he asks the class to brainstorm all of the things that the volunteer could do, knowing about this more positive way to understand the protagonist's behavior. Finally, Mr. Lee asks the volunteer to select a course of action based on one of the options the class has provided and to think through how she or he would know if that course of action were successful. What kind of evidence would demonstrate success?

Engendering Competence (criteria: authenticity and effectiveness)

Are students becoming more effective in learning that they value and perceive as authentic to their experiences?

Mr. Lee asks students to work with a partner to repeat the process, using either partner's blame cycle. The lesson concludes with blame similes (e.g., Blame is like a gun with a barrel pointed back at you because when you use it you hurt yourself most).

Closing question: In what ways might the blame cycle be valuable inside and outside of school?

The Four Motivational Conditions Work Together

The snapshot of a lesson about blame in Exhibit 2.2 illustrates how the four motivational conditions constantly influence and interact with one another. Without *establishing inclusion* (normalizing the tendency to blame and asking students to work with a partner regarding a situation in which they were blamed) and *developing a positive attitude* (working with a relevant problem, e.g., blame creates a cycle of defeat for everyone who is involved), *enhancing meaning* (students practice reframing using a

Exhibit 2.3 Circular Framework With Map of the Lesson

How can this learning experience . . .

. . . help students feel respected by and connected to other students and to the teacher?

Teacher shares personal story about blame.

Establishing Inclusion:
Respect and Connectedness

. . . promote choice and personal/cultural relevance?

Students do a quick-write exercise based on their own experiences; teacher uses a student's example to demonstrate how to map a blame cycle; students map their blame cycles.

Developing a Positive Attitude:
Choice and Personal Relevance

. . . enhance students' understanding that they are becoming more effective in authentic learning that they value?

Students work with a partner to reframe each other's blame cycles. They also write blame similes and respond to a closing question.

Engendering Competence:
Authenticity and Effectiveness

. . . engage students in challenges that are so compelling that students lose their sense of time?

Students learn reframing through active participation, working with the teacher as a class to reframe a sample blame cycle.

Enhancing Meaning:
Challenge and Engagement

volunteer's blame cycle) might not have occurred with the ease and energy it did. Also *engendering competence* (what students learned from practicing with their own blame cycles) might have been less productive without a relevant and engaging learning process). In short, enhancing student motivation is a systemic process. Removing any one of the four motivational conditions would likely affect the entire learning process.

The motivational framework in Exhibit 2.3 allows for as many strategies and activities as the teacher believes are needed to develop each motivational condition and a coherent lesson plan. The teacher's knowledge of the learners' motivation and culture, the subject matter, the setting, authentic assessment, the technology available, and time constraints determine the nature and number of learning strategies. A fundamental goal is to enhance the motivation to learn that all people possess, with the teacher as a valuable resource and vital partner in learning.

A HIGH SCHOOL EXAMPLE OF THE MOTIVATIONAL FRAMEWORK*

Ms. Galván teaches "Introduction to Social Science" at Jefferson High School in Chicago. She begins each class with 15-minute cooperative base groups (*motivational condition: establishing inclusion*). The primary goal is to ensure effective peer support for all of the students in her class. Ms. Galván has worked with students so that each base group member has a clearly defined role (e.g., facilitator, timekeeper, recorder, reporter, process observer). She has also worked with students to create agreed-upon norms for collaboration and, in particular, positive ways to encourage all group members to participate in base group dialogue. Today's base group task is to solve problems that several students have had with the most recent homework assignment. Last week's task was to share notes and summarize a challenging journal article from a previous class session (*motivational conditions: developing a positive attitude, enhancing meaning, and engendering competence*).

Ms. Galván organizes all of her teaching around authentic problems, opportunities, and issues. For example, students are currently investigating the question: "How can urban neighborhoods influence the safety and health of residents?" She has selected this focus in the aftermath of the deadliest summer in Chicago's history as well as a number of other gun violence–related deaths across the country, including the slaughter of students at Sandy Hook Elementary School in Connecticut (*motivational condition: developing a positive attitude*). In addition to analyzing the dilemmas that are inherent in the Second Amendment, students investigate social and economic conditions that suggest a relationship to gun violence. Further, they learn how local stewards of peace and justice facilitate non-violence in their communities. With the assistance of Cure Violence, a local organization formerly known as CeaseFire, students identify and analyze documents from a range of programs whose mission is to create or maintain safe and peaceful neighborhoods. They also observe meetings, probe statistical databases, and interview informal and elected community leaders such as the police chief, former gang members, and members of an organization whose specific focus is to build the capacity of youth in the area of restorative justice (*motivational condition: enhancing meaning*). Having decided to become experts in restorative justice (*motivational condition: developing a positive attitude*), students plan to draft funding proposals for a restorative justice program in their high school. Their concept is to build the leadership capacity of youth with truancy records so that they can receive academic (social studies) credit for developing their skill as justice-minded leaders (*motivational conditions: enhancing meaning and engendering competence*).

Students understand and appreciate Ms. Galván's feedback. She provides clear descriptions of her expectations and she is consistently encouraging. Her typical feedback cycle includes accomplishments, questions, resources to assist with questions, and encouragement. An A means "Outstanding job! You could teach this"; B means "Good. You are almost there"; C means "Additional practice needed. You can do it on your own with more attention to detail"; NGY stands for "No grade yet" and means "Propose a time to meet with me for additional assistance with your goals." Ms. Galván expects assessment to guide as well as monitor learning (*motivational condition: engendering competence*).

*Adapted from the Polaris Charter Academy (PCA) Peacekeepers Project (www.youtube.com/watch?v=1wqB6dPTeVc).

CONNECTING TO OTHER FRAMEWORKS

Over the past decade, a number of frameworks have appeared on the landscape of instructional resources, and some have become tools for teacher evaluation. The four conditions of the motivational framework encompass most if not all of other frameworks' pedagogical foci. For example, the 5 Dimensions of Learning (5D) framework from the Center for Educational Leadership (Fink & Markholt, 2011) focuses on (1) purpose: setting a clear, meaningful course for student learning; (2) student engagement: encouraging substantive, intellectual thinking; (3) curriculum and pedagogy: ensuring that instruction challenges and supports all students; (4) assessment for student learning: using ongoing assessment to shape and individualize instruction; (5) classroom environment and culture: creating classrooms that maximize opportunities for learning and engagement. Each condition from the 5D framework relates to a set of academic concerns about learning. With the Motivational Framework for Culturally Responsive Teaching, a primary concern is cultural diversity and the framework is explicitly grounded in intrinsic motivation theory. Further, because it has been developed for higher education as well as K–12, it is relevant to dual-enrollment programs that bridge high school and college. In this way, high school and entry-level college courses are consistent in their attention to learners' motivation and academic success. Finally, many instructional frameworks are proprietary ones for which users pay a fee, and users are expected to implement the ideas as they have been conceived.

The Motivational Framework for Culturally Responsible Teaching has never been marketed as a commodity or scalable mandate. It is not intended for teacher evaluation nor precise implementation because it is a malleable tool for planning, reflecting on, and strengthening instruction based on a teacher's, school's, or discipline's instructional priorities. Its underlying epistemology deliberately avoids fixed decisions about teachers' usage. In many ways implementing the framework is a matter of co-authorship because its effective implementation requires teachers' nuanced understanding of students, curriculum, and the broader community. An underlying principle is that learning resides within the "webs of significance" that human beings create together. Although educational research can shine a light on instructional practice, with empirical investigation, expert teaching and learning differ in nature from the precise laws of experimental science (Geertz, 1993, p. 5).

As is true for many frameworks, the motivational framework is a guide to significant learning with students. Its particular virtues reside within its concern for intrinsically motivating and culturally responsive teaching and its respect for the imagination and knowledge of teachers. Exhibit 2.4 shows one of several ways that schools have adapted the framework to their specific priorities, for example, project-based learning.

Exhibit 2.4 Cleveland High School Instructional "Look-Fors"

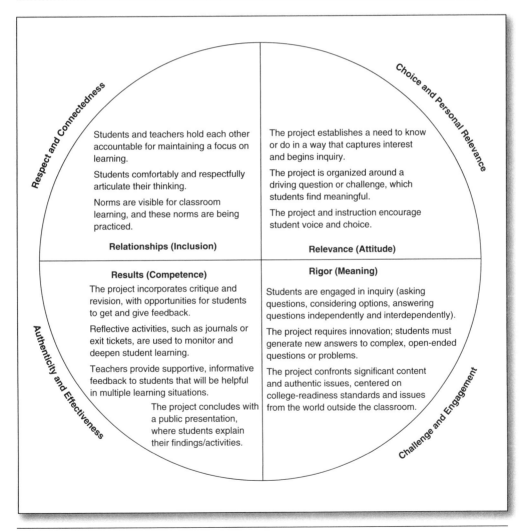

Source: created in collaboration with Catherine Brown & colleagues at Cleveland High School in Seattle, WA. Used with permission.

INTRODUCING THE MOTIVATIONAL FRAMEWORK TO OTHER TEACHERS

If you are interested in sharing the motivational framework with your colleagues, one way to introduce it is to show a video that provides context for each of the four motivational conditions. An advantage of teaching the framework to other educators is that it enhances your own understanding. An example of a 45-minute introduction to the framework follows.

Part I: Looking for the Four Conditions of the Motivational Framework (15 minutes)

After welcoming your colleagues to this opportunity for shared learning (motivational condition: establishing inclusion; applied criterion: connectedness) introduce Handouts A.1 and A.2 (see pages 248 and 249 in the Appendix) and provide adequate time for participants to read and discuss these visuals of the motivational framework. Explain that Handout A.1 is a format to apply the framework to lesson design and Handout A.2 is a rubric that provides a set of "look fors" for each motivational condition in the framework. Handout A.2 is useful as either a personal reflection tool or a peer observation form for non-evaluative confidential feedback from a trusted colleague.

Ask participants to consider the following questions: When you plan a lesson, which of the conditions do you usually begin with? Which of the motivational conditions challenges you the most (motivational condition: developing a positive attitude; applied criterion—personal relevance)?

Next, ask teachers to share activities that they might use throughout a unit or learning experience that exemplify each of the four motivational conditions, noting that the framework can be used for a single lesson and for an entire unit (motivational condition: developing a positive attitude; applied criteria: choice and personal relevance).

Use the following questions in each group to stimulate examples for each of the four conditions:

Condition 1: Establishing Inclusion

What activities do you use that contribute to developing as a community of learners who feel respected and connected to one another and to the teacher?

Condition 2: Developing a Positive Attitude

What activities do you use that offer meaningful choices and promote personal relevance to contribute to a positive attitude?

Condition 3: Enhancing Meaning

What activities do you use that engage students in challenging learning that has social merit?

Condition 4: Engendering Competence

What activities do you use that develop students' understanding that they are becoming more effective in authentic learning that they value and will use?

Part II: Using a Video to Identify "Wows" and "Wonders" (15 minutes)

Show a 10- to 15-minute video segment of a teaching example, and ask participants to observe teacher and student interactions, taking note of "wows" and "wonders" for each condition using Handout A.4 on page 254 of the Appendix as a format. Note: Some teachers prefer to watch the video and make notes with a colleague following the viewing. Regardless, the goal is to familiarize teachers with the framework by filling in instructional examples from the video that correspond to the various motivational conditions.

Explain that a single teaching strategy might be relevant to more than one condition and that participants are encouraged to use their own judgment since there will be some overlap. Also explain that strategies do not occur in a linear order. Participants may, for example, see a strategy that applies to attitude prior to a strategy that applies to inclusion.

After viewing the video and noting observations on Handout A.4, ask participants to form triads to share examples of how the teacher created each condition. Tell them that although they may want to make note of some "wonders" (questions they might ask the teacher in the video), the primary goal is to focus on "wows" (positive examples). Ask each group to select a reporter to share one example that they mutually agree created a particular condition from the framework.

Part III: Wrap-up and Conclusion (15 minutes)

Distribute Handout A.3, a Frayer Model (see Appendix, p. 251). Ask each participant in a group of four to use the graphic to explain one of the four motivational conditions. Provide time for participants to teach their motivational condition to their group members using the graphic organizer.

As a final step, review the session objectives and address any questions that participants may have. Also review ideas that participants intend to implement, and assuming that the group will continue to convene, indicate possible next steps.

CONNECTING CULTURAL AWARENESS TO THE FRAMEWORK

Although educators generally understand the motivational significance of the framework, the cultural significance may be less obvious. The concept of culture cannot be fully examined without considering the role of power and race in educational disparity, a helpful starting point for deeper conversations is the research of sociologist Robin M. Williams Jr. (1970) discussed in Chapter 1. The range of considerations found in Williams's cultural themes can be helpful as we think of questions to ask ourselves about our own assumptions and as we construct reflective questions that can enhance the learning experience we are creating with our students.

A second resource that many people have found profoundly valuable for examining their assumptions is Chimamanda Adichie's "The Danger of a Single Story" (www.youtube.com/watch?v=D9Ihs241zeg). It is approximately 19 minutes long, and it was first presented as a Ted Talks on October 7, 2009. In my own teaching, many important discussions have evolved from comparing the message of Chimamanda Adichie with this quote from Peggy McIntosh (1989):

> As a white person I had been taught about racism as something that puts other people at a disadvantage, but had not been taught to see one of its corollary aspects, white privilege, which puts me at an advantage. . . . I was taught to see racism only in individual acts of meanness, not in invisible systems conferring dominance on my group. (p. 10)

The research on culture can seem daunting. Yet to be mindful of one's own values, beliefs, and assumptions is foundational to teaching that is intrinsically motivating to students from across a cultural spectrum. This can be particularly challenging to educators who are raised in privileged communities where their implicit assumptions about achievement, success, and other cultural values were accepted as the norm.

Cultural pluralism and the struggle for educational equity requires unpacking and, in some instances, reconsidering long-held beliefs. The discoveries we make along the way may be quite different than what many of us, across our different backgrounds, believed as new teachers. However, one thing that effective educators among culturally diverse students hold fast to across their lifetime is the inseparability of educational equity and social justice, and the idea that the essence of teaching is to inspire dreams.

SUMMARY

This chapter provided a discussion of intrinsic motivation as it relates to student learning in culturally diverse classrooms. It introduced the Motivational Framework for Culturally Responsive Teaching as an instructional model that teachers can use to plan and reflect on lessons they design for intrinsically motivated learning. Culturally responsive educators understand the vital connection between intrinsic motivation and academic achievement. Further, they teach in ways that stimulate a deep concern for the perspective of others, curiosity, creativity, persistence, and commitment to lifelong learning. This chapter provided examples of how the motivational framework might contribute to such learning, its application in three different learning contexts, and an intrinsically motivating approach to introduce the framework to colleagues. It concluded with a reminder that the means we use to foster student learning must be consistent with value for a conscientious and satisfying life.

The following four chapters correspond to the four conditions of the motivational framework. In particular, the next chapter, "Establishing Inclusion," provides strategies that contribute to respect and connectedness. These strategies have been field-tested across grade levels, disciplines, and geographical locations as a way to promote safe and welcoming learning environments. In the words of Jean Anyon (2005, p. 45), "Where there is a way, there is a will."

3 Establishing Inclusion

Remember the sky you were born under,
know each of the star's stories.

—Joy Harjo (poet)

Although he has been interested in the reading material, Damean Matthews is thinking about dropping his 11th grade U.S. history course taught by Roberta James at Woodward High School. Academic learning generally comes easily to him, but he feels socially isolated and has become disinterested in the course. Ms. James is enthusiastic and sincere. She expects that no one will fail the course, all assignments will be clear, and she will be available to help anyone who needs it. Thus far, these are promises she has kept: Read Chapter 6, make appropriate notes in your journal, pass the quiz on Friday, complete a small-group assignment, and you will succeed. However, the group of students with whom Damean has been assigned for the small-group assignment feel overwhelmed by the amount of work they have in other classes. In addition, with parents who are alumni of well-respected universities, they are confident about their futures. Their goal for an otherwise interesting assignment is, as one student expressed, "Get the grade and move on. You won't even think of this course next semester." On the other hand, Damean believes that successful completion of a course assumes a certain level of learning has occurred; yet to push himself and members of his group to a higher level of expectation might further alienate him from a peer group in which he already feels uneasy. In addition, Damean is the only African American student in his predominantly European American group.

Damean wishes some of his classmates had taken the course on marginality that was offered last summer as part of the Upward Bound Program. One of the initial exercises was for students to remember a moment in the recent past (a week to a month) when they felt marginal, excluded, or discounted—"the only one like me in a group, not understood or, perhaps, unaccepted." After they reflected on this, students paired off and discussed the following questions: How did you know? How did *you feel? How did you behave? Next, the instructor asked students to recall a moment when they felt that they mattered, were included, or were regarded as important to a group. Once again, they were given time to reflect and then paired off to discuss the questions: How did you know? How did you feel? How did you behave? Finally, students were asked to reflect on both situations and discuss the patterns of thinking, feeling, and behaving that emerged, the influence of those patterns on their motivation and enthusiasm, and how the changes in motivation and enthusiasm might relate to learning and teaching. Within this culturally diverse classroom, Damean and most of his classmates were able to see for themselves how motivation across cultural groups is influenced by the degree of a person's inclusion in a learning environment. Together they were able to see that when human beings do not feel safe, complex information can be difficult to learn, frustration is predictable, and in some cases it leads to withdrawal or conflict.*

With the road to success in Ms. James's course otherwise clear, Damean is not sure what to do. It would be easier to address his concerns if her requirements were not so clear about how to complete the course. But with limited direction on group work and limited motivation among his peers, he feels trapped.

Throughout the four chapters on the conditions of the motivational framework, readers will find a brief scenario and an explanation of the motivational condition, followed by related sets of strategies. As is true for the initial brief scenarios, examples of the importance of a motivational condition and related motivational practices range from high school to primary education. While some practices are directly connected to a particular educational level or subject area, most can be easily adapted for older or younger students and for different subjects. In addition, each of the chapters concludes with a list of strategies for quick reference. The practices associated with establishing the motivational condition of inclusion are those that foster *respect* and *connectedness*. This chapter provides a host of ways teachers and students can build mutually supportive relationships.

As the introductory scenario suggests, a fundamental need that learners of all ages share is to become part of an environment in which they and their instructors are respected by and connected to one another and, as Damean's situation indicates, to know their opinion matters. This is the challenge of the first condition of the motivational framework: establishing inclusion. It requires teachers to thread learning experiences throughout the lesson that support social and academic risk taking. Although in education the concept of emotional safety is frequently an introductory activity or warm-up, a single strategy rarely creates a milieu in which students from a range of backgrounds are comfortable together as learners.

From a research perspective, when an environment encourages students to use their own social and cultural strengths, they can develop ways to connect to new ideas that make knowledge relevant and within their personal control (Vygotsky, 1978). In doing so, students become knowledge builders rather than knowledge resisters. Everyday reason as well as research indicates that students who feel alienated achieve less than those who do not. Most of us can easily recall what became of our motivation within a context in which we felt alone or excluded. We are social beings and our feelings of inclusion or exclusion are enduring and irrepressible. This is a primary reason that Damean avoided expressing his interests to his small group. In a classroom, as in civic life, a sense of community that encourages comfortable communication establishes a foundation for learning and participation.

A basic assumption of this chapter is that a supportive learning community depends as much on an instructor's capacity to promote cooperative interactions as it does on instructional effectiveness for individual learners. These practices take the form of innovative presentations regarding personal stories (see the section "Opportunities for Multidimensional Sharing," p. 48), small-group work structured to promote equitable participation and learning, and "historians" or note-takers who post their notes on a webpage so that students and teachers have a way to compare and contrast their recollections. Since motivation and learning are influenced by culture, the most effective teaching strategies may require adaptation for different learners and contexts.

ALLOW TIME FOR INTRODUCTIONS

No matter how obvious this suggestion may seem, it is worth the reminder. Students become more comfortable with one another when they have a chance to learn about each other's lives and interests. Regularly include why you or others in the room are excited about a particular topic, learning strategy, or course. This is always a good opportunity for people to share their own history as learners and aspects of the learning experience that make a situation distinct or important.

At the beginning of the year (even in high school), name tents that students personalize are a valuable way to ensure that everyone learns and pronounces each other's names correctly. Some teachers accompany the name tent exercise with initial introductions that ask students to introduce themselves and recommend one thing they have read (such as an article, story, or book) or one thing they have seen (such as a piece of art, TV or Internet program, or film) that has had a strong and positive influence on their lives, with each student stating the reason for the recommendation. An alternative exercise asks students to (a) introduce themselves, (b) name one, or up to five, of the places they have lived, and (c) offer one expectation, concern, or hope they have for a learning experience in a particular subject area, course, or in the year ahead.

In general, an introduction of any sort is most inclusive and motivating when it helps people learn each other's names, validate individual and collective experiences, relieve the normal tension that most new groups feel in the beginning of a school year or class, and establish a sense of affiliation.

Learning about each other is a continuous process. The more natural and appropriate such opportunities feel, the more likely a genuine sense of community will evolve. In the beginning of a course, these activities can contribute to the initiation of sustainable relationships for personal and academic growth.

Scores of books and websites describe exercises to help people become acquainted in new learning contexts. For example, Edutopia (www.edutopia.org) and Teaching Channel (www.teachingchannel.org) provide a treasure trove of free and easily accessible ideas. Several other possibilities appear in the section of this chapter titled "Opportunities for Multidimensional Sharing."

Because establishing inclusion means that students are part of an environment in which they and their teacher(s) are respected by and connected to one another, agreed-upon classroom norms (see Chapter 4) are essential to general classroom interactions and group work. Norms not only diminish feelings of cultural isolation that can undermine motivation to learn, they help to establish an environment that encourages students to be their authentic selves and, consequently, to take risks that are fundamental to personal development and academic performance.

When students do not feel included, they are far more likely to guard their resources, strengths, and perceived weaknesses. Inclusion, therefore, is at the core of genuine empowerment, agency, and academic success. One might simply say that establishing the condition of inclusion allows students to tell and hear their stories and to make sense of things without fear.

OPPORTUNITIES FOR MULTIDIMENSIONAL SHARING

Opportunities for multidimensional sharing are those occasions, from introductory exercises to personal anecdotes to classroom rituals, that provide a chance for people to see one another as complete and evolving human beings who have mutual needs, emotions, and experiences. These opportunities give a human face to a class, break down assumptions and stereotypes, and support the identification of oneself with another person. It is important to note that multidimensional sharing differs from many icebreakers in that it is less game-like and students can control the content and format. Except where noted, the examples of multidimensional sharing given in this chapter work effectively within a small- or large-group format.

There are many ways to provide opportunities for multidimensional sharing depending on the history, composition, and purpose of the group. If there is a caution, it is to guard against intrusiveness, providing ways for people to self-disclose personal information only to the extent that it feels appropriate and comfortable for the students that are involved. Many students are from backgrounds that value modesty. Further, many of us have learned hard lessons about inauthentic trust that is developed in artificial ways. Multidimensional sharing should always be approached with respect for the privacy of others.

Meals and extracurricular activities offer people ways to be themselves and to reduce self-consciousness. As mentioned earlier, activities that help people learn each other's names and laugh together can also be worthwhile. As educators, not taking ourselves too seriously reveals our humanity and suggests that the way we teach allows for a range of feelings and perspectives.

Following are specific exercises and activities that help members of a group become familiar with one another. They provides ideas that contribute to classrooms where everyone knows they belong and can safely offer their perspectives and take risks in order to learn. Several of these activities can be adapted to complement the curriculum. For example, the following Venn diagram exercise works well for younger students who are also learning to compare and contrast ideas. Language arts teachers could extend this exercise to three characters from a novel. The possibilities are endless.

ACTIVITY 3.1

Venn Diagram Sharing

Purpose: To learn about each other, to identify commonalities and differences, to personalize the concept of culture, and to identify options related to instruction that support the intrinsic motivation of all students

Time: 30 minutes

Format: Triads and large group

Materials: Newsprint and markers

Process

Ask the entire group to consider the concept of culture and to name factors that might influence a person's cultural identity. People normally suggest such possibilities as gender, socioeconomic class, ethnicity, language, music, religion, food, and country of origin. Write down approximately seven to ten words that people call out.

The large group divides into triads, and each group draws a Venn diagram as shown in Figure 3.1. Each triad member selects one of the three circles to represent herself or himself. Triad members then select topics from the list of words that the large group has generated and begin to identify ways in which they are similar and different from one another in regard to each topic. Distinctive qualities such as languages spoken and ethnicity are entered on the portion of the person's circle that does not overlap anyone else's circle.

Some characteristics will be shared by only two group members, and in different pairs—for example, having siblings for the first and second students, and a community with significant influence on their lives for the second and third students. These are entered in the space intersected by the two circles belonging to the two people who share that particular characteristic. When all three triad members have a quality in common, they locate it in the center of the diagram, where all three circles intersect. Participants are encouraged to share information only on those topics that are comfortable for the triad.

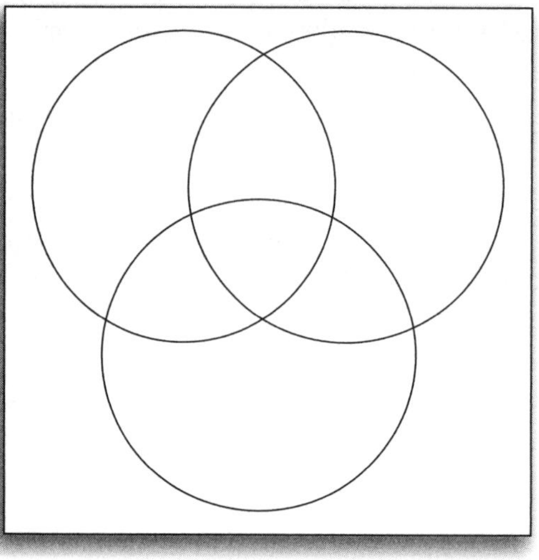

Figure 3.1 Venn Diagram

Source: Ginsberg (2011).

After 15–20 minutes, participants take a short time to publically reflect on something that they learned as a consequence of participating in the exercise. Some generalizations occur more frequently than others, for example, "We realized that we had more in common than we might have predicted" or "The more information people have about each other, the more open their conversations become." This activity is often a good beginning for establishing a sense of community.

Note: Older students are often interested in understanding additional influences on their cultural identity. Figure 3.2 illustrates four dimensions that interact as a significant part of a person's identity. Students will notice that Loden and Rosener (1991) view personality as central. The next layer delineates characteristics that are often considered to be consistent across a lifetime. The third and fourth layers tend to be more variable. One way to help facilitate a conversation among students is to ask three thought questions: What does this diagram attempt to communicate? To what extent does this model of cultural diversity make sense to you? What, if anything, would you change?

Figure 3.2   Four Layers of Diversity

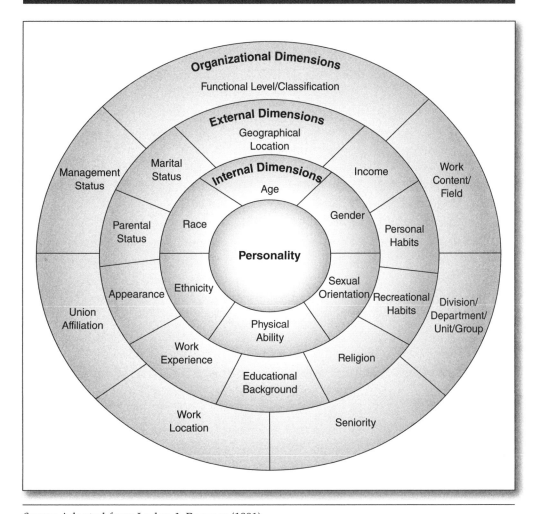

Source: Adapted from Loden & Rosener (1991).

ACTIVITY 3.2
Our Stories

Purpose: To create a strong sense of community that recognizes each student's strengths and to practice introducing oneself and another person

Time: 5 minutes per person plus a 2-minute introduction from a peer

Format: Presentation to the entire class

Materials: Students are encouraged to integrate technology and/or the arts into their presentations

Process

As part of this ongoing series of introductions, students sign up with a partner for a 15-minute block of time. Although students present their own story, for roughly 5 minutes they begin by introducing each other. This provides an occasion for students to become sufficiently well acquainted with their partner to create a thoughtful introduction. It also provides practice introducing other people, which is a skill students can use throughout life. To exemplify the process, the teacher and a volunteer introduce each other and then one of them steps back for the other to share significant aspects of his or her life in a creative way.

Among teachers and students, the narratives have taken a variety of forms. Students have created PowerPoint presentations with photos organized around a theme such as people who stand behind me, places that taught me something important, my extended family, and so forth. The diversity of approaches has been as intriguing as the stories. One student shared a collection of textiles that represented significant memories, for example, a childhood quilt and a kitchen tablecloth. A middle school teacher who used the theme of places where he had learned important things showed his middle school bus stop where he learned about bullying, the naval ship where he learned about racism in job assignments, and the college that prepared him to teach. A particularly significant influence was his childhood home, where he learned lifelong values from a mother who had played a pivotal role in reparation to Japanese American families interned during World War II.

Through "Our Stories" students and teachers laugh together, listen to music, watch simulations, learn of great places and moments, and discover a variety of lives and perspectives. In addition to the ways in which this activity creates a stronger sense of community, it provides insight into how students' personal and cultural experiences can be woven into the curriculum. It also contributes to an environment primed for risk-taking and collaboration, setting the stage and creating a human safety net for rigorous academic challenge.

Here are a few suggestions for assisting students in the preparation. Ask students to (1) have a plan for making sure their presentations are no more than 5 minutes long, (2) choose a theme and make an outline, (3) practice with a partner, (4) set the stage in advance to maximize time, (5) provide visuals to enhance their stories, and (6) include things that make one's life distinct.

You may also want to remind students that good stories are memorable, personal, simple, and powerful. They have emotional appeal and inspire others. Like good teachers, good storytellers use symbols and analogies to bring stories to life. They rarely rely on just one method of communication. This opportunity for multidimensional sharing requires time and would need to be adapted to different timeframes.

ACTIVITY 3.3
Two Wishes and a Truth

Purpose: To personalize the concept of culture and to identify options for instruction that supports the intrinsic motivation of a range of students

Time: 30 minutes

Format: Triads and large group

Process

Ask each participant to write down three statements about himself or herself: one that is true and two that he or she might wish to be true. For example, a high school student might write that (a) she met Jay-Z in his dressing room, (b) she challenged Donald Trump to get a makeover, and (c) she played in a polka band at her cousin's wedding. Triad partners take turns listening to each other's statements and try to guess which of the statements is the truth.

In situations with older students, the debriefing includes these questions: What occurs to you as a consequence of participating in this activity? When you guessed which one of your partner's statements was true, how did you make that decision? (If appropriate) What is the difference between a generalization and a stereotype? Can you imagine a situation where your guess would be influenced by a stereotype?

ACTIVITY 3.4

Decades and Diversity

Purpose: To learn more about the diversity among students

Time: 45 minutes

Format: Small groups with large group debrief

Materials: Note-taking materials for each group and a chart with five questions

Process

Ask students to interview and record the answers of an older family member about that person's high school experience, specifically related to the topics covered in questions a through h below. (With younger students this may need to be revised.) In middle and high school classes with a large number of students from different geographical regions, this can be adapted to a place they have lived that had a strong influence on their development. After students interview a family member (or gather in groups according to places they have lived), they discuss the answers they recorded. Students form discussion groups according to the decade of their interviewee's last year of high school. For example, if it was 1980, the student would join the decade group that is 1980–1989, if it was 1993, the student would join the decade group that is 1990–1999, and so forth.

a. What year was your last year of school? (Refer to this year for the rest of the questions.)

b. What did you like to do for fun on Saturday night?

c. What music or musical groups did you listen to?

d. What kind of clothes and styles were in fashion?

e. What were important world events that occurred during this time?

f. What behaviors were strongly considered to be wrong or taboo?

g. What food did you most enjoy?

h. What family or community events did you look forward to?

Decade groups (or geographical groups) share and record their interview data. Afterward, ask each group to report out question by question, revealing the range of responses for each question. For example, when asked what the person they interviewed did for fun on a Saturday night, each decade group shares its responses to only that particular question. This allows for clear comparison across groups. Final debrief questions include the following: What generalizations can you make from the range of responses to each question? What connections can you make between this activity and the diversity among us? What does this activity help us understand about each other culturally? What questions did this activity raise for you?

ACTIVITY 3.5

Photo Scavenger Hunt

Purpose: To promote relationships, teamwork, and familiarity with a school

Time: 1 hour

Format: Groups of three

Materials: One digital camera or smartphone per triad and a checklist of items to capture

Process

Print out a list of people, places, and things that teams need to find, photograph, and explain. A sample list follows. It can be easily adapted for younger students.

- A staff member in the front office (Who is the person, and what does she or he do?)
- Someone who works in the cafeteria (What is this person's name and what does he or she like about his or her work?)
- Someone who keeps the school clean (What is this person's name and what does she or he do?)
- An interesting display of student work (What is the theme of the display and why is it interesting?)
- An encouraging sign or poster
- Three book titles that sound interesting
- Something healthy to eat in the cafeteria
- Eyeglasses that are round, oval, and square
- Something that you enjoy about school
- Something you'd like to change about school
- Something you'd like to further explore in school

> ## ACTIVITY 3.6
>
> ## Pair-Share, aka Elbow Partners or Turn and Learn Exercises (all are similar and can be adapted for other purposes)

Purpose: To learn more about each other and each other's perspectives

Time: 15–20 minutes

Format: Dyads with large-group debrief

Materials: Whiteboard, flip chart, markers, paper and pens

Process

For the purposes of reflection and sharing, select *one* of the following questions and ask students to briefly think to themselves, share the response with a person near them, and then summarize their ideas. During the large-group debrief, record students' responses or ask a volunteer to do so.

1. What is the significance of any part of your name to you?

   Debrief Questions: What are one or two thoughts that occur to you as a consequence of reflecting on this question? What can we learn about each other and ourselves from this exercise?

2. What is one thing about our class (or school or community) that an outsider might not realize at first glance?

   Debriefing Questions: What are the implications of this exercise for our classroom or school? What are the implications of this exercise for you?

3. Draw a metaphorical illustration of a concept (such as motivation or another concept that is relevant to a learning experience) to share with your partner. [The teacher may want to create a "gallery" on a spare wall so that after students share images with a partner, the illustrations can be viewed by everyone.]

   Debriefing Questions: How do you understand the picture that you drew? What can we say about our group as a whole when we reflect on the illustrations that were shared?

ACTIVITY 3.7

"Ask Me About . . ." Posters

Purpose: To learn more about each other and each other's perspectives

Time: 30 minutes

Format: Triads with large-group debrief

Materials: Construction paper, markers, scotch tape, or glue sticks

Process

Ask students to share something about themselves or an experience they have had that they value by creating individual posters that elicit others to ask them about the personal meaning of their drawing, symbol, or attached item(s). For example, a student who had recently traveled to Guatemala and who had in her possession a bean that can be found only in a certain region glued it to her paper. Across the top of the paper above her bean, she wrote "Ask me about" and concluded the sentence with the bean she glued to her poster.

Note: This activity provides a good way for students to share experiences and can be adapted to projects students have already completed.

ACTIVITY 3.8

Multicultural Inventory

Purpose: To learn more about each other and to gain respect for the diversity one finds within any group

Time: 30 minutes

Format: Large group

Materials: Handout 3.1 (p. 58)

Process

Distribute the Multicultural Inventory sheet and then ask students to move around the room to introduce themselves to each other and to identify any statements on the inventory that connect to the other person's attributes or experience. You may want to consider limiting the number of connections found with any single student to two statements.

HANDOUT 3.1

Multicultural Inventory

Please see if you can identify people who have attributes that correspond to the following statements.

1. Speaks more than one language

2. Born in a country other than the United States

3. Raised by someone who was born in a country other than the United States

4. Has more than three siblings

5. Has a family member who speaks more than two languages

6. Is good at (or enjoys) something that isn't typical for his or her gender

7. Is friends with someone who is over 80 years old

8. Enjoys reading books by an author who is from a background that is different from his or her own (give an example)

9. Enjoys listening to music by a musical artist who is from a background that is different from his or her own (give an example)

10. Traveled to a country where people speak Arabic, Urdu, Hindi, or a Mandarin dialect

11. (Create an attribute of your own)

ACTIVITY 3.9

Bio-Poems

Purpose: To learn about other people while simultaneously expressing one's own needs and concerns. A bio-poem is a formulaic structure to create a poem expressing what the writer sees as significant or meaningful about the subject's life (Gere, 1985, p. 222).

Time: 45 minutes, including presentations

Format: Individuals and small or large groups (small groups if there are many participants)

Materials: Handout 3.2 (p. 60)

Process

Discuss how students are going to use bio-poems to build community among themselves. Mention that the method is particularly useful for helping students in upper elementary, secondary, and postsecondary settings to see the personal dimensions of important figures. For example, students could write bio-poems about Barack Obama, Jane Adams, Julius Caesar, or Frankenstein's monster. Or students could visit a nursing home or a homeless shelter and create a bio-poem that lets them enter the life of a person in one of those particular environments. In math or science class, students could write a bio-poem about an equation, a formula, or an approach to solving a problem (Bean, 1996). The formula for writing a personal bio-poem and an example are provided on Handout 3.2 (Bio-Poem).

ACTIVITY 3.10

View From a Window

Purpose: To find commonalities with others

Time: 10 minutes

Format: Asynchronous class blog

Materials: Individual computers

Process

Tell students that they will contribute to a class blog for introducing themselves to others. Explain that this exercise requires them to write a

HANDOUT 3.2

Bio-Poem

Line 1: First name

Line 2: Four traits to describe a character (in this case, yourself)

Line 3: Relative of _____ (brother of, sister of, and so on)

Line 4: Who feels _____ (three items that relate to how you feel in in this class)

Line 5: Who needs _____ (three items that express what you need to be successful)

Line 6: Who fears _____ (three items related to this class or to your experiences as a learner)

Line 7: Who gives _____ (three items that indicate what you can contribute to others or to the class)

Line 8: Who would like to _____ (three items related to goals for this class)

Line 9: Last name

Example

I am Kendra

Gardener, musician, determined, intense

Aunt of baby girl twins, youngest of four sisters, granddaughter of Victoria and Rasmea

Who feels curious, cautious, and connected

Who needs feedback, flexibility, and free time

Who fears ambiguity, deadlines, and bad grades

Who gives good listening, deep thinking, and laughter

Who would like to get my homework done in school, learn things to solve environmental problems, work with others

Last name, Young—forever

description of the view from a favorite window and to weave some autobiographical information into their description. For example, "I am looking out at a parking lot where people who come to visit us leave their cars. Although I lived downtown in Seattle, living downtown in Chicago is even better." They will read what others have written and respond to two peers' postings, explaining why they would like to trade places for a day.

Source: Adapted from Conrad & Donaldson (2004, p. 56).

ACTIVITY 3.11
Check-in Adjectives

Purpose: To connect with another person

Time: 10 minutes

Format: Synchronous chat room entry

Materials: Individual computers

Process

Students think of a word that describes how they are doing in the class or course. They post their word in the chat room as you call their name at the beginning of a class. Once all the names have been called, students review the words and send a private message to someone whose word resonates with their own. Together they try to find additional adjectives that they have in common.

Source: Adapted from Conrad & Donaldson (2004, p. 54).

ACTIVITY 3.12
Interpretive Community Maps

Purpose: To personalize the concept of culture, especially as it relates to students' experience in the community, and to identify options for instruction that support students' intrinsic motivation to learn

Time: 30 minutes

Format: Dyads, triads, or small groups

Materials: Chart paper, colored markers, masking tape for posting maps

Process

Ask students, in dyads, triads, or small groups, to think of the history, places, people, services, customs, and resources in their community that support learning about or enjoying cultural diversity. Ask students to propose a list of possibilities to include on a comprehensive map. Because time constraints are generally a concern, ask students to narrow their lists to a few key sites. On a mural-sized sheet of paper, use colored markers to construct a collectively designed interpretative map. It does not need to conform to a standard scale or cardinal directions. Students may, however, want to develop symbols or landscaping to enhance their contributions.

To extend the activity, divide the map into sections. Ask students to get into groups to design the sections of a guidebook for the sections of the map. Guidebooks might include descriptions, lists, stories, illustrations, interviews, and so forth. In addition to information on various sites, they might offer community history, a community time line, personal time lines, a local language survey, oral histories, discussion of social issues, and different people's beliefs about various community issues.

ACTIVITY 3.13

Dialogue Journals

Purpose: To enhance peer dialogue on issues related to a course or any other learning experience

Time: As needed

Format: Dyads

Materials: A journal or notebook

Process

Participants pair themselves (or are asked to pair) with another person. At least once a week, partners are asked to write a reflective response to a question or experience as framed by you. For example, you may say, "Please use your dialogue journals this week to reflect on your experiences of creating your senior biology projects." At a designated time each week, dialogue partners exchange journals, read each other's entry, and respond in writing in the part of the partner's journal that is reserved for such responses. Some students wish to have their partner write a response on the same page. Others reserve a section in the back of their journal, or in a separate journal, for their partner's response.

Entries to a partner's reflective response may include but are not limited to (1) asking for clarification or further support for an idea, (2) adding support or evidence for an idea, (3) extending examples of an idea, (4) offering related ideas, (5) raising alternative views, and (6) noting similarities or contrasts to a partner's response.

ACTIVITY 3.14
Response Cards

Purpose: To provide an opportunity for participants to equally express their response to a perspective, statement, or mini-lecture

Time: 1–2 minutes

Format: Individuals

Materials: Three 3 × 5 cards (one yellow, one red, one blue) for each participant

Process

Students write "Interesting!" on the yellow card, "I have a different perspective" on the red card, and "I'm confused" on the blue card. When asked to hold up the response card that best reflects their response to a perspective, statement, or mini-lecture, students hold up the yellow card if what has just transpired is interesting, the red card if they think there is a different perspective to consider, or the blue card if clarification is needed. This provides you with a way of connecting with the perspectives of a group and knowing if a presentation needs to be modified to respond to students' interests or concerns.

ACTIVITY 3.15
Fist-to-Five

Purpose: To check in with the perspectives of a group by using five fingers of a hand to give a scale response to a question. This strategy avoids forcing people to respond with a simple "yes" or "no" answer.

Time: 1–2 minutes

Format: Individuals

Materials: None, except one's hand. Individuals who are physically unable to use a hand as a scale may wish to write—or have someone write—a number from one to five on a piece of paper and position it in a visible location near where they are seated.

Process

Ask students to raise the number of fingers on one of their hands that reflects their understanding or agreement to a given idea or perspective. Five fingers means "I understand so well, I could teach the concept myself"; four fingers means "I have a good understanding"; three fingers means "I understand, but not clearly"; two fingers means "I have some questions"; one finger means "I'm confused"; and a fist means "I need another opportunity to learn this idea."

You might check for understanding after much discussion of an idea, saying, "Let's do fist to five," and explain the categories. After surveying the students' hands, you can make appropriate decisions about how much clarification is needed.

ACTIVITY 3.16

Class Historian

Purpose: To provide an online record of topics and issues that have been examined along with learning activities, assignments, and resources so that students who were not in attendance have reliable information about what occurred in their absence. With a class historian, all students can check the accuracy of their own notes and records, and instructors can have a port- folio that reflects the course as a whole.

Time: As needed

Format: Individual students who rotate in and out of this assignment

Materials: An individual computer

Process

At the beginning of a course or institute, ask students to sign up to serve as the class historian on a specific date. The format of the class record (see page 65) can vary, but participants use their notes and the materials provided by you as a guide. In some instances, a class editor reviews and compiles sub- missions for enhanced reliability and consistency. A sample format follows:

Class Record

Date:

Topics Discussed:

Key Points:

Learning Activities:

Handouts:

Websites and Other Resources:

Upcoming Assignments and Due Dates:

Personal Comments:

For additional information, contact _____ (name of class historian).

ACTIVITY 3.17

Class Review

Purpose: To provide group memory of and/or perspectives on topics and issues from the previous session and to support all students in verifying that they have a reliable record of prior learning upon which to build

Time: 15–30 minutes

Format: Triads and large group

Materials: Notes from the prior session

Process

At the beginning of the learning experience, each triad identifies two to three of the most important points, concepts, or ideas from the previous session. Then a reporter from each triad joins a panel of experts at the front of the room and presents a key point discussed in the reporter's triad. Two volunteer scribes take turns recording the contributions of the panel of experts so that there is a written record to which any student may refer for additional information.

ACTIVITY 3.18
Bean Experiment

Purpose: To provide context in which students can examine whether all participants have had an opportunity to comfortably participate in group work

Time: 10–20 minutes when a small-group discussion is part of the learning process

Format: Small groups of five to six students

Materials: A small container of 20–30 beans

Process

Ask each student who participates in a small group to take a bean after speaking. At the end of the learning experience, group members discuss how many beans each person has and the implications of any disparity in numbers. They set personal and team participation goals to support the opportunity for all group members to make meaningful contributions.

ACTIVITY 3.19
Class Agreements or Participation Guidelines

Purpose: To provide an environment for all students to feel respected by other students as well as by their teacher in order to offer their perspectives

Time: 30 minutes

Format: Individuals, triads, and large group

Materials: Handout 3.3, note paper, and pens

Process

Ask students to work individually to review sample guidelines and select, modify, and add other kinds of classroom agreements or guidelines that might help people construct a positive and productive learning environment. Ask students to begin by underlining on Handout 3.3 what they can agree to, modifying what they want to change, and adding addition possibilities. After students discuss their choices in triads, collect the handouts and make a large chart based on students' perspectives. At a follow-up class meeting, students put a star next to what they like, a check next to what they can live with, and a question mark next to what they want the class to reconsider. Class agreements are carefully discussed to ensure mutual understanding of each item. For example, "listen carefully" does not necessarily mean "don't interrupt." Depending on students' backgrounds, especially students from multicultural urban communities, interrupting can be a sign of active listening. However, often students from white, European American communities view interruption as impolite. These are cultural norms that need to be discussed and negotiated.

HANDOUT 3.3

Sample Class Agreements

1. Listen carefully to others.
2. Share air time.
3. Approach conflict as a problem that can be solved.
4. Speak from one's own experience, to say, for example, "I think . . ." or "In my experience I have found . . ." rather than generalizing one's experiences to others, as in "People say . . ." or "We believe . . ."
5. Diminish the temptation to blame others by offering constructive insights and ideas related to a topic or issue.
6. Contribute to the learning of others in ways that are respectful and supportive.

Some schools have schoolwide agreements to promote respect throughout the school. When this is the case, classroom agreements are often focused on collaborative projects and group work.

ACTIVITY 3.20

Note Cues

Purpose: To provide an opening for participants who are cautious about speaking in class, so they can begin to hear their voices and participate in a discussion group

Time: Variable

Format: Individuals

Materials: 3 × 5 note cards with sample questions and comments

Process

Note Cues tell students who are reluctant to speak publically *what* they might say in class discussion, leaving them to think only about *when* they might say it. To encourage their participation, give students who seem consistently reluctant to speak publically a note card with questions or comments that might be made during class discussion. For example, a note card might have the question "Would you please provide an example to clarify that point?" The person with the note card then decides at what point he or she will make this contribution to the discussion. The reading of teacher-prepared notes may seem like mindless parroting, but it can help students feel more competent by helping them practice situationally appropriate ways to participate in discussion. This strategy can also be designed to foster progressively greater forms of independence in question posing—for example, encouraging a student to ask a certain kind of question, such as a question that asks for another perspective (Wilson, 1995, p. 29).

Source: Adapted from Manzo & Manzo (1990).

ACTIVITY 3.21

Cooperative Groups

Purpose: To provide a setting in which students can construct and extend their understanding of a topic through group discussion, joint resolution of a problem, or feedback about how effectively procedures are performed. An example of this strategy is peer editing, in which each person looks for specific attributes in the written work of group members.

Cooperative learning is a form of rigorous collaborative learning. Its fundamental components are positive interdependence, individual accountability, promotive interaction, social skills, and group processing (Johnson & Johnson, 2006).

Time: Variable, according to the task

Format: Typically groups of three to five students

Materials: Variable, according to the task

Process

There is a wide variety of cooperative learning methods, and most emphasize students' exploration and interpretation of course material to an equal or greater extent than they do the teacher's explication of it. One way to introduce cooperative learning to students is to divide the class into four research groups using the jigsaw strategy. As an initial introduction to the process, proceed through the following steps for structuring a jigsaw lesson.

1. *Cooperative groups:* Assign a different cooperative learning website to each member of a four-person group. For example, one group member might be directed toward research on cooperative learning that is based on Robert and David Johnson's work at the University of Minnesota (see www.context.org/iclib/ic18/johnson). Another group member might be assigned to Elizabeth Cohen, Rachel Lotan, and colleagues' complex instruction work that originated at Stanford (see http://cgi.stanford.edu/group/pci/cgi-bin/site.cgi). Another student might focus on project-based learning as organized by Edutopia (see www.edutopia.org/project-based-learning). The fourth student might begin with a whole-school model such as Expeditionary Learning, which crosses grade levels and content areas (see http://elschools.org/best-practices and http://elschools.org/student-work). High school teachers might prefer to direct students to Work That Matters (www.innovationunit.org/sites/default/files/Teacher's%20Guide%20to%20Project-based%20Learning.pdf). This comprehensive guide to project-based learning grew out of a partnership between New Tech High Schools in San Diego and the Learning Futures Project in England. Another website that may be helpful is author and prolific blogger Larry Ferlazzo's "Best Sites for Cooperative Learning Ideas" (http://larryferlazzo.edublogs.org/2010/04/02/the-best-sites-for-cooperative-learning-ideas).

    Note: A valuable international resource, especially for teachers working with ethnically and linguistically diverse students, is the International Association for the Study of Cooperation in Education (www.iasce.net). This professional organization publishes a newsletter and is dedicated to educators who research and practice cooperative education and democratic social processes across the globe.

2. *Preparation pairs:* Assign students the cooperative task of meeting with someone else in the class who is a member of another cooperative group and who has the same topic and website. They are to complete two tasks: (a) learning and becoming an expert on their material and (b) planning how to teach the material to the other members of their groups.

3. *Practice pairs:* Assign the pair of students the cooperative task of meeting with another pair who have learned the same material and share ideas as to how the material may best be taught. These "practice pairs" review what and how each student in each pair plans to teach her or his group. The best ideas of both pairs are incorporated into each student's presentation.

4. *Cooperative groups:* Assign students the cooperative tasks of (a) teaching their area of expertise to the other group members and (b) learning the material being taught by the other members.

5. *Evaluation:* Assess the students' degree of understanding of all the material.

Source: Adapted from Johnson, Johnson, & Smith (1991, p. 4:17).

Note: Amid the many collaborative learning possibilities, cooperative learning has a particularly strong research base, including a meta-analysis of 375 relevant experimental studies (Johnson, 2003) in which research participants varied in age, economic class, and cultural background.

Over two decades of studies suggest that well-designed collaborative and cooperative learning impacts academic content knowledge, grade point averages, student retention, and preparation for college. Across cultural and linguistic groups, cooperative learning researchers have found that this approach to learning

- provides students with social support and encouragement for taking risks in increasing personal competencies,
- encourages accountability among peers for practicing and learning procedures and skills,
- offers students a pathway to new attitudes about learning,
- helps students establish a shared identity with other group members,
- helps students find effective peers to emulate, and
- provides a means for students to validate their own learning.

As Jenny Nagaoka and colleagues (2012) at the University of Chicago point out, many school reform efforts are unsuccessful because they are based on the values of relentless individualism and competition. Collaborative and cooperative learning represent another value system, one that holds cooperation and community to be as important as academic achievement. These approaches invite learners to offer their perspectives and to listen to the voices of others, to deliberate and to build consensus, and to find academic learning a model of an equitable means to civic life.

These are foundational skills for both K–12 and postsecondary success. Although collaborative and cooperative learning may be particularly effective for students who are from communities that have been historically underserved in schools, and especially for students who are learning English along with academic content, almost everyone benefits (Zakaria, Solfitri, Daud, & Abidin, 2013).

From a motivational perspective, cooperative learning is particularly effective when teachers (1) help students develop relationships; (2) promote a genuine need to understand high-level content and skills in order to solve rigorous problems; (3) ensure that problems or projects are authentic, creative, and interdisciplinary; and (4) assist students in learning the art of project management. Excellent online examples of project-based and inquiry-focused collaborative and cooperative learning are widely available. Chapter 6 further explores collaborative learning with a focus on feedback, revision, and public presentations that matter to students and their communities. Exhibit 3.2 provides a simple form to help organize cooperative learning groups.

Exhibit 3.2   Cooperative Lesson Planning Guide

Step 1: Select an activity and desired outcome(s).

Step 2: Makes decisions.
   a. Group size:
   b. Assignment to groups:
   c. Room arrangement:
   d. Materials needed for each group:
   e. Roles:

Step 3: State the activity in language your students understand.
   a. Task:
   b. Positive interdependence (i.e., how each person is invaluable to completing the task):
   c. Individual accountability:
   d. Collective accountability:
   e. Criteria for success:
   f. Specific behaviors or agreements to encourage among group members (especially in heterogeneous groups where status issues could interfere with shared respect and learning):

Step 4: Encourage.
   a. Evidence of cooperative interactions:
   b. Potential assistance needed:

(Continued)

Exhibit 3.2 (Continued)

Step 5: Evaluate outcomes.
       a. Task achievement:
       b. Group functioning:
       c. Ways to strengthen support for individual students:
       d. Feedback to offer:

Step 6: Determine specific ways to enhance individual accountability, including the following:

- Keep the size of the groups small (typical size is two to four members). Keep the role of each learner distinct.
- Assess learners individually as well as collectively.
- Observe and encourage groups while they are working.
- Randomly request that individuals present what they are learning to you or another group.
- Request periodic self-assessments and outlines of responsibilities from individual group members.

Source: Adapted from Johnson et al. (1991, pp. 4:35–4:36).

Note: A simple and positive way to support individual accountability and prevent related conflict among group members is to brainstorm answers to the questions: How would we like to find out if someone in our cooperative learning group thought we were not doing enough to contribute to the total group's benefit? What are some acceptable ways of letting us know? Then write the possible actions on the chalkboard and discuss them. Such a procedure can go a long way toward avoiding unnecessary suspicion or shame (Wlodkowski, 2008, p. 146).

ACTIVITY 3.22

Cooperative Base Groups

Purpose: To develop heterogeneous, cooperative learning groups that meet regularly, last for the duration of a course, have a stable membership, and provide support, encouragement, and assistance in completing assignments and to hold each other accountable for striving to learn (Johnson et al., 1991). The larger the class and/or the more complex the subject matter, the more base groups can provide a sense of connectedness and reduce feelings of isolation or frustration. Such groups also increase the probability that diverse perspectives will be shared, increasing the understanding and intrinsic value of a learning experience.

Time: Variable, according to the task

Format: Typically groups of four to five students

Materials: Variable, according to the task

Process

To effectively establish base groups, I suggest the following guidelines and goals adapted from the work of Johnson et al. (1991).

1. Before assigning base groups, use cooperative learning groups from the very beginning of the course for class activities and instructional purposes until the five essential components (see the section on cooperative learning in this chapter) are understood and some expertise in using cooperative learning is evident among the learners.

2. Have a reasonable awareness of your students, and wait for class membership to stabilize before assigning base groups.

3. Set base groups at four to five members to allow for more diversity and lessen the pressure of initial interdependence.

4. Schedule regular meetings of the base groups during class time. (The beginning and/or end of class often works best.)

5. Ensure the purposes of the base groups are well understood.

6. The following goals for base groups can be modified according to course and learners' needs:
   - To clarify learning goals, class content, and/or homework assignments
   - To provide feedback, support, and encouragement for mastering course content and skills
   - To develop expertise in intellectual controversy
   - To complete work done on time
   - To apply new learning to one's own life and other contexts
   - To develop trustworthy "critical friends" throughout the course and as a means for trying out collaborative learning procedures and skills
   - To provide a structure for managing course procedures, such as homework, attendance, and assessment
   - To share the rewards of the members' talents and experiences

To ensure adequate structure, especially in the beginning phase, provide an agenda for base group meetings. Developing an agenda that considers what students believe to be most important to discuss at this point in their learning experience has the additional benefit of helping you develop a regular system to learn from students' perspectives on their needs. For example, regularly and in advance of constructing a home group agenda, you might briefly conference with three students—a student who is currently low performing, a student who falls somewhere in the middle, and a student who is currently high performing.

Depending on student needs, an agenda could include the following:

1. Check in, using such questions as: How are group members doing? Is everyone prepared for this class period? Has everyone read the assignment? Has everyone done the problems?

2. Focus on academic support by checking what assignments each member has yet to complete and what help she or he may need to understand or complete the work.

3. Prepare for tests and review them afterward.

4. Help each other practice skills (during or outside of class) by sharing expertise.

5. Summarize, review, or critique what students have written.

6. Share resources students have found regarding course content and assignments.

Some base groups face relationship challenges. Some take longer to cohere. Teacher patience, periodically assessing how base groups are functioning with a short survey, and being available to meet with groups to enhance relationships are ways to ensure the effectiveness of this structure from the beginning to the end of a course.

STRENGTHENING STUDENT-TEACHER RELATIONSHIPS

Across ethnic, linguistic, and socioeconomic groups, there are four basic assurances that students would like to receive from their teachers.

- The teacher is going to respect and value students.
- The teacher is going to keep students' safety and well-being in mind at all times.
- The teacher is going to do everything he or she can to help all students become responsible, caring, and well-educated people.
- The teacher is a skillful educator.

While these assurances are essential, they are only part of a comprehensive approach to strong relationships with students. Effective two-way communication is fundamental as well.

Positive communication and mutual trust are often strengthened by thoughtful email messages, brief phone calls, or postcards that arrive before a school year or prior to the start of a course. Open-ended questionnaires to elicit students' perspectives on their learning experiences and occasional lunches with students also help to forge valuable connections. The main idea is to let students know that, first and foremost, you as a teacher value students as human beings and are accessible.

Here are some questions (always age-appropriate) that allow students to know they are valued and that you are accessible: What do you like most about school? What would make school more interesting or enjoyable? What activities does your family enjoy together? What, in general, gives you strength? What skills or knowledge might you be able to share with other students? What are some questions you haven't had a chance to ask and would value information about?

Even when questions are focused on strengths, the purpose should be clear, including how a teacher will use information and whether it will be kept confidential. Finally, students should always have the option of not participating in conversations and activities that are personal or in which they may feel they will have limited control.

Experienced teachers often have important information about the following questions that new teachers may want to ask:

- How do you maintain a flexible and accessible approach to meeting with students? How, if at all, do you set aside personal time for getting to know students?
- How do you create a welcoming environment that encourages authentic informal conversation with students? What ideas do you have for posting pictures of students or people who matter to students and to you? Posting student work? Posting signs in multiple languages? Having an abundance of books that are written by people from the various cultural groups represented in the school or community? Helping students feel comfortable throughout the school?
- What have you learned about being a good listener? What are some basic norms of respect you try to abide by? What ideas do you have for good conversation starters? Prompting deeper conversation? Inviting different perspectives? Being careful about clichéd responses? (Sometimes older students find the active listening technique to be clichéd or tedious. You may want to ask colleagues about how they communicate with students to make sure that they have been heard.)

- What suggestions do you have for sharing information in ways that are sincere, specific, and hopeful? What have you learned about praise that is culturally relevant and that avoids being controlling or contrived?
- How do you ensure that students have equal access to resources?
- What have you learned about concluding communication on a hopeful note? When you discuss students' mistakes or challenges, how do you also discuss ways that students can apply other forms of skill and competence to improving their work? How do you set goals so that they are valued and realistic?

Strong two-way communication is essential to acceptance when, later in the relationship, there is miscommunication or a mistake has been made. In such instances, it is also helpful to have an approach to solving problems.

Solving Problems

Many students are gifted problem solvers. However, because of what's at stake, strong emotions are often just below the surface when a problem arises. Skillful teachers know that a one-size-fits-all, step-by-step approach to work through problems is likely to lead to more problems. In our most troubling moments, none of us wants to be reduced to or controlled by a formulaic sequence. That said, it is advisable to have a basic protocol that can be easily adapted to the nuances of different situations.

In problematic situations, an advisable first step is to offer a sincere expression of empathy, such as "This is an issue I care about as well" or "I can relate to your frustration." Insinuating that you *know* how a student feels is most likely a step too far. This is especially important when a teacher is white and a student is from a non-white community that has been historically marginalized. No matter how much a teacher from a dominant culture may care about students, white educators do not personally know the ways in which race, racism, and issues of power are interacting—or not—in any given situation.

Following an empathic start, a wise next step is to invite a student(s) to sit down with you to share information and think through possible solutions. Beyond the courtesy of reaching out, an invitation helps to ensure that students are ready to talk. Finally, if the time is right to set some goals, you may want to remember that this is a shared, creative process in which you as the teacher do not need to, nor should you, have all the answers.

If the situation allows for goal setting, a simple approach usually works well. Clarity, alignment, and evidence of success are three objectives that problem solvers keep in mind. In other words, make sure the problem you are trying to solve is clear, and be clear about the solution. Then, ensure that the solution is aligned with the problem so that you have a tight "if-then" sequence. To put it another way, you want to be able to say, "*If* we do this, *then* this will happen." Finally, identify the specific kind of data you will collect to show evidence of progress.

Evidence doesn't need to be numerically measurable; it can be anecdotal. For example, if a child has been having troubling interactions with another child, keeping some notes about what you are doing to help with the situation and what results you see can constitutes a credible form of data that can provide evidence of success or of the need to reconsider a course of action. Whether you conclude your conversation with a better understanding of a problem or a plan to resolve things, try to follow up as soon as possible. In a challenging situation, a simple note that says, "I appreciated the chance to understand the problem, and here is what I am doing about it," shows concern and responsiveness. This is often the beginning of a loyal two-way partnership for learning.

Rethinking Homework

The topic of homework is included here because it is too often a cause of frustration for teachers and students and it can interfere with mutual respect and connectedness. Although teachers (and students) may have entirely different perspectives than the ones in this section, the goal is to contribute to conversations about this understandably complex issue.

Homework is an intriguing word. For students who have welcoming homes, it combines the comfortable thought of "home" at the end of a long day with the dissonance of more "work." For students who have responsibilities that take them away from their homes, it can be a source of constant anxiety. And for students who are without support or means to complete homework, it can erode a hopeful orientation to a promising future.

Although teachers and parents commonly believe that homework is fundamental to academic success, its relationship to high grades is somewhat counterintuitive. In fact, in recent years researchers have become aware that often the students who already are high achieving are the students who are most likely to turn in their homework. Because of this, many teachers have become more conscientious about assigning meaningful homework and many teachers have stopped grading homework. Instead, they encourage completion without penalizing students' grade point average by providing time in class for students to share what they have learned through homework assignments, writing comments on homework that show evidence of the impact of the assignment on student learning, and allowing students to use their homework on open-book tests.

It is interesting to note that in a study of 50 countries, those that are seen as being the most educationally effective are the least likely to grade homework. While 70% of U.S. teachers said they calculate homework into students' final grade, only 14% in Japan and 9% in Singapore do so. In fact, the study found a negative correlation between grading homework and increased achievement (D. Baker & LeTendre, 2005). *Homework's value lies not in a grade but in the student's value for learning.* To create motivationally and academically effectively homework assignments, consider the following:

- Make the assignment directly relevant to a classroom learning experience.
- Give assignments that are clear.
- Create interesting assignments, including assignments about which you are enthusiastic.
- Develop assignments that are challenging and stimulating and that require skills and knowledge that are within the range of students' current capabilities.
- Implement a cooperative telephone network among older students so that everyone has access to a peer or support person who can provide assistance.
- Brief students—and parents—on your system of homework. How much do you typically assign and how often? What is its function? Understandably, students value knowing that teachers do not use homework to control their behavior. Homework is for learning, and there are more effective ways to help students learn responsibility than rewarding or penalizing them for work they have or have not completed.

Meaningless homework bears a relationship to mindless videogames or television. It can override rich curiosity, creativity, and social responsibility and contribute to a student's desire to just get it done in ways that don't require intellectual responsibility or courage. In fact, you may want to provide a gentle reminder to parents to try to avoid offering television viewing as a reward for homework completion. Instead, they might create family experiences such as cooking, sharing a book, exercising, playing games, doing puzzles, enjoying the arts, or simply engaging in conversation. These are activities that are rewarding in ways that enhance emotional, physical, and cultural well-being. On this note, when adult family members are willing to share some of what they are learning—from work, their community, or their child—it communicates the importance of education as a shared enterprise. Most students are curious about what parents or family members are learning, especially when they assist with school activities. Such a conversation topic can be a valuable ending to finishing homework.

Recognizing that school success or failure is often a social and political challenge as well as an educational one, the need for partnerships with students that provide a sustained focus on their well-being and academic success is imperative. Data that point to persistent gaps in learning outcomes among diverse student groups suggest that helping students feel valued as human beings and learners can require reexamining historical assumptions about homework.

Dealing With Resistance

Learning experiences that are new and complex can provoke some version of "We don't need this" or "This is going to be a waste of time." Chapter 4, on the second condition of the motivational framework (developing a positive attitude toward learning), provides specific strategies to effectively introduce new challenges to students. Regarding respectful and inclusive relationships, which are the topic of this chapter, when resistance occurs, it is usually best to openly acknowledge it and the possible feelings that may be occurring in the group. Then you can plan or engage in learning that emphasizes immediate relevance and choice for students (discussed in the next chapter). These procedures have a good chance of moving the group forward.

Of course, resistance can also occur at any time during a learning experience. Most resistance appears to stem from apprehensions about vulnerability or control. Although this book advocates changing conventional teaching practices, many students (and teachers) have formed habits and expectations that run counter to some of our suggested approaches. To negatively label concerns or reluctance to maintain an open mind as "resistance" is usually ineffective. It can divert attention from real goals and concerns such as the need for emotional safety or greater clarity regarding learning goals and processes. In addition, labeling other people can lead to thinking that immobilizes a teacher's creativity.

One way to think about resistance is as a concern about difficult realities. For example, if a student in a learning situation maintains that there is not enough time to discuss a controversial topic when the time is actually available, he or she is probably being resistant. However, if there is really not enough time for an adequate discussion, the student is judiciously expressing a realistic concern.

A formulaic set of guidelines for dealing with resistance can exacerbate frustration. Tense situations are contextually determined (who, what, where, when, and so forth) and a lockstep process that does not consider the complexity and variation in a scenario may delay, but does not often resolve, tension around an issue. It is wise to focus on a positive interpretation of resistance, respectfully listen, and elicit information about the nature of a student's concerns. It can also be helpful to request examples and evidence of "the problem" as well as suggestions for other courses of action. One approach to communication is to use *suppose* or words to that effect to introduce ideas, to probe a comment, or to keep a conversation more open ("Suppose we . . .").

In closing this chapter it is important to acknowledge that a mere strategy does not create a milieu of emotional safety and respect. Inclusion is the result of complex interactions. The options and considerations in this chapter are meant to contribute to a teacher's nuanced repertoires for working with students from a range of backgrounds. Although the four conditions of the motivational framework (establishing inclusion, developing a positive attitude, enhancing meaning, and engendering competence) work in concert and are interdependent, the specific practices in this chapter can vitally contribute to inclusive classrooms where students take important risks as learners.

If we reconsider the scenario that began this chapter, we now see that Roberta James has several options that could positively influence Damean's comfort in his small group. First, she can select from the set of multidimensional sharing options to promote relationships that allow students to more comfortably communicate their concerns to one another and with her. She could use the Cooperative Lesson Planning Guide (Exhibit 3.2) to plan, discuss, and support group work. In addition, she might consider which assignment each group member is responsible for and find time for brief personal check-ins with individuals. She can also assess how groups are functioning with a short survey, share the data with students, and facilitate a large-group conversation about effective collaboration. She might begin the conversation about effective collaboration by asking each group to create a visual representation titled "The Secrets of Our Success."

The challenge for Ms. James and all teachers is to consistently model respectful practices from the beginning to the end of every class session, course, and personal interaction. Of course, we all make mistakes and let time get the better of us in ways that interfere with the goals we would like to achieve. An attribute of great teachers is their refusal to allow mistakes to thwart their vision and imagination for developing a classroom that is welcoming, supportive, and productive for every student. In education, rich and authentic relationships between students and teachers are the foundation for student success. In a broader sense, they suggest to students that respect and interdependence are achievable goals.

SUMMARY

This chapter emphasized a fundamental need that all learners share—the need for a safe and supportive environment in which to learn. It provided strategies for teachers to build mutually supportive relationships among students and between students and teachers in which every person feels respected and connected. This is the challenge of the first condition of the motivational framework: establishing inclusion.

Chapter 4 introduces the second condition of the motivational framework: developing a positive attitude. As is true for all for motivational conditions, establishing inclusion and developing a positive attitude are interdependent. In the absence of trustworthy relationships (establishing inclusion), human beings are less likely to engage with opportunities for choice and relevant learning experiences (developing a positive attitude). A safe and unthreatening environment is foundational to a positive attitude toward learning. Teachers appreciate that many of the strategies in the following chapter can be adapted to enlarge their repertoires for establishing inclusion *and* developing a positive attitude toward learning.

LIST OF ACTIVITIES AND
MAJOR TOPICS FROM CHAPTER 3

The following checklist can serve as a guide to teachers, providing considerations for creating the conditions of respect and connectedness for establishing inclusion. The subsequent list includes the activities in this chapter that have been described with attention to time, materials, and a reasonably precise process for carrying them out.

Establishing Inclusion

How does the learning experience contribute to developing as a community of learners who feel respected and connected to one another?

Routines and rituals are visible and understood by all:

_____ Rituals are in place that help everyone feel that they belong in the class.

_____ Students and teacher(s) have opportunities to learn about each other.

_____ Students and teachers(s) have opportunities to learn about each other's backgrounds.

_____ Classroom agreements/rules and consequences for violating agreements are negotiated.

_____ The system of discipline is understood by all students and applied with fairness.

Evidence

All students are equitably and actively participating/interacting:

_____ Teacher directs attention equitably.

_____ Teacher interacts respectfully with all students.

_____ Teacher demonstrates to all students that he or she cares about them.

_____ Students talk to/with a partner/small group.

_____ Students respond to the lesson by writing.

_____ Students know what to do, especially when making choices.

_____ Students help each other.

_____ Student work is displayed

Evidence

Opportunities for Multidimensional Sharing (Narrated Information, p. 48)

Allow Time for Introductions (Narrated Information, p. 47)

Venn Diagram (Activity 3.1)

Four Layers of Diversity (Figure 3.2)

Our Stories (Activity 3.2)

Two Wishes and a Truth (Activity 3.3)

Decades and Diversity (Activity 3.4)

Photo Scavenger Hunt (Activity 3.5)

Pair-Share (Activity 3.6)

"Ask Me About . . ." Posters (Activity 3.7)

Multicultural Inventory (Activity 3.8)

Bio-Poems (Activity 3.9)

View From a Window (Activity 3.10)

Check-in Adjectives (Activity 3.11)

Interpretive Community Maps (Activity 3.12)

Dialogue Journals (Activity 3.13)

Response Cards (Activity 3.14)

Fist-to-Five (Activity 3.15)

Class Historian (Activity 3.16)

Class Review (Activity 3.17)

Bean Experiment (Activity 3.18)

Class Agreements or Participation Guidelines (Activity 3.19)

Note Cues (Activity 3.20)

Cooperative Groups (Activity 3.21)

Rethinking Homework (Narrated Information, p. 77)

Solving Problems (Narrated Information, p. 76)

Dealing With Resistance (Narrated Information, p. 79)

4 Developing a Positive Attitude

Any human anywhere will blossom in a hundred unexpected talents and capacities simply by being given the opportunity to do so.

—Doris Lessing, author

Although she has above-average grades, Maria Chou feels her positive attitude and her grade point average are slipping away in her eighth-grade science class taught by Beverly Kubiak. Maria was proud to get off to a good start. Because her mother was raised in a small Malaysian community that struggled with waterborne illnesses, Maria wants to be the first person in her family to attend college and she plans to become an environmental engineer. Ms. Kubiak began the course with small-group experiments just like what geologists do when they study sedimentary rocks. However, now Ms. Kubiak's assignments come directly from the textbook, with a lot of information and facts but very little that seems relevant to Maria. She reads and memorizes to pass the tests but has lost her interest in the topics she is studying.

In a hallway conversation, Maria tells Ms. Kubiak how much she enjoyed the beginning of her course. Then she asks Ms. Kubiak if she could make a suggestion. As Ms. Kubiak listens attentively, Maria wonders if there could be more experiments and maybe even a chance to do group projects on some of the environmental issues the textbook explores. Maria explains that this might help her and other students make an even stronger connection between the material they study and to important future interests.

In response to Maria's suggestion, Ms. Kubiak explains that there simply isn't enough time for everything she would like to do. The course standards and the text require her to focus on a specific sequence of skills and knowledge. To alter that pattern would complicate what she is expected to teach as well as significantly increase her workload. With a polite smile, Ms. Kubiak thanks Maria for stopping to talk. As Maria walks along to her next class, Ms. Kubiak reminds her of something Maria has been hearing a lot about lately: Doing well in school requires grit. In life, you can't always have what you want.

The previous chapter explored the first condition of the motivational framework for culturally responsive teaching: establishing inclusion. It provided a rationale and activities to create a welcoming and safe learning environment where students are respected and connected to each other and to their teacher(s). Using a format similar to the previous chapter, this chapter provides a rationale, research-based theory, and activities teachers can adapt to achieve the second condition of the motivational framework: developing a positive attitude. The checklist at the end of the chapter provides considerations for teachers who seek peer support for enhancing students' attitudes about a learning experience.

As addressed earlier in the book, schools today serve many students who have historical and daily experiences that undermine positive beliefs about the significance of school. Yet a favorable predisposition toward a learning environment, a teacher, or a course is a condition for academic success. It supports our ability to effectively interact with unfamiliar people and different approaches to learning. It strengthens our determination to make sense of things.

Nonetheless, developing a positive attitude is a motivational condition that is frequently overlooked by educators. Some of us assume that students simply ought to be "ready to learn" when they enter a classroom. Others try to talk students into learning by accessing their own enthusiasm and ability to persuade, and by teaching about perseverance and grit. Still others believe that as soon as students experience success, a positive attitude will follow. At the end of the day, how we teach has the most enduring impact on students' attitudes. If we expect students to have a positive attitude toward learning, our instructional practices must take into account students' perspectives, interests, and strengths.

All students benefit from relevance and choice, two of the attributes that research associates with a positive attitude toward learning. When relevance and choice are present, most students perceive learning to be appealing and valuable (Deci & Ryan, 1991; Gardner, 2006). Relevance, both personal and cultural, is the degree to which students see their needs, perspectives, values, and experiences in the content, discussion, and methods of learning. Relevant learning opportunities are connected to who students are, what they care about, and how they perceive and make sense of new information.

Choice, the second criteria for developing a positive attitude, connects to the notion of relevance. When students find learning relevant, they are more naturally interested in what they are learning and they then pursue answers to questions of authentic concern. Such self-determination or choosing contributes to a heightened sense of endorsement of and satisfaction from learning. Global history and social science are two areas of study that support this observation: People consistently struggle to determine their lives as an expression of their beliefs and values. Learning is no exception to this desire.

Motivating learning opportunities for diverse students include relevant learning experiences, multiple ways for students to access and demonstrate knowledge, and opportunities for genuine choice. Although there may be certain nonnegotiable expectations, there are many options for shared decision making and personal choice. Examples of choices include how to learn, what to learn, where to learn, when a learning experience will be considered to be complete, how learning will be assessed, with whom to learn, and how to solve emerging problems.

In recent years, relevance and choice have become associated with differentiated learning. This process for teaching dates back at least to ancient Greece and, in more modern times, the one-room schoolhouse in the United States. According to Carol Ann Tomlinson (2014) in *The Differentiated Classroom*, differentiation has come to mean consistently using a variety of instructional approaches to modify content, process, and/or products in response to the learning readiness and interest of academically diverse students. Two excellent resources for differentiating instruction in ways that are culturally responsive and promote relevance and choice are *Reach Every Student Through Differentiated Instruction* (www.edugains.ca/resourcesDI/Brochures/DIBrochureOct08.pdf) and *Culturally Responsive Differentiated Instructional Strategies* (http://steinhardt.nyu.edu/scmsAdmin/uploads/005/120/Culturally%20Responsive%20Differientiated%20Instruction.pdf).

An unfortunate reality for some of us is that we entered the teaching profession with limited knowledge about ways to encourage choice. Offering choice was seen as equivalent to "anything goes." Because of this, the students who dominated were not necessarily the students who manifested a democratic orientation toward learning. What many educators have come to understand is that choice is not a value in and of itself. Its value is meaningful according to the purposes it serves.

As educators, we continuously grapple with the tension between listening to the perspectives of others and maintaining a purposeful agenda of our own. For culturally responsive educators, the challenge is to provide choices that are in harmony, not only with high-quality learning opportunities for all students, but also with a powerful vision of a pluralistic democracy. In other words, the framework within which choices occur must be one that unites academic success with concern for others and responsible participation in local and global communities.

Respect for the authority of students includes helping students learn to use their authority well. One of the best ways a teacher can accomplish this is through communicating which decisions are negotiable and which ones are not. Clarity about decision making helps avoid confusion and mistrust. This is one of the reasons for working with students to establish class agreements, as described in Chapter 3. Such agreements contribute to a respectful and responsible learning environment within which shared and autonomous decisions are encouraged.

The following section of this chapter outlines some practices and activities that contribute to a positive attitude toward learning through relevance and choice. Several of the practices help students apply ideas about relevance and choice to inquiry projects or groupwork. In the 21st century, many schools are organizing themselves around inquiry-focused projects and groupwork that help students learn how to work well with others. This approach requires both theory and strategy because when students understand both sides of the coin, they can construct or elaborate on a host of purposeful activities and perspectives. Without a doubt, one of the most powerful things that teachers do is help students develop positive attitudes toward learning as competent decision makers and motivated architects of opportunity.

MAKING INITIAL LEARNING ACTIVITIES APPEALING AND COLLABORATIVE

The first time students experience anything that is new or that occurs in a different setting, they form an impression that will have a lasting impact. In learning, first impressions are important and we need to make them as positive and motivating as possible. We can achieve this when the learning activity meets the following five criteria adapted from a strategy for creating relevant learning experiences from the work of Raymond Wlodkowski (2008):

1. *Safe:* There is little risk of students suffering any form of personal embarrassment from lack of knowledge, personal self-disclosure, or a hostile or arrogant social environment.

2. *Successful:* There is some form of acknowledgment, consequence, or product that shows that students are effective or, at the very least, that their effort is worthwhile.

3. *Interesting:* The learning activity has some parts that are novel, engaging, challenging, or stimulating.

4. *Self-determined:* Students are encouraged to make choices that affect the learning experience (e.g., what they share, how they learn, what they learn, when they learn, with whom they learn, where they learn, how they are assessed), basing those choices on their values, needs, concerns, or feelings. At the very least, students have an opportunity to voice their perspectives.

5. *Personally and culturally relevant:* The teacher uses students' concerns, interests, or prior experiences to create elements of the learning activity or develops the activity in concert with the students. At the very least, a resource-rich learning environment is available to encourage students' selections based on personal interest. For example, students can easily access a library, the Internet, or a community context for learning.

Brainstorming a topic or inquiry question in small groups is an example of this strategy when

- all answers are initially acceptable (*safe*),
- a list is created and acknowledged (*successful*),
- creative examples from personal experience occur (*interesting*),
- answers are voluntary and self-selected (*self-determined*), and
- the topic is selected by the teacher and students because it is relevant (*personally relevant*).

The following activity is an example of how teachers can apply and teach the criteria for such a positive learning experiences to students. Although the focus of this particular example is group projects, the activity can be adapted to other forms of learning.

ACTIVITY 4.1

The 360-Degree Turnaround for Working Together on Projects

Purpose: To assist students in creating motivational conditions for small-group projects

Time: 1 hour

Format: Large and small group

Materials: Four movable chairs, paper, pens

Process

Step 1   Begin by referring to a multidimensional sharing activity (Venn diagram, two wishes and a truth, etc.), a brainstorming activity, or carousel graffiti, and clearly describe how it met each of the five criteria: safe, successful, interesting, self-determined, and personally relevant (*model* and *think out loud*).

Step 2   Provide a checklist with the five criteria along with prompts and cues. Here are examples of prompts for each criteria:

Safe: To what extent was the learning experience safe for (inclusive of) all group members? Are there ways it could be even more inclusive?

Successful: To what extent was the learning experience successful for all group members? How might it have been more supportive of everyone's success?

Interesting: To what extent was the learning experience interesting for all group members? Are there ways it could have been more interesting?

Personally relevant: To what extent was the learning experience personally relevant to all group members? Are there ways it could have been more relevant?

Self-determined: To what extent was the learning experience an opportunity for everyone to make choices? Are there ways it could have been more supportive of each person's decision making?

Invite three volunteers to join you in front of the group. One represents the safety criteria, one represents the successful and interesting criteria, and one represents the personally relevant and self-determined criteria. Regulate the difficulty by narrating (a video example would be great!) an example of a learning experience that exemplifies the five criteria but *do not* use the words *safe, successful, interesting, personally relevant,* and *self-determined* when describing the activity. Then each volunteer tells you and the other students in the demonstration group how the criteria he or she represents was met by the activity you described. Have a large-group discussion afterward to emphasize and elaborate insights from this round robin process.

Step 3   Explain to students that the next task is to analyze their groupwork in order to make it even stronger. Ask students to form small groups (no more than four people) to repeat a version of the process they have just witnessed. Groups begin the activity by reflecting on groupwork that they have done in this class or another class that meets these five criteria. Each person takes a turn sharing his or her learning activity and the other three participants offer feedback for the criteria each of them represents (as in Step 2). By rotating the role of the teacher who shares the learning activity in the small group, each student can give and receive *reciprocal feedback* about a learning activity. This is an entirely supportive process with students coaching each other to refine their understanding of the five criteria.

Step 4   Now students group themselves in project groups that have been formed for the purpose of investigating a particular topic. Ask group members to apply the five criteria to how they will work together on their project. Their ideas will become a written agreement for how the group will work together based on these criteria.

Note: The architecture of the round robin activity can be used for different teaching purposes when a teacher wants to facilitate the sharing of different perspectives for commonly experienced phenomena. For example, students hear a story or historical event and offer different possible perspectives of various characters (e.g., father, mother, child), political views (e.g., Republican, Democrat, Socialist), or ethnic groups (e.g., Latino, Chinese American, European American, African Americans). In a science course students might review an ecological event from the perspective of a chemist, geologist, or physicist. This exercise can also be used for students to provide supportive peer feedback on a piece of student work using specific criteria for excellence.

As mentioned earlier, many positive learning experiences meet the five criteria for making initial learning activities appealing and collaborative. When an activity or group experience does not go well, the criteria help to critique, refine, and improve it—often through a conversation with a trusted friend. Teachers are wise to resist the temptation to simply throw away imperfect new ideas that are still in the process of being learned. It takes practice to effectively use a new strategy. This is one of the reasons why the second volume of this two-part series can help educators construct a humility-friendly environment in which we are able to maintain a positive attitude toward our own learning.

STRATEGIES TO ELICIT PRIOR KNOWLEDGE AND CURRENT INTERESTS

The KWL process, originated by Donna Ogle (1986), is another example of a positive initial learning strategy. It helps students construct meaning and set personal goals for a new topic or concept based on their prior knowledge. The National Council of Teachers of English, in partnership with the

International Reading Association, provides a colorful and easy-to-use read/write/think KWL creator for students and teachers at www.read-writethink.org/files/resources/interactives/kwl_creator.

ACTIVITY 4.2

KWL

Purpose: To help students build on prior knowledge and personal inter-ests to set learning goals

Time: 20 minutes

Format: Large group

Materials: Whiteboard or PowerPoint with three columns

Process

In the first phase of a KWL process, for example, prior to solving double-digit division problems, students identify and list what they think they *know* about the new topic, a range that can cover anything from things that students think they know about the topic to the topic's relationship to a mathematical formula. This safe and successful approach creates an interesting array of perspectives and historical contexts. It can be elaborated on by asking students to express their ideas outside of the conventions of oral and written discourse. For example, students may relate their experience with a topic through metaphors or art, depicting how they see their comfort in relation to a topic. For example, a student might say she is a newly planted field in need of water when it comes to technical innovation in her life.

In the second phase, the students suggest what they *want* to know about the topic. This self-determined and relevant information may be listed as questions or considerations for exploration and research. In the case of reading a section of text, students would keep their *want* questions in mind, identifying key points but also gaps in what the narrative provides so that they can follow up on their curiosities later. In the last phase, the students identify discoveries and what they have *learned*. This is also an opportunity to discover what has not yet been learned that is of interest.

SETTING GOALS WITH STUDENTS

There are many different methods of goal setting. Strategies like KWL can get the ball rolling. Afterward, teachers become involved in the task of helping students investigate their interests. The following activity is an eclectic adaptation of various models in the literature on assisting students in ways that support a positive attitude and commitment to learning.

ACTIVITY 4.3
Setting and Supporting Students' Goals

Purpose: To help students sustain positive attitudes toward learning throughout a challenging project

Time: 20–60 minutes

Format: Large group

Materials: Case study, which can be adapted for different grade levels and subject matter

Process

To ensure that learning goals have a good chance of being achieved, you can work from or adapt the following case study and criteria to discuss with students. It is adapted from *Diversity and Motivation* (Ginsberg & Wlodkowski, 2009).

Case Study: Leticia George

Leticia George, whose tribal affiliation is Yakima, is a student in an inquiry-focused 11th-grade social studies course. She wants to design, conduct, and report a research study in an area of personal interest that relates to the question: "What motivates students to learn in U.S. schools?" Leticia has questions about the concept of learning styles, especially as it is applied to American Indians. She wants to carry out a study to understand if urban American Indian high school students, when compared to members of their families who live in rural Indian communities, are similar in terms of preferred ways of learning. This is an ambitious study for a high school student. Let's begin the goal-setting process by examining the criterion of achievability.

Achievability: Can the learner reach the learning goal with the skills and knowledge at hand? If not, is there any assistance available, and if so, how dependable is that assistance?

Leticia feels confident, and her competent completion of exercises in class substantiates that confidence. She is also a member of a class cooperative learning group and values her peers as knowledgeable resources. She and her teacher work out a plan that includes a preliminary conference with peers to garner their support and a follow-up email from Leticia to the teacher. Is there enough time to reach the goal? If not, can more time be found, or should the goal be divided into smaller goals? This is a bit tricky. Although Leticia will limit her study to a small sample, this will mean involving, at minimum, two high schools. Can she get the necessary permission? Whom will she interview or survey and when? This could complicate the study and take a lot of time.

Measurability: *How will a student specifically be able to gauge progress toward the goal and its achievement? In many circumstances this can be done quantitatively, in terms of problems completed, pages read, or exercises finished. To respect different conceptualizations of how to accomplish long-range goals, scheduling intervals to talk about evolving student experience is important.*

Leticia and her teacher decide the most important next step is for Leticia to draft a research proposal using an outline her teacher has provided. Then they will work out a schedule for her completion of the study.

Desirability: *Why is the goal important? A student may have to do it or should do it, but does he or she want to do it? If not, then the satisfaction level and sense of self-determination for a student will be less. Goal setting can be used for required tasks, but this is best handled if students are clear about it and teachers admit to students the reality of the situation to avoid any sense of manipulation.*

Leticia wants to do this study. She believes certain teaching practices derived from learning-styles research may not apply to some Northwest Indian tribes or members of urban Indians communities. Because these methods are so often advocated by educators for teaching Indians, she believes more caution about their use may be necessary.

Focus (optional): *For many people, to avoid forgetting or procrastination, it is important to have a plan to keep the goal in the learner's awareness. For others, such an idea may seem oppressive. Possible reminders are a prescheduled set of text messages from a peer, personal outlines, electronic messages to oneself, sticky notes on a timeline, and daily logs.*

Based on prior experience completing complex tasks, Leticia found this option unnecessary.

Identify resources and learning processes with the student. *Engaging students in a conversation about how they would like to reach the learning goal can be a very creative process. This is the time to consider various talents and preferred ways to learn. Will accomplishing the learning goal involve media, art, writing, or some other possibility? What form should it take—a story, a research project, or a personal multimedia presentation? Identifying outside resources, such as library materials, local experts, exemplary models, or films, aids and sometimes inspires the entire learning process.*

Leticia decides to review the literature on learning styles, especially as it refers to American Indians and other indigenous peoples. She also chooses to interview a university professor and an Indian administrator at a local school district. She decides the format for reporting her study should be a conventional and brief research thesis outline.

Commitment: *A formal or informal gesture that indicates a student's acceptance of the learning goal is a valuable part of the goal-setting process. It can range from a shared copy of notes taken at the meeting to a contract. This affirms the student's self-determination and acknowledges the mutual agreement between the student and the teacher, building trust, motivation, and cooperation for further work together.*

> *Leticia composes a contract that can be agreed on at her next meeting with her teacher.*
>
> Review schedule: *Some time for contact between a student and teacher to maintain progress and refine learning procedures is usually necessary, even when students are part of a peer learning community to which they are accountable. Because of the way time varies in its meaning and feeling to different people, contact can be along regular or irregular intervals. The main idea is that support continues.*
>
> *If progress has deteriorated, reexamine the criteria. Also, it may be helpful to search together for informative feedback (Brophy, 2004) with questions such as these: What's working and why? What needs to change (or improve) and how?*
>
> *Leticia and her teacher have three meetings at irregular intervals prior to completion of an excellent study. To find a large enough sample for her research, Leticia eventually involved three high schools. Her research suggested the possibility that previous research conducted on American Indian learning styles is inconclusive across tribal communities and regions. She also learned something valuable about research: When you enter the unscripted realm of authentic research, anticipate that unexpected information or obstacles will occur.*

The activities in the following section provide additional ways to help students develop a positive attitude toward learning through relevance and choice. They are group oriented and can be adapted to any subject matter or grade level.

SCAFFOLDING COMPLEX LEARNING AND ENGLISH LANGUAGE DEVELOPMENT

Lev Vygotsky (1978) is widely recognized for demonstrating that there are many problems and skills a person can solve or master when given appropriate help and support. The following activity is an example of what has become known as assisted learning. It provides scaffolding—giving clues, information, prompts, reminders, and encouragement at the appropriate time and in the appropriate way. This gradually supports independent learning.

Most of us naturally scaffold when we teach someone to drive a car, play a card game, or learn to use a personal computer. By making the implicit explicit, we provide similar support to students who are learning to solve a math problem, conducting an experiment, or writing a clear and cohesive paragraph. The key is to assess where a student needs assistance and structure for ongoing success.

Historically, classrooms in the United States have been highly competitive, favoring students who are independent learners with a high tolerance for abstraction and ambiguity. However, many talented students have not had adequate opportunity to participate in academic discourse, acquire confidence in their writing, and develop different modes of creative self-expression. To do so requires opportunity and support that is concrete, immediate, and relevant to students' needs and perspectives.

The following methods can be used to scaffold more complex learning. The description of each method includes an example of how to assist middle or high school students with writing a research report. It includes some of the principles of the Sheltered Instruction Observation Protocol, commonly known as SIOP (Echevarria, Vogt, & Short, 2004), to ensure that students who are learning academic English in addition to learning how to write a research report have adequate assistance.

ACTIVITY 4.4

Building on the Strengths of English Language Learners

Purpose: To help students who are learning English as well as challenging content sustain positive attitudes toward learning throughout a learning experience

Time: Varies according to the task

Format: Large group

Materials: Varies according to the task

Process

Step 1 *Preview key vocabulary, concepts, and how the text is organized:* Help students understand a few essential vocabulary words and concepts that are part of the lesson. Also preview an article students will read by reviewing the organization, section headings, and illustrations of the article. Then provide a handout with sentence starters that students can use for a guide while reading as well as complete in a small-group discussion of the article.

Step 2 *Model:* Demonstrate how to begin a research paper while students observe, or offer examples of learning outcomes, such as completed papers or solved problems. You could ask students to read two previously submitted reports. One is excellent, the other is satisfactory. They discuss criteria for an excellent paper.

Step 3   *Think out loud:* Articulate your thought processes while performing the demonstration. Talk to yourself—out loud—about some of your goals related to reading another person's research report on a topic about which you are interested. Also think out loud about features of a strong report and ways in which you can create one yourself. This, in fact, is often a good time to check in with students and ask why they think one report might be considered excellent and the other only satisfactory. When modeling, supplement the students' perceptions with your own. To assist English language learners and English-dominant students when thinking out loud, use a Venn diagram or another graphic organizer to help everyone think about their thinking. For example, ask students to consider their own points of view as they read an article or report, and show how they can use a basic Venn diagram to compare their own thinking with an author's thinking. One circle of the Venn diagram is "I think . . ." and the other circle is "Author thinks. . . ." The overlapping circle in the center is where you note some of the overlapping ideas that you and the author share.

Step 4   *Anticipate difficulties:* Discuss with students areas in which mistakes seem more likely to occur and where support may be needed. Because the sections of the report that discuss findings and analyses seem most challenging to students, carefully point out these sections in the two reports and tell students that when they start to write these sections, you will be their consultant and provide prompt feedback. Also invite three former students from different backgrounds and language groups who did excellent work in different ways to come and talk about their research and writing process, including challenges they encountered and what they learned from those challenges. Save time for current students to ask questions, which they anonymously write on 3×5 cards and submit to the panel via you so that people who are less confident when asking questions publically can also participate.

Step 5   *Provide prompts and cues:* As students examine other students' work (or your work), highlight critical features of the report(s) and personalize procedural steps that respond to individual learner strengths and challenges. Being careful not to overwhelm, help students clearly identify accomplishments and their importance to the learning task while limiting suggestions to two or three key opportunities for improvement. Provide an outline for each assignment and for the final research report with exemplars from previous student reports to increase clarity and promote success.

Step 6 *Regulate the difficulty:* As students master initial skills and gain confidence, introduce a more complex task and perhaps offer some practice with it. Give students a very basic research scenario, a hypothesis, data, and an analysis scheme, and ask them to write a brief research report in class with this information. Ask students who are strong in Spanish and are learning English to sit next to students who are strong in English and respectful of linguistic challenges that peers may experience.

Step 7 *Use reciprocal teaching:* Students rotate the role of teacher with one another. While you observe and provide support when needed, students present their brief research report to a learning partner who acts as the teacher and gives supportive feedback, identifying—along with specific accomplishments—no more than two to three suggestions. Then they reverse roles.

Step 8 *Provide a checklist:* As previously mentioned in the discussion of prompts and cues, students use self-checking procedures to monitor the quality of their learning. Provide a checklist of questions and criteria to consider as students write their reports. Consider the possible metaphors for a provider of assisted learning: respectful tutor, experienced coach, wise friend—all of whom are people who tell us just enough, what we need to know when we need to know it, trusting us to chart the rest of our journey to learning. The image of the student is not one of the rugged individualist or the solitary explorer. Assisted learning embraces a vision of students as competent learners nurtured by a supportive community.

HELPING STUDENTS ATTRIBUTE THEIR SUCCESS TO THEIR CAPABILITY, EFFORT, AND KNOWLEDGE

Students frequently think about the consequences of their behavior. If they experience success, they will typically reflect on a reason or cause for that success, for example, "I think I did well in this debate because I put a lot of work into preparing for it." Educational psychologists call these inferred causes *attributions* (Gordon & Graham, 2006). When students experience success—complete a fine project, solve a challenging problem, earn a high score on an important test—their attitude toward learning is generally enhanced if they believe the major causes for this success are their capability, effort, and knowledge (Weiner, 2000). This positive effect on their motivation occurs because such beliefs lead to feelings of personal control and possession of the causes of their success. Unlike other possible attributes such as luck or an easy task, successful students know that when they exert effort through study and practice, they will become more knowledgeable. Because capability has a stable quality to it (it lasts), students tend to feel more confident when approaching similar learning experiences in the future. Also, attributions to effort provide realistic hopes when learning outcomes are not successful. Students are more likely to believe that trying harder and seeking new strategies for learning will make a positive difference.

ACTIVITY 4.5

Practices That Help Students Attribute Success to Effort and Knowledge

Purpose: To help students attribute their success to their effort and knowledge

Time: Varies according to the task

Format: Large group

Materials: Varies according to the task

Process

Step 1 Provide students with learning tasks suitable to their current skill level. "Just within reach" is a good rule of thumb. These kinds of tasks challenge students' capabilities and require knowledge and moderate effort for success.

Step 2 Before initiating a learning task, remind students of the importance of their effort and knowledge in pursuing success.

Step 3 End verbal and written messages in ways that accentuate students' perceptions of effort and knowledge in relation to their success. Here are a few examples: "That's a perceptive performance." "Great to see your hard work pay off." "Your effort was strategic and it made a real difference."

Step 4 When learning tasks are suitable to students' current skill level, help them understand that effort and knowledge are the path to improving learning outcomes. For example, "I realize you are disappointed with how this assignment turned out, but there is evidence throughout your work that with continued effort you will achieve a rewarding outcome. I hope you will keep on going! Here are some additional strategies to consider."

ACTIVITY 4.6

Finding Numbers: A Strategy for Students to Understand Effort With Strategy

Purpose: To help students realize how important effort with strategy are for effective learning and performance

Time: 20 minutes

Format: Large group

Materials: Sets of three papers per participant with apparently random numbers on each of them

Process

Prior to meeting with students, prepare a sheet of paper with numbers from 1 to 50 on it. Begin by folding the paper in half and then in half once more. You now have four quadrants. Write the number 1 in the upper left quadrant and then continue clockwise: 2 in the upper right quadrant, 3 in the lower right quadrant, 4 in the lower left quadrant, 5 in the upper left quadrant, and so on up to 50. Write the numbers at different angles so that when you make a copy of this master sheet, the numbers appear random and scattered. Create enough copies so each participant can receive three.

During class, pass out three copies to each student and issue the following directions: "This is an exercise that allows us to see the benefits of applying effort and strategy to learning. This is especially important when we are frustrated and decide we are just not smart enough to accomplish a challenging task. Please take out your first sheet of paper and wait until I signal you to begin. When I give the signal, quickly circle numbers in order from 1 to 50. We'll see how many you can consecutively circle starting with 1, then 2, then 3, and so forth in 30 seconds. Okay, please begin. (wait 30 seconds) Please stop."

Take a few moments to see which students had the highest amount of numbers consecutively circled, but do not discuss why. Now indicate that the first try could be considered a practice round; in the second round appeal to students' effort and ask them with good humor to "try harder" using the second sheet. Proceed as before, timing the round at 30 seconds and seeing who had the highest amount of numbers consecutively circled. Ask how many people improved (had more numbers consecutively circled in the second round) as a result of "trying harder." Usually, a few people will actually do less well. Note this, but at this point don't discuss it.

Tell students that the third round demonstrates the advantages of combining effort with an effective strategy. Have them fold the third sheet in half, then again, so that there are four quadrants. Show how the pattern of numbers emerges by looking clockwise for numbers in each of the four quadrants. For example, the number 1 is in the top left corner, 2 is in the top right corner, 3 is in the bottom right corner, and 4 is in the bottom left corner. With this knowledge, ask students to once again consecutively circle as many numbers as they can in 30 seconds, beginning only when you signal them. Afterward, ask how many students improved their performance and by how much. For example, how many doubled the numbers they circled? The improvement should be vast for most people.

Conclude with a whole-group discussion of how this activity relates to the theory that being smart is not something that is fixed. People become smarter by knowing how to learn and putting forth effort. Perhaps, ask how "working smarter" has made a difference in their lives outside of school. The following activity helps students see themselves as having the capacity to be capable, creative, and joyful. It helps them recall and analyze experiences and feelings associated with their own resources for being intrinsically motivated.

ACTIVITY 4.7

All People Are Motivated!

Purpose: To show students that *all* people are motivated and that there are ways in which we can make our motivation even stronger

Time: 30 minutes

Format: Dyads with large-group debrief

Materials: PowerPoint slides or whiteboard

Process

Using the think/pair/share structure, ask students to think silently about a time in which they were learning something and felt capable, creative, and joyful at the same time. Also ask them to think about the situation in which these feelings occurred: with whom, where, when, and under what conditions.

After 1–2 minutes, ask students to share their experience with another student, focusing on what was happening that supported them in feeling capable, creative, and joyful. After a few minutes, ask students to share what they discussed and post this information electronically or on the board. Possible responses include "I didn't feel worried" or "I was involved in a task that was a good challenge." After compiling a list of conditions, point out that this exercise helps them identify the conditions of intrinsic motivation that enhance their motivation and skill as learners. When the right conditions exist, intrinsic motivation emerges. Just as important, we can create these conditions when we are learning something new.

Debrief: Ask students to consider what this means with respect to their effectiveness as learners. Depending on the context, this activity can serve as a segue to a deeper discussion of the difference between intrinsic and exclusively extrinsic motivation and to the Motivational Framework for Culturally Responsive Teaching. In some schools students learn the four conditions of the motivational framework so that they can work with their teachers to create optimal conditions for learning (Chopra, 2014).

CREATING A LEARNING ENVIRONMENT WITH A BLAME-FREE AND REALISTICALLY HOPEFUL VIEW OF PEOPLE AND LEARNING

Justice and equity inhabit a hopeful consciousness. They resist cynicism and accusation. Often when people experience frustration or difficult challenges, they attribute the responsibility for these circumstances to others rather than themselves. Commonly, this is known as *blame.* Although the tendency to blame, especially when one is frustrated, is tempting, it reduces our sense of responsibility, drains energy away from problem solving, and is damaging to relationships among people, especially culturally different people with fragile trust relationships. The following exercise can help students explore blame and develop a strategy to turn blame around when it occurs.

ACTIVITY 4.8

Understanding Blame

Purpose: To show students how to convert blame to hope

Time: 30 minutes

Format: Large group

Materials: PowerPoint slide with a blame cycle (see Exhibit 2.2 in Chapter 2)

Process

Explain to students that the blame cycle in Exhibit 2.2 graphically represents the series of outcomes that seem to emerge automatically with devastating impact on the relationship of the people involved. In this instance the cycle occurs in the relationship between a teacher and student.

Let us say that in this case the student has done poorly on a weekly quiz. At the top of the cycle the teacher wants to help because the student appears to be struggling and sincerely wants to improve. The teacher's normal procedure is to encourage persistence, greater effort, and study habits that might include reviewing notes and outlining chapters. The student sees the problem as the quizzes containing irrelevant material that she has to memorize without a meaningful context or personal application. The teacher acknowledges the student's comments but with little empathy or validation. The teacher continues to emphasize his previous advice. When the student leaves class, her frustration is noticeable.

When the student again comes to see the teacher because her quiz scores have not improved, the teacher provides a variation on his former advice, telling the student to join a study group. Because the quizzes, in the student's opinion, remain largely irrelevant, her participation in the study group is cursory. When the student's performance on the next quiz shows little improvement, both teacher and student feel less competent and frustrated. Each feels justified in blaming the other for the student's continued poor performance, confirming reasons that each should simply lower her or his expectations of the other. Now both teacher and student begin the search for ways to label each other—"lazy," "unprepared," "unfair," "insensitive." They have become hostile, allowing themselves to stereotype and dismiss each other with such comments as "He just doesn't get it. I've seen this before with people like him." And so the cycle maintains itself. It can be quite disturbing to listen to faculty talking about students who don't perform well in their classes and to students in those classes who talk about the faculty with whom they are frustrated. The conversations are often a mirror image of blame.

In difficult matters between people who do not know each other well, blame often occurs after only one negative encounter. People are particularly vulnerable when ways of understanding and interacting with one another have not had a chance to develop. This is one of the primary reasons why some school reform programs, such as the one pioneered by James Comer (1993), have a "no-fault" agreement. Meeting time is not used to blame others. *The focus is on solving problems and taking advantage of opportunities.* The blame cycle is prevented by simply not allowing blame to occur. Teachers can model this approach, teach it to their students, and provide it as a norm for behavior in the classroom.

Ridding a learning environment of blame does not mean to stop telling the truth or to avoid conversations about unethical or contradictory behavior. What this does mean is that students and teachers accept that the purpose of disagreement or another viewpoint is to provide perspectives that lead to shared understanding, to find common ground, and to establish a clearer path to open communication in the future. The goal is to agree that even though I may see it differently from you, I do not withdraw my support from you as a person.

ACTIVITY 4.9

Reframing to Change a Blameful Situation Into a More Hopeful Situation

---

Purpose: To teach students an effective way to promote change in problematic relationships in which the cycle of blame may have occurred, eroding trust and mutually supportive problem solving

Time: 45–60 minutes

Format: Large group and small group

Materials: PowerPoint, Handout 4.1 (p. 105), Handout 4.2 (p. 106)

Process

Adapt the following written material for developmental appropriateness.

By avoiding blame, reframing offers an excellent process to generate effective solutions to teacher-student conflicts. Part of this method's success is due to how well it invites the creativity of teachers. It also can invite the creativity of students. The example of reframing in Handout 4.2 involves a sixth-grade student trying to come to terms with his grandmother's attempts to help with homework. It can be shared as a handout for educators who would like to teach reframing to younger students.

DIFFERENT WAYS TO LEARN A SUBJECT BASED ON THE MULTIPLE INTELLIGENCES OF DIVERSE STUDENTS

When we understand intelligence as the capacity to solve problems or to fashion products that are valued by one's culture or community, we realize intelligence cannot be conceptualized apart from the context in which people live. There is always an interaction between students' personal inclinations and the opportunities for learning that exist in their cultural milieu.

HANDOUT 4.1

An Overview of Reframing

Reframing is based on the view that human behavior can be legitimately interpreted in a variety of ways and that people tend to view their behavior as appropriate to the situation as they perceive it (Molnar & Lindquist, 1989). Consider this example. A teacher regards a student as too aggressive and sees the student's repeated blurting out of answers in class as proof of this estimation. The student considers it necessary to blurt out answers because he believes the teacher ignores him. Their perceptions are mutually reinforced when the student suddenly raises his voice to get the teacher's attention and the teacher ignores the student to discourage his behavior. And on it goes, with the likelihood of consequent labeling and stereotyping between both individuals.

Reframing means realizing that people with whom we have a problematic relationship may hold a different idea about their experience than the one we hold. If the teacher in our example were able to interpret the student's blurting out answers as impassioned involvement in the learning experience instead of a hostile act to gain attention, then responses other than ignoring the student would suggest themselves, along with a change in the teacher's demeanor. This might even be an opportunity for disarming humor.

Reframing is finding a plausible, positive alternative interpretation of the problematic behavior followed by acting in ways that are consistent with that interpretation. Elements of reframing are embedded in the exercise that follows (Molnar & Lindquist, 1989, p. 61):

Awareness of your current interpretation of what you consider to be the problem behavior. A teacher volunteers a recurring problem that she is having with a particular student. She offers her interpretation as to why the student "acts" as he does.

Creation of positive alternative interpretations of the behavior. The rest of the group brainstorms plausible, *positive* alternative interpretations of the student's behavior. These are listed for the whole group.

Selection of a plausible positive interpretation. The teacher indicates which of the brainstormed positive interpretations might hold some "truth" and why. Then she selects the one that seems most realistic and truthful.

Formulation of a sentence or two that describes the new positive interpretation. The teacher offers in her own words the new positive interpretation that she will use. This is publicly recorded.

Action that sincerely reflects this new interpretation. The group brainstorms possible strategies for the new interpretation. These are listed. The teacher selects from among them to create a plan to use with the student.

HANDOUT 4.2

Reframing Activity

1. Think through a series of interactions with another person toward whom you feel blameful and map them. What did or does this person do? How did or do you respond? What happens next? Then what happens? And so on. (You are trying to describe what happens in the problem situation, how you respond, and what the usual result is.)

    Example: *I live with my grandmother and she tries to help me understand a math homework problem. But the way she explains it is confusing. I respond by telling her I am still confused. She tries to teach me another way, but it is a lot like the first time. I get very frustrated. I stop listening and tell her she is no help at all. She gets angry and says that I have a bad attitude and that I need to care enough to patiently figure things out. I start to think that my grandmother doesn't know much about how to figure out math. I get mad at her for making my life more difficult. I go to my room and close the door.*

2. What is your **current explanation** of why the person behaves this way?

    Example: *My grandmother is nervous about my future. She thinks if I am not a perfect student then I won't have a good life.*

3. What **positive** alternative explanations might there be for this behavior?

    Example: *My grandmother really cares about me and wants to help. She wants me to have more choices about my future than she had. The fact that we get angry at each other shows that we are really comfortable with each other and secure enough to know that deep down we love each other.*

4. Based on one of your positive explanations, how can you respond differently than you have previously? What might you actually say or do differently?

    Example: *When I feel myself getting frustrated, I am going to try to count to 10 in order to stay calm. Then I will tell her that I know she is trying but it isn't working even though I really do care about doing well in math. I will tell her that I am going to try Plan B, which is to call a friend for help. I will tell her that I will try to learn how to do my math homework so well that I can teach her how to do it.*

Thus, there exist multiple ways to be capable and to demonstrate intelligence. According to Howard Gardner (2006), people have the capacity for at least eight intelligences, and people differ in the strength of these intelligences. For example, some students perform best when asked to manipulate symbols such as words and numbers, while others demonstrate their understanding best through a hands-on approach where they build or create a concrete representation or product. Rather than possessing a single intelligence, students have a profile of intelligences that combine to perform different tasks.

Although the theory of multiple intelligences includes the idea that people have preferences for learning, as does the concept of learning styles, multiple intelligences theory locates intellectual processing in a specific location of the brain and across a much wider context of experiences. Gardner (2006) proposes that any concept worth teaching can be approached in numerous different ways that give *all* students relevant access. Let us look at each of the eight intelligences to understand its meaning (Gardner & Hatch, 1989), related career choices, and relevant action words to inspire lesson planning (Handout 4.3).

Notice that there are action words to create something especially relevant for each intelligence. For teaching any topic or concept, we can use a variety of approaches to respect and accommodate the wide range of profiles of intelligence found among diverse students. For example, rather than only presenting the concept of photosynthesis as a series of steps reflecting chemical changes (logical-mathematical), we can also examine relevant transformative experiences of our students in their families and communities and compare them with the process of photosynthesis (interpersonal) or look for musical transformations that parallel photosynthesis.

HANDOUT 4.3 Eight Multiple Intelligences

Logical-Mathematical: Sensitivity and capacity to discern logical and numerical patterns; ability to handle long chains of inductive and deductive reasoning

Careers: Scientist, accountant, engineer, economist, physicist, and programmer

Action Words: Sequence, rank, prove, conclude, judge, assess, critique, analyze

Verbal-Linguistic: Sensitivity to the sounds, rhythms, and meanings of words; sensitivity to the different functions of language, written and spoken

Careers: Author, journalist, teacher, salesperson, actor, translator, politician

Continued

HANDOUT 4.3   Continued

Action Words: Write, speak, read, narrate, talk, e-mail, script, translate, create a metaphor

Visual-Spatial: Capacity to perceive the visual-spatial world accurately and to effectively transform one's initial perceptions and images

Careers: Designer, navigator, sculptor, cartographer, architect

Action Words: Imagine, draw, dream, graph, design, visualize, video, create

Musical: Ability to produce and appreciate rhythm, tone, pitch, and timbre; appreciation of the forms of musical expressiveness

Careers: Musician, composer, disc jockey, music critic, dancer, sound engineer, singer

Action Words: Sing, rap, play, rhyme, compose, create a jingle, beat, melody, opera

Bodily-Kinesthetic: Ability to know, use, and control one's body movements and to handle objects skillfully

Careers: Athlete, actor, juggler, physical therapist, dancer, coach, performance artist

Action Words: Express, enact, perform, dance, mime, create a game, play, drama

Interpersonal: Capacity to discern, intuit, and respond appropriately to others as well as to communicate the moods, temperaments, motivations, and desires of other people

Careers: Therapist, politician, teacher, manager, executive, salesperson

Action Words: Collaborate, process, communicate, empathize, lead, create a plan, interview, policy, law

Intrapersonal: Access to one's own feelings and inner states of being with the ability to discriminate among them and draw on them to guide behavior; knowledge of one's own strengths, weaknesses, desires, and intelligences

Careers: Philosopher, spiritual leader, inventor, researcher, author, computer expert

Action Words: Plan, envision, reflect, write, invent, propose, investigate, study, create a philosophy, credo, new way, research plan, software package

Naturalist: Capacity to recognize, classify, and use plants, minerals, and animals, including rocks, grass, and all variety of flora and fauna

Careers: Botanist, farmer, oceanographer, park ranger, geologist, zookeeper

Action Words: Classify, grow, develop, find, search, create a terrarium, aquarium, field trip, classification system

In this way we improve the chances that diverse students with different ways of knowing can find engaging ways of learning.

ACTIVITY 4.10

Using Multiple Intelligences to Learn

Purpose: To help students be aware of and apply multiple intelligences in their learning

Time: 60 minutes

Format: Large group and small group

Materials: Paper and pencils and handout of the multiple intelligences (Handout 4.3, p.107)

Process

Step 1 Ask students to peruse the handout and begin with an interesting story (linguistic) from your own history about someone (yourself, your child, student, friend, or relative) who exemplifies and thrives on using his or her multiple intelligences (at least three). Then, narrate (linguistic), draw (visual-spatial), or enact (bodily-kinesthetic) how you know which three of the intelligences are dominant in your own profile.

Step 2 Have students individually analyze (logical-mathematical) the handout to determine which three intelligences dominate their own profile of intelligences. Then, as you modeled in Step 1, ask students to narrate, draw, or enact to a partner how they know which of the three intelligences are dominant in their own profile.

Step 3 Ask students to find one or two other people in the group who have the same or nearly the same three intelligences in their profile. After these groups have assembled, have each choose one relevant concept or topic they have to teach. Each group then brainstorms and invents ways (intrapersonal) to teach this topic or concept in a manner that compellingly accommodates their three intelligences.

Step 4 Groups report out, post, or dramatize the activities that teach the concept or topic.

The following activities are simple ways to incorporate visual-spatial, interpersonal, and intrapersonal intelligences in student reflection on learning.

┌───┐
│ **ACTIVITY 4.11**   │
│ **Story Posters**   │
└───┘

Purpose: To focus on prior experiences and learning in order to develop shared understandings and a foundation upon which to build

Time: 45 minutes

Format: Small group

Materials: Poster board or newsprint, glue sticks, precut symbols, Handout 4.4 (p. 111)

Process

Note: This activity can be adapted for students to imagine the experiences and perspectives of fictional or historical characters.

Students review the handout and identify symbols that allow them to discuss issues in which they are most interested. As members of the groups share their experiences related to selected symbols, they glue them on their poster board or newsprint with whatever pattern they choose. Groups also summarize their dialogue related to the symbols they have selected and write a few words on the poster to clarify the meaning of the symbol. In this way, people who are looking at their finished product will understand the significance of the symbols. While some groups paste their symbols on the poster randomly, others prefer a more deliberate pattern.

Debrief: Groups share their posters "gallery style" on a wall and appoint a reporter to discuss one or two features of the poster with the whole group.

┌───┐
│ **ACTIVITY 4.12**   │
│ **Blue Skies**   │
└───┘

Purpose: To create a vision of an ideal product related to an ideal classroom for students' learning and supporting their success

Time: 1 hour

Format: Individuals or small groups (depending on the size of the whole group)

Materials: Poster board or newsprint, colored markers, masking tape, a large sign that says "Draw, map, or use words to describe an ideal classroom, where every student feels respected and can learn"

HANDOUT 4.4

Story Posters

HEART

What holds particular value for you when you think of _____?

JAGGED HEART

What has disappointed you related to _____?

FOG

What are some of the things that confuse you about _____?

GIFT

What are some treasured times of celebration or success related to _____ (work or life)?

GREEN PEOPLE

Who are some of the people that you personally know who currently inspire _____ (work or life)?

BLUE PEOPLE

Who are some of the people that you have personally known who have inspired you even though they are no longer present in your life? _____

THUNDER CLOUDS

What are some of the storms related to the topic of _____ that you have had to endure and learn from?

LIGHTNING

What are some unexpected things that have happened as a consequence of _____?

SUN

What makes you feel hopeful? _____

Process

On large newsprint or poster board, students draw, map, or use words to describe an ideal classroom that supports the success of *all* students. The goal is to be as creative as possible. Each poster ought to have a few words beneath whatever has been created that describe the ideals represented in each student's product (e.g., "class agreements that help us respect each other," "all kinds of literature," "a publishing center," "a place where students can go at any time to build, paint, or create something using lots of different media," "a media center," "peer coaches who provide support when we need it," "projects that make the world a better place," "learning by doing," "time to work with and learn from each other").

Next, all of the posters are hung around the room and students stroll, gallery style, to take note of themes for a shared vision statement. Finally, work with the group to shape a few sentences that represent the themes about which the group feels strongly. For example, a sample vision statement might be *"Our classroom will be a place where students and teachers work together to create learning experiences that build strong academic and interpersonal skills in ways that are meaningful to students and provide different ways for students to creatively express themselves. In addition, our classroom will maximize the use of community resources, inviting outside experts to work with students to create meaningful projects that are an integral part of the academic program. We will not put down our peers if they are not succeeding and will, instead, provide support to encourage motivation and success for everyone."*

After a rough draft has been generated, students work in small groups to suggest revisions that might make it stronger or more representative. Finally, a small committee nominated by the whole class integrates suggestions into a final draft. Using fist-to-five, where fingers are used as a Likert scale (five is high, one is low, and fist means "I can't live with it"), students respond to the final draft.

Note: A vision statement ought to be a working document. Periodic class review of how to strengthen the application of the vision helps ensure that the goals and ideas manifested in the vision statement are taken seriously.

ACTIVITY 4.13

Metaphorical Ecosystems

Purpose: To recognize strengths in order to identify needs

Time: 30 minutes

Format: Collaboratively in teams

Materials: Newsprint, colored markers

Process

Ask students to examine the "whole picture" related to their role in implementing a particular goal—for example, implementing a project. Students work collaboratively to design and draw a metaphorical illustration that highlights the conditions and situations that have, continue to, and will impact their project in relation to a set of standards for high-quality learning. The picture ought to address the following:

- *Blooms:* What actions have we taken that still need tending in order to strengthen our work?
- *Seeds:* What are the ideas for ways to enrich our work?
- *Nutrients:* What resources or support do we need to achieve our goals?
- *Clouds:* What challenges might lie ahead? How might we overcome these challenges?
- *Sun:* How might we sustain our energy as we continue down the road?

A spokesperson for each group displays and briefly explains the group's poster.

Debrief: Ask students what insights they have from creating their picture or listening to other groups. How might they use these insights to strengthen their work?

ACTIVITY 4.14
Creating Time for Collaboration Among Students

Purpose: To encourage students to make collaboration a priority

Time: 30 minutes

Format: Triads

Materials: One copy per student of a handout based on the information in Exhibit 4.1 (p. 115)

Process

Ask students to consider the following:

1. How do you currently try to find time to collaborate on school work outside of class?

2. What norms or traditional ways of organizing time make it challenging for you to collaborate with other students outside of class?

3. What might you do to find more time?

Present the handout based on Exhibit 4.1 to help students consider ways to allocate time for enhanced collaborative learning. Ask students, working in groups of three, to discuss these questions: What is one idea you would like to try in support of greater collaboration? What would you need to do to make your idea a reality?

> **ACTIVITY 4.15**
>
> ## Establishing Norms for Groupwork

Purpose: To define how groups will work together

Time: 30 minutes

Format: Individuals, then triads, then teams of six

Materials: Handout based on Exhibit 4.2 (p. 116), sticky notes

Process

Explain that in some ways, a classroom is an organization. Effective organizations tend to have collaborative teams that investigate, solve problems, and create products. Students review the handout based on Exhibit 4.2. They use three different sticky notes (one idea on each) to identify the three most important things from the *entire* matrix that they need to happen in order to effectively work as a learning team. After a few minutes, individuals form triads and the triads lay their sticky notes out on a table and group them according to similarities.

Note: The matrix has redundancy between categories, for example, the theme of collaboration. It is easy for triads to find overlap in priorities.

Each triad merges with another triad to become a six-person team. They repeat the process of grouping their priorities for common and distinct themes. Next, they prioritize their themes in order to identify the top three to five norms they would like to have in place. Then the teams work together on a final statement that represents norms that will guide their teamwork.

Finally, ask the teams to create a procedure to regularly review and strengthen their agreed-upon norms. They write their norms and their procedure to review on two 3 × 5 cards along with the names of two people who will co-chair each team. They give one card to you and save one card for themselves.

The following activity is a way to build a shared understanding among teams and within an entire class. It provides an example of how an

Exhibit 4.1   Strategies to Expand Time for Collaboration

Think of a situation in which you might need to collaborate.

Assess when there is time during the school day that you can free up.

Assess when there is time before or after school that you can free up.

What are you doing in electives such as art, music, and clubs that might support groupwork (projects) in this class?

When does your school schedule overlap with other people's schedules? How much time does this allow you to work together?

Are there any ways that family, friends, or community members can free you up one day a week before or after school?

Are there ways to rearrange the class schedule to include longer blocks of time for collaboration?

To what extent are you using your transition times, class time, and lunch time to solve problems related to issues of immediate and long-range importance so that you can be productive with independent work?

Would it help to have one "collaboration day" per week in this class? What would that look like?

Exhibit 4.2 Profile of an Effective Learning Team

The categories as well as the items for consideration are an integration of research on effective teams and themes/needs for creating change in institutions. Please rate your responses in terms of highest and lowest priorities.

General Direction of the Team						
	Low	Middle		High		Examples
1. The team has a shared vision and mission that focus on working together in ways that are highly motivating.	1	2	3	4	5	
2. The team develops a manageable work plan with clear goals.	1	2	3	4	5	
3. The team focuses on activities that have a positive impact on all team members.	1	2	3	4	5	
4. The team participates in the development and implementation of an assignment plan.	1	2	3	4	5	
5. The team ensures that everyone respects student diversity.	1	2	3	4	5	

Meetings						
	Low	Middle		High		Examples
1. The team meets enough times to accomplish its goals.	1	2	3	4	5	
2. Team meetings are scheduled in advance and members are notified of and expected to remember meeting times.	1	2	3	4	5	
3. Team members have an opportunity to contribute to the formation of the agenda.	1	2	3	4	5	

	Low	Middle		High	Examples
4. Team members arrive on time and have regular attendance.	1	2	3	4	5	
5. Minutes are kept of all meetings and, when appropriate, are made available to others.	1	2	3	4	5	
6. Team members conduct work as needed between meetings, with the necessary support to make decisions that effectively follow through on responsibilities.	1	2	3	4	5	

Ability to Work as a Team					
	Low	Middle		High	Examples
1. Team members communicate well with each other.	1	2	3	4	5	
2. Team members agree on a way to make decisions and fully participate in discussions as well as decisions.	1	2	3	4	5	
3. The team uses members' skills and areas of expertise.	1	2	3	4	5	
4. Team members support each other in fulfilling responsibilities.	1	2	3	4	5	
5. Team members resolve conflicts and problems effectively.	1	2	3	4	5	
6. The team works to ensure that all members feel included and valued.	1	2	3	4	5	
7. The team regularly assesses itself.	1	2	3	4	5	

Continued

Exhibit 4.2 (Continued)

Leadership						
	Low		Middle		High	Examples
1. The leaders work with team members to clarify roles and responsibilities.	1	2	3	4	5	
2. The leaders work collaboratively with all team members.	1	2	3	4	5	
3. The leaders act as facilitative leaders in team decision making.	1	2	3	4	5	
4. The leaders ensure that all team members have the timely information they need to make decisions.	1	2	3	4	5	
5. Members of the team share leadership and responsibility for the team's work.	1	2	3	4	5	
6. The leaders encourage diversity of opinion and ideas.	1	2	3	4	5	
7. The leaders encourage creativity and risk-taking.	1	2	3	4	5	

External Communication						
	Low		Middle		High	Examples
1. In an equitable manner, the team seeks input from the teacher, students, community members, and other constituencies.	1	2	3	4	5	
2. The team effectively communicates with people outside of the team about relevant issues.	1	2	3	4	5	

	Low	Middle		High	Examples
3. The team keeps the teacher informed about its activities, challenges, and outcomes.	1	2	3	4	5	
4. The team uses an external as well as internal communication plan so that team members know who will be a liaison for connecting with people such as the teacher, other students, community members, and so forth.	1	2	3	4	5	

Source: Adapted from the National Staff Development Council's *School Team Innovator*, edited by Stephanie Hirsh.

establishing inclusion exercise can also be a *developing a positive attitude* exercise. In other words, some activities contribute to respect and connectedness (establishing inclusion) in way that promote choice and relevance (developing a positive attitude). As Chapter 3 discussed, many of the conditions overlap with each other and are mutually reinforcing because implementing a single strategy—even when it is aligned with a particular motivational condition—can blend into other motivational conditions because their boundaries are not absolute and may contain elements of the other conditions. For example, imagine trying to develop a positive attitude toward learning (the second condition of the motivational framework) without also creating a situation in which the environment felt safe for students to take risks (a criteria for establishing inclusion, the first condition of the motivational framework).

ACTIVITY 4.16
Carousel Graffiti

Purpose: To elicit prior knowledge, different perspectives on a topic, and shared understandings as a foundation upon which to learn

Time: 45 minutes

Format: Small group

Materials: Newsprint, markers, tape for posting graffiti responses

Process

Step 1   Select approximately five questions that are relevant to a learning experience. For example, if a class is studying fractions, one question might be "What are some of the ways fractions appear in everyday life?"

Step 2   Using bright markers, write each of the questions you have selected for group brainstorming across separate pieces of newsprint. Each piece of newsprint should contain only one question, so if there are five questions, there are five pieces of newsprint.

Step 3   Ask students to count off so that they form small groups. The number of groups corresponds to the number of questions. When groups have been formed, give each group a piece of newsprint with a question on it.

Step 4   Tell the groups that in just a minute they will be asked to collectively address their questions. The process is called "graffiti" because students record their responses to their question in any way they choose, including symbols or other artistic representations, to the extent that others can understand their thinking. You may want to suggest that each group select a scribe to write down everyone's thoughts throughout the brainstorming because consensus is not necessary for this activity. You may also want to let students know that this process involves being interrupted, sometimes in the middle of a thought, because the process moves along quickly. Even if a group has more to say about the question to which they are responding, there is a chance that the next group that offers its contribution to the same question will provide such information.

   After each group has had approximately five minutes to discuss and respond to its question, the timekeeper (perhaps this is you) directs groups to pass their questions (newsprint) clockwise. Each group then considers its new question, underlining what it agrees with, modifying what might be changed, and adding to the graffiti of the previous group. After another five minutes, the timekeeper cues students to pass their question clockwise. This process continues until each group has had an opportunity to respond to all of the questions.

Step 5   Ultimately, each group will end up with its original question. At this point, the task is to briefly summarize all of the contributions written on the newsprint. Because everyone has had an opportunity to think about each of the questions, the summaries should be concise statements or artistic representations that express identifiable themes or that draw a conclusion. Each group appoints a reporter to share his or her group's summary, limiting the report to 1–2 minutes. If space permits, graffiti responses can be posted around the room. Later, the information can be transcribed for further study.

The following are carousel graffiti questions that a high school social studies teacher created for students at the beginning of a unit on cultural diversity in the United States. We suggest that you first check to ensure that all participants interpret the questions in the same way and that their interpretations are consistent with your own.

1. In our school, do you think that students who look or act a certain way are more likely to be seen as "normal"? (Why or why not?)

2. What is a valuable lesson you have learned, either directly or indirectly, from a person who is from a background that is different from your own?

3. How might a school or community look if it was truly respectful of cultural diversity?

4. What are some ways to build understanding and respect among different groups of people?

5. What is a question related to cultural diversity that you would like to explore?

The following activity helps students examine the concept of change. Although school curricula often focus on changes in the lives of people that students study, students do not often have an opportunity to examine the implications of change in their own lives. This activity can be adapted to situations in which students work together as a group for the first time or to changes they experience in the school or community.

ACTIVITY 4.17
Roundtable Dialogue on Change

Purpose: To share insights and lend perspectives related to the process of change

Time: 30 minutes

Format: Individuals and small groups

Materials: Handout 4.5 (p. 123)

Process

Although the issue of change is complex, when a new approach to learning is introduced it is a good idea to "normalize" some of the caution and ambiguity that people feel as they begin to work together. Distribute Handout 4.5 and ask students to underline the issues that speak to their own experiences or that make sense for other reasons. Next, ask students to identify a challenge that they feel because of their involvement in this process and one or two strategies for productively working with it. Then ask students to count off so that small groups of four people are formed. After groups have been formed, request that each group identify a facilitator (who keeps things moving), a recorder (who records key points), a reporter (who will provide a 1- to 2-minute summary for the large group by noting insights and recommendations), and a process observer (who will help group members remember to share "air time" so that all people have an opportunity to comfortably participate). The process observer will also be the timekeeper.

Have groups discuss these dialogue questions:

1. As you reflect on the handout, what are some of the things that you can relate to from experience?

2. How does the information on change apply to you (e.g., a new and potentially ambiguous approach to learning)?

3. As you think about _____ (e.g., the experiential group project you are about to do), what are some insights about change to keep in mind?

SUMMARY

This chapter introduced theory and strategies for the second condition of the motivational framework for culturally responsive teaching (*developing a positive attitude*) by applying the two criteria of *relevance* and *choice*. Many of the strategies aim to help students feel control over their learning, participate in open-minded dialogue, and persist in times of uncertainty or challenge. Generally, students appreciate relevant information that invites participation in shaping the conditions that influence learning. In fact, in recent years, many schools have been partnering with students to create compelling instruction schoolwide. This is a topic for discussion in a forthcoming volume that applies the motivational framework to leadership for school transformation.

As you tailor the resources in this chapter to your own setting, you will likely do so with the understanding that strategies are important but

HANDOUT 4.5

Caveats About Change

Change is a complex, nonlinear process that requires an open exchange, participation from all who are concerned, validation of important work, time to plan and reflect as a part of work and daily life, and support from a range of people. What caveats might team members consider in advance of their work to be better prepared? *Note:* The following bullets were adapted from the research of Carl Glickman (Glickman, Hayes, & Hensley, 1992) while he worked with the League of Professional Schools.

- Conflict will increase when members of teams take their responsibilities seriously.
- Assessment information will cultivate dissatisfaction and possibly blame if student learning and attitudes do not match with "the cardiac approach" to believing that "in our hearts we're doing fine."
- Without new information, decisions will be made that reinforce the status quo.
- With immediate success, pressure for more short-term success will increase at the potential cost of long-term student gains.
- Decisions about dreams will be easier than decisions about how to attain one's dreams.
- Criticism will develop from the outside, especially as a team attains success and recognition.

According to Rosabeth Moss Kanter (1992), these are some of the frequently mentioned reasons that people resist change:

- Loss of control
- Excess uncertainty
- Concerns about competence
- More work
- Past resentments

We also know that:

- Change is a process that occurs over time
- Ultimately change is an individual act
- The more complex the new idea/behavior, the longer it takes for change to occur
- Change efforts must be directed not only toward the new idea itself, but also toward individuals and the time and assistance they need to implement a new idea

not completely sufficient to create learning environments where students have a positive attitude toward learning. Teaching well is technically, psychologically, and culturally complex. For teachers as well as students, a positive attitude toward learning is influenced by how we see ourselves as learners, cultural beings, and community members in relation to curriculum and instruction. A positive attitude toward new ideas that push us to do things a bit differently than we might prefer requires a tolerance for doubt and humility. This is one of the reasons why the first condition, establishing inclusion, works in concert with the second, developing a positive attitude. The environment must be safe for everyone—teachers and students—to take risks and persevere until new learning feels confident. However, even when we are equipped with years of teaching experience and wonderful memories of the moments that mattered to a young learner, teaching is demanding and it can seem easier to justify detachment than to experiment in ways that might be relevant to others but are outside of our own comfort zone. Although research and experience can help, the genesis of many of our best instructional practices is listening carefully to students.

The next chapter explores how to challenge ourselves and students in making sense of things in ways that compel deep immersion in learning.

The set of research-based considerations on page 123 can assist teachers in planning and carrying out activities that contribute to students' attitude toward learning and teachers' desire to strengthen their instructional repertoires.

The following list can serve as a guide to teachers, providing considerations for creating the conditions of choice and relevance for developing a positive attitude toward learning. The subsequent list includes the activities in this chapter.

Developing a Positive Attitude

How does this learning experience promote personal relevance and offer meaningful choices that contribute to a positive attitude?

Teacher works with students to personalize the relevance of course content:

_____ Students' experiences, concerns, and interests are used to develop course content.

_____ Students' experiences, concerns, and interests are addressed in responses to their questions.

_____ Students' prior knowledge/learning experiences is/are explicitly linked to course content and questions.

_____ Teacher encourages students to understand, develop, and express different points of view.

_____ Teacher encourages students to clarify their interests and set goals.

_____ Teacher maintains flexibility in pursuit of teachable moments and emerging interests.

Evidence

Teacher encourages students to make real choices such as:

_____ how to learn (multiple intelligences, including the arts)

_____ what to learn

_____ where to learn

_____ when a learning experience will be considered to be complete

_____ how learning will be assessed

_____ with whom to learn

_____ how to solve emerging problems

Evidence

LIST OF ACTIVITIES FROM CHAPTER 4

Following is a list of the activities from this chapter.

5 Enhancing Meaning

The formulation of a problem is often more essential than its solution, which may be merely a matter of mathematical or experimental skill. . . . To raise new questions, a new possibility, to regard old problems from a new angle, requires creative imagination and marks real advances.

—Albert Einstein

Vladimir Price loves adventure. He also likes performance art. Today, in his eighth-grade physics class at the Science and Math Academy, he tells students that one of the best things about teaching physics is doing live experiments as a way for students to generate their own questions. He says, "I know you love social media and find interesting videos to share with friends. In this class, you are going to see a lot of live performance." To remind students of something he said the first day of class, he declares, "You are going to have a great time learning physics!"

Next, Mr. Price sits down on a desk chair with wheels. With his arms outstretched he asks Matt, a student in the front row, to spin him around with all the might Matt can muster. Matt spins his teacher, and as Mr. Price brings his arms in toward his chest he asks, "What just happened?" Matt looks perplexed so Mr. Price calls on Dan, another student who is sitting near the front of the classroom. Dan says that it looked like Mr. Price was trying to keep his balance while spinning. Mr. Price says, "Good try," and turns his attention back to Matt. He tells Matt to point to another student to assist with the next part of the experiment. Matt chooses Raymond, a member of the rodeo club. Mr. Price tells Raymond that they will repeat the experiment but this time Mr. Price will add weight to his outstretched arms with two cans of soup. After a hefty spin, he asks Raymond, "Now what's going on?" Raymond says, "You slowed down."

Turning his attention to the class as a whole, Mr. Price tells the class to use their cell phones to research what this experiment has to do with physics. Almost immediately, Amanda, a student in a middle row, calls out, "It was a demonstration of the conservation of angular momentum!" Surprised by the quick response, Mr. Price inquires about Amanda's research strategy. She explains that her grandmother is a physicist and they often discuss things that happen in everyday lives that demonstrate scientific principles.

Moving on, Mr. Price tells students that their homework is to define the meaning of *conservation* and *angular* within the context of the conservation of angular momentum. In other words, what do the words *conservation* and *angular* have to do with momentum? He also challenges students to see if they can find another example of the conservation of angular momentum on the web. As students exit the classroom, Mr. Price thanks Matt, Dan, and Raymond for their contributions to his experiment.

The previous two chapters focused on creating a safe and supportive learning environment (motivational condition: establishing inclusion through respect and connectedness) and promoting a willing disposition among students toward learning (motivational condition: developing a positive attitude through choice and relevance). These conditions are fundamental to the focus of this chapter, which requires students to challenge themselves in ways that require exploration, experimentation, creativity, and thoughtful application of new ideas to relevant problems. When we challenge ourselves to learn something new, we are vulnerable to mistakes. In the absence of respect and relevance, human beings are reluctant to risk a deep dive into new territory. This is why all of the motivational conditions are interdependent and, under the best circumstances, occur simultaneously.

Although the introductory scenario may expose some flaws in Mr. Price's pedagogy, it is an example of a promising teaching strategy that needs to be more fully developed. For example, this chapter speaks to the importance of teaching in ways that challenge and engage a range of students. In this regard, to what extent was Mr. Price's experiment effective and what might he do differently to create meaningful learning for all of his students? Regarding the motivational conditions of the previous two chapters, to what extent did Mr. Price establish inclusion so that all students felt respected and connected to their teacher and classmates? To what extent did Mr. Price help students develop a positive attitude toward learning? If you were a trusted colleague, what might you do to help Mr. Price strengthen his teaching methods? These are ethical and pragmatic considerations because, in this scenario, Mr. Price seems more inclined to interact with male students. In addition, one might wonder how often Mr. Price focuses on performance rather than engendering inquiry among students. To what extent does he accomplish his desire to help students generate relevant and substantive questions?

Of course, one might surmise that Mr. Price seeks to stimulate students' curiosity. Further, he may know all too well that of all the challenges educators face, student indifference or resistance to carefully developed plans for learning is disheartening. Perhaps his performance attempts to outmaneuver what he perceives as student apathy. One thing is certain: For learning to matter to students, it must hold meaning.

Meaning penetrates our hearts and minds, to the "eyes of our eyes." This chapter probes two essential questions: What is meaning? How can we create it in schools? It provides examples of learning activities that teachers have adapted to a range of subject areas and grade levels.

MAKING SENSE OF MEANING

One way to think about meaning is as the ordering of information in ways that provide basic understanding. For example, when we say the word *castle* we know it means a large fortified residence. Or when our telephone number is in a listing we can discern it from others. This kind of meaning contributes to our awareness of how things operate or are defined, but in a way that doesn't deeply touch us. In the words of Whitehead (1929), this is *inert knowledge,* sometimes necessary but often of little emotional importance.

When meaning provides a connection or pattern that links our perceptions to important goals or questions, it intensifies motivation for *all* students because there is obvious relevance. This deeper meaning accesses strong feelings that are intertwined with the ways in which we have been socialized in our families and communities. As the philosopher Susanne Langer (1942) has posited, there is a basic and pervasive human need to invest meaning in one's world, to search for and find significance everywhere. It cannot be separated from who we are as cultural beings, nor can it be separated from our sense of purpose. Across many cultures, achieving purpose is fundamental to a satisfying life (Csikszentmihalyi, 1997).

To exalt the significance of students' lives, to assist them in realizing what is truly important in their communities and world, educators generally rely on language. Language can serve as a powerful mediator between deep meanings, awareness, and expression. But it is not the only mediator. There appear to be deeper structures within human beings that process meaning (Fischer, 2009). Many of these connections are made through creative, artistic, spiritual, and manual experiences involving music, dance, theater, the visual arts, meditation, and service to others. Creative and contemplative forms of cognition contribute, in pivotal ways, to students' interest in and interpretation of opportunities to learn. In essence, they help students experience harmony in their feelings, thoughts, intentions, and actions. This fusion of feeling, wishing, and thinking has been described as *flow* (Csikszentmihalyi, 1997), "being in the zone," or, at times, "ecstasy." (To hear Professor Csikszentmihalyi discuss the concept of *flow*, see www.ted.com/talks/mihaly_csikszent mihalyi_on_flow.)

The Concept of Flow

Flow is the feeling and concentration that often emerges when a musician is playing a challenging score, a weaver is designing a complex tapestry, or athletes are experiencing a closely contested athletic competition. But flow also can occur while reading an appealing book or having a deep conversation with an old friend. In such activities we feel totally absorbed. Often, we are in a state of exhilaration in which time quickly passes.

Flow occurs in learning when the students' goals are desired and clear, feedback is immediate and relevant, and the level of challenge is in balance with the required skills or knowledge. A visual representation of this phenomenon might be a student absorbed in creating a photographic journey of her neighborhood, solving a compelling math problem, or working on a new computer program. Because flow can be found across cultures, it may be a sense that humans have developed to recognize patterns of actions that are worth preserving and transmitting over time (Delle Fave, Bassi, Cavallo, & Stokart, 2007). When it occurs as part of the process of learning, it makes learning an end in itself. Students who experience flow have not only a better chance of learning but also a better chance of *wanting* to learn more. All of the activities that follow in this chapter have the potential to elicit deep engagement in learning.

Flow requires *engagement* on the part of the student, an action that might involve searching, evaluating, constructing, creating, or organizing some kind of learning material into new or better ideas, memories, skills, values, feelings, understandings, solutions, or decisions. Critical to engagement are the voices of the students and teacher in dialogue with one another, creating meaning as they develop and meet a learning *challenge.* This challenge often has a goal-like quality such as solving a problem or completing a project and requires some degree of capacity, skill, or knowledge on the part of the student. At its core, motivating instruction is the co-creation by teachers and students of challenging learning experiences in engaging formats about relevant topics. The following activities support this ideal.

USING METAPHORS AND STORIES TO ENCOURAGE DIFFERENT PERSPECTIVES AND DEEPEN RELEVANCE AND MEANING

Metaphors allow us to create meaning with students and educators in ways that are often not possible through academic language. For example, to say that being a teacher in a school that is being threatened with closure is enormously challenging is logically clear, but to say it feels like swimming in a hurricane expands meaning to a deeper and more emotional level. When we encourage students to use their own metaphors, they not only construct their own knowledge but also contribute diverse perspectives to classroom dialogue and learning.

An enjoyable starting place for students to explore creative metaphors comes directly from the music they enjoy. For example, the Flocabulary website includes a section on metaphors and similes in hip-hop (www. flocabulary.com/hiphopmetaphors). Creative metaphors are also common in the titles of popular articles. For example, a website with compelling metaphorical titles is The Authentic Voice—The Best Reporting on Race and Ethnicity (http://theauthenticvoice.org/mainstories); two of several articles on this site are "Broken Trust," which examines American Indian land rights, and, on the topic of large-scale immigration, "The Rim of the New World."

An alternative to written metaphors is illustrated metaphors. At the conclusion of a course or unit, a teacher might ask students to draw a metaphorical illustration of a concept they studied. For example, after a lesson on the concept of blame, one student drew a desert oasis with poisoned water while another sketched a pin in search of a balloon.

Stories are also a way that people construct meaning. Ask anyone to tell their favorite family story and you may gain personal understanding of a person that profoundly alters previous assumptions. When we tell stories about what matters to us, our voice and perspectives become discernible. Whether it is an academic problem, a political event, or a childhood memory, when people tell how something happened in their family, their community, or their world, their narrative provides a context for the fundamental desire to make meaning. The following activity uses poetry as a medium through which to engage students in telling a story about their personal histories.

ACTIVITY 5.1

Where I'm From

This iconic teaching strategy by Linda Christensen (2000; used with permission) originally appeared in *Reading, Writing, and Rising Up: Teaching About Social Justice and the Power of the Written Word.*

Caveat: Some students, especially those with traumatic pasts, have a difficult time with this activity. Because of this, students should be forewarned and have the option of an alternative assignment that doesn't require nostalgic images of childhood.

Purpose: To share aspects of students' lives in ways that surface creativity and promote meaning making about influences on their identities

Time: 1 hour

Format: Individual and large group

Process

Step 1 Read the following poem by George Ella Lyon out loud together. (Note that some poems use a hook to "link the poem forward" like a repeating line so the poem can build momentum.)

Step 2 Using the line "I am from" (or creating another phrase), ask students to think about their past. Have them write lists to match the details that Lyons remembers about her past and share their memories as they wish.

- **items found inside** whatever you called "home" when you were a child (e.g., bobby pins, stacks of newspapers, discount coupons for a Mercedes); you don't have to tell the truth
- **items found in your yard** if you had one (e.g., hoses coiled like green snakes, dog bones, broken rakes)
- **items found in your neighborhood** (e.g., the corner grocery store, the "home-base" tree)
- **names of relatives**, especially ones that link you to your past (e.g., Uncle Charlie, Aunt Selma)
- **sayings** (e.g., "Do as I say, not as I do")
- **names of foods and dishes** that recall family gatherings (e.g., matzo ball soup, black-eyed peas, tamales)
- **names of places where you kept your memories** (e.g., diaries, boxes, inside a family album)

Step 3   Have students share their lists out loud as everyone brain-storms. Recommend that they try to make their lists "sound like home" by using the names and voices of their home, their family, their neighborhood; let sounds, smells and languages emerge (e.g., bubbles of chicken fat on hot soup, pink tights crusted with rosin).

Step 4   Once everyone has specific lists of words, phrases, and names, have them begin writing, using some kind of phrase like "I am from . . ." to weave the poem together. They should end the poem with a line or two that ties their past to their present, which ties them to their family history. For example, in Lyon's poem, she ends with "Under my dress box/spilling old pictures . . . I am from those moments . . ."

Step 5   After students have written their first draft, they join in a "read around" to share poems. As they listen, they write comments about each reader's piece. Tell them, "Pull out a piece of paper, write the name of the reader, and then as each person reads, write what you liked about his or her piece. Please be specific. Write down what words or phrases that made their poem work. Did they use a list? A metaphor? Humor?"

Step 6   Seated in a circle, each person reads her or his poem. After a person reads, people raise their hands to comment on what they liked about the piece. The writer calls on people to speak.

Where I'm From

George Ella Lyon

I am from clothespins, from Clorox and carbon-tetrachloride.

I am from dirt under the back porch.

(Black, glistening

it tasted like beets.)

I am from the forsythia bush,

the Dutch elm

whose long-gone limbs I remember

as if they were my own.

I am from fudge and eyeglasses,

    From Imogene and Alafair.

I'm from the know-it-alls

    And the pass-it-ons,

from perk up and pipe down.

I'm from He restoreth my soul

    With a cotton ball lamb

    And ten verses I can say myself.

I'm from Artemus and Billie's Branch,

fried corn and strong coffee.

From the finger my grandfather lost

    to the auger,

the eye my father shut to keep his sight.

Under my bed was a dress box

spilling old pictures,

a sift of lost faces

to drift beneath my dreams.

I am from those moments—

snapped before I budded—

leaf-fall from the family tree.

Source: Linda Christensen. Used with permission.

The following excerpts are from a student's poem that Lyon's piece provoked:

I am from bobby pins, doo rags, and

    wide tooth combs.

I am from prayer plants that lift their

    stems

and rejoice every night.

I am from chocolate cakes and deviled

  eggs

from older cousins and hand-me-downs

to "shut-ups" and "sit-downs."

I am from Genesis to Exodus,

Leviticus, too.

church to church, pew to pew

I am from a huge family tree that begins

  with dust

and ends with me.

USING STORIES AND CASE STUDIES

A case study is a narrative of real events that presents provocative questions in a way that compels students to deliberate, analyze, and advance informed judgments to integrate an array of perspectives and concepts (Marsick, 2004). Although some cases focus on "What would you do?" and others on detailed descriptions that call for careful data analysis, the hallmark of all cases is their lifelike, concrete details and characters. They bring to life otherwise abstract and ambiguous concepts. The same can be said of stories. Combining case studies and stories for high school science educators, the work of Herreid, Schiller, and Herreid (2012) gives life and substance to a topic too often far removed from real life.

Stories and case studies have been linked with increased student motivation and interest in a subject (Christensen, 2011–2012; Mustoe & Croft, 1999). When teachers use stories that are someone else's, yet are relevant to students' lives, students tend to be more open-minded and less defensive in their analysis. In addition, the opportunity to think through a relevant predicament with others often contributes to a sense of solidarity with others and different perspectives can be safely communicated. Further, powerful stories with complex issues encourage inquiry, imagination, and vision because students can see that opinions are insufficient as a way to build knowledge.

As in the discussion of other strategies in this chapter, a goal is to be specific enough about the ways to use stories as a learning tool so that you can make use of this method in your own setting, and to offer guidelines that are general enough to work in different contexts.

When stories (or case studies) are a teacher's primary approach to teaching a subject, it is particularly effective to present them in a sequence that lets the narrative unfold with additional information and complexity. Whether a primary or occasional learning tool, guiding questions scaffold students' ability to make meaning. The most effective questions for critical thinking ask students to critically analyze a situation in a way that requires students to clarify what they need to know, distinguish facts from assumptions, identify issues, prioritize and research issues in ways that include multiple sources and different perspectives, and identify possible solutions based on research as well as experience. One way to extend learning at the end of a learning experience is to ask students to critically analyze each other's solutions, exploring both the process their peers used to solve the story and the solution itself.

Two of the primary decisions a teacher faces in using stories as a learning tool are selecting or creating engaging stories and developing purposeful guiding questions.

Selecting or Creating Engaging Stories

- tells a "real" story
- raises a thought-provoking issue that is relevant to students
- has elements of conflict
- promotes empathy with the central characters
- lacks an obvious or clear-cut right answer
- encourages students to think and take a position
- demands a decision
- is relatively concise

Developing Purposeful Guiding Questions

- What is the situation?
- How does it relate to your own experience?
- What issues (or problems) does this story address?
- Evaluate the pros/cons and underlying assumptions of issues (or problems) in the story in relation to (learning goals).
- What problems need to be solved? What problem(s) will you focus on? What are some possible ways to solve the problem(s)?
- What information do you need? Where/how could you find it?
- What criteria will you use to evaluate your solution?

WORKING WITH YOUNGER STUDENTS

At all levels of education, there is significant opportunity to customize story-telling for different academic, social, cultural, and developmental purposes. For example, with listening skills as a Common Core standard, and the 21st century learning goals of collaboration and communication, teachers of young students often share stories that include student accountability for listening well. In a blog post on Edutopia, Rebecca Alber (2013) provides simple and helpful listening strategies. For example, although teachers want students to hear what they say the first time they say it, many students have very active minds. The idea of *ask three, then ask me* helps students draw on each other's knowledge when they lose track of something a teacher has said.

In addition to teaching students to ask peers for assistance, the process of *turn and talk* or *turn and learn* and other kinds of frequent response opportunities are common across grade levels. To introduce the practice of *turn and talk*, teachers of younger students explain, "I'm going to describe the process of 'turn and talk' and show you what it looks like. I will pause along the way and ask you to turn to a partner and explain to them what you heard. You and your partner will decide who speaks first. As you talk to your partner, I will walk around to listen. This helps me understand how you and your partner are talking and listening to each other. It also helps me assess what you are learning." It is especially important for teachers to check in with English language learners since they are learning two sets of skills at once: English and academic content.

To encourage concentration, teachers might also ask students to think of questions to ask other students about different sections of a story. This encourages deep listening because students have to consider what is interesting or important as they listen. Further, being accountable to peers generally supports motivation, especially when the learning environment is respectful and friendly.

Regardless of age, searching online using the key words "using stories to teach" provide links to freely available web-based resources for many disciplines and purposes.

WORKING WITH OLDER STUDENTS TO WRITE THEIR OWN STORIES

Because there are many online resources for teachers regarding how to use stories to teach, this section focuses on an exercise Linda Christensen (2012) uses with older students to write their own stories. As she works with students to explore the legacy of racism and classism in the United States, she integrates standards from several subjects through powerful vignettes that students read and write. In this case, she uses storytelling to unite history, civics, and language arts while working with students to analyze what makes a compelling personal narrative about how race and class function in society. She draws from two primary sources: Brent Staples's (1986) beautiful essay "Just Walk on By: Black Men and Public Spaces" and Nobel Laureate Chimamanda Ngozi Adichie's poignant and entertaining TED talk titled "The Danger of a Single Story" (www.ted.com/talks/chimamanda_adichie_the_danger_of_a_single_story?language=en). A full description of Christiansen's purposes and approach is available at www.rethinkingschools.org/archive/26_04/26_04_christensen.shtml.

The motivational significance of using stories with middle and high school students to personalize the consequences of intractable social problems is best conveyed through Christiansen's (n.d.) own words:

> Give students meaningful assignments that they want to write and revise. When I interviewed a group of Latina/o and African American juniors after one of our first essays, I said, "I noticed at some point you stopped doing this because it was an assignment, and you became passionate about writing the essay." Their answer: We got to write about issues that were real in our lives, and someone listened and cared. ("Writing and Revising Vignettes," para. 3)

Using Case Study to Engage English Language Learners in Analyzing a Student's Experience of School in the United States

The following activity is adapted with permission from the work of a graduate student at the University of Washington in Seattle. It focuses on the high school experience of an English leaner and is intended for use in an ESL class. However, it can be adapted for other purposes and grade levels. A primary goal of this activity is to exemplify a case study approach to learning.

ACTIVITY 5.2

Case Study: Working With English Language Learners to Analyze the School Experience of an English Language Learner

Purpose: To examine the experience of English language learners in schools and their communities

Time: 45 minutes

Format: Individuals and small groups

Materials: Case study

Process

Step 1   Explain that students are going to read a fictionalized account of a high school student named Filad who immigrated to the United States from Somalia with his family. The case study was written by a teacher who wanted to understand Filad's experience at school and home so that she could make her own teaching more culturally relevant. With permission from Filad, other teachers, and Filad's family, the teacher followed Filad around for a day. She attended his classes and visited his home after school.

Step 2   Explain that there are two goals to this case study. The first goal is to develop reading and thinking skills among high school youth. The second goal is to elicit perspectives from students who are English language learners about their experiences at school and home.

Step 3   Distribute the Filad case study that follows. Explain the goals of this activity.

Step 4   Ask students to make notes as they read about connections between Filad's experiences and their own.

Step 5   Ask students to put a box around passages they would like to discuss as a class. When they are through reading, they will return to these passages and write questions to prompt class discussion. You should demonstrate the process using a think-aloud strategy so that students can hear what someone might say to himself or herself while reading a relevant passage and drafting a question for the class to probe.

Step 6   Explain that students will discuss their work with a partner before the whole-class discussion. You may want to provide a specific discussion guide.

Case Study: Filad

If I had to choose one word to associate with Filad, it would be *basketball*. Filad is rarely seen without a basketball in his hand. Almost every day the first thing he does upon entering my math classroom is hand me his basketball and ask me to put it somewhere safe until the end of class. He is frequently late to each of his classes because he stops by the gym to shoot baskets and is caught skipping his advisory class several times a week because he is involved in a basketball game in the gym during lunch.

Filad is from Mogadishu, Somalia. Now 16 years old, he was born right at the start of the war in Somalia and is the second youngest child in a family with five boys and six girls. The early years of Filad's life were chaotic, and he remembers only bits and pieces of his childhood. He is hoping to be able to go to Somalia and visit this summer, and he has dreams of joining a Somali Olympic basketball team.

Filad has been enrolled in the same school district since arriving in the United States 5 years ago with his mother, father, and two of his sisters, and he has struggled with school ever since. Although his verbal skills in English are far above the rest of the students in my math class, which is made up of mostly intermediate-level English language learners, the same is not true for reading and writing. This is a reason he is in the school's Read-Right program, which is designed to accelerate students who are significantly below grade level in reading. In addition, Filad is in an advanced language arts class for English language learners in which the students work primarily on writing.

Most of Filad's teachers are frustrated with him, his frequent tardiness, his talent at avoiding work in the classroom, and other behaviors that suggest a lack of academic effort. Since coming to the United States he has been recommended for special education by nearly every teacher he has had. His parents however, will not allow him to be tested because they see this as a weakness and they want Filad to be strong and work hard to achieve success. Filad was placed in my math class for English language learners by the school as an alternative to a special education program.

ELL Program at School

The ELL program at school is divided into four levels: beginning 1, beginning 2, intermediate, and advanced. Students who complete the advanced level of classes but cannot pass the language proficiency test to be officially exited from ELL are mainstreamed and checked on periodically by the bilingual tutors at the school. The ELL department is made up of five teachers. Four of the teachers teach a combination of reading, language arts, and communication classes to the various language levels. I am the fifth teacher and I teach math to beginning and intermediate ELL students, split into two classes. There are also three bilingual tutors, two Spanish tutors, and one Vietnamese tutor who work as aides in the

ELL classrooms and around the school. In most of the classes students seem to sit in groups according to whether they are pushing themselves and planning to go to college.

The beginning ELL classes are almost exclusively Latino, and the intermediate and advanced classes are around 60% Latino, the rest being a combination of students from Asia, Africa, and the Pacific Islands. Students can stay in the public school system until they are 21 years old, which means that the ELL classrooms have students varying in age from 14 to 20 years old, all with very different education backgrounds in their home countries. Most of the non-Latino students seem to learn English more quickly, because they have fewer people at school to converse with in their home language. There seems to be a split in many of the classrooms between students who come to school primarily to socialize and to learn some English and those who are concerned with academics and have dreams of graduating and going to college.

A Day in the Life of Filad

I see Filad for 80 minutes a day, 5 days a week. I often hear stories about the rest of his school day both from him and from his other teachers. In fact, one of Filad's favorite things to do seems to be to start up a conversation with me after class about his school day in hopes that we will talk long enough for me to write him a pass out of advisory. I also know quite a bit about Filad's activities around school from the emails circulated by other teachers.

Despite what I thought I knew about Filad and his education, shadowing him to other classes for an afternoon was an eye-opening experience that highlighted for me both how much potential Filad has and also the risks he faces of being inadequately prepared for the future. The school operates on a four-period day, which means that Filad has my math class along with three other classes, an advisory, and a lunch period; all classes are one semester long. The Read-Right program that follows my math class requires a student-teacher ratio of no more than 4:1. Filad is in a lower level of the three stations, which means he and one other student read out loud with a teacher from their assigned level picture book. The books in the classroom are divided by bin based on reading level. All of the books, even those at higher levels, are picture books geared toward very young children.

The students are assigned specific books and move through them based on their progress in the program. Filad shows me the system for the books and seems relatively confident about where he is in the process. The room appears to be a safe environment for him; he does not try to hide his reading struggles like I have seen him do in my class. The teacher working with Filad and the other student at his level has established a positive relationship with the students and insists on an environment that focuses on the progress they were making rather than problems.

As the day began, it was immediately apparent that I was influencing the environment. Filad made quite a few mistakes during the first few minutes and the teacher commented that he was not thinking about his reading as carefully as he normally does. Filad became quieter and quieter each time he made a mistake. I decided that I should leave, as he was clearly embarrassed to have me in the room.

Some initial questions immediately came to my mind as I waited for Filad's session to finish. He was obviously embarrassed by his lack of skill. However, he is not fully literate in his home language of Somali, and because he started school in the United States in sixth grade Filad, like many of his peers from similar backgrounds, missed the years in school that lay the foundation for the rest of a student's education. I wonder if the experiences we are providing students like Filad at the secondary level are rich enough educational experiences to fill in the huge gap in their learning. Is the education we are providing meaningful? As I followed Filad through the rest of his day, these questions remained in the forefront of my mind.

After 45 minutes in Read-Right, Filad moved next door to a writing class that is designed to complement the Read-Right program. The class had 10 students, one of whom appeared to be a teacher's assistant. The TA was the only girl in the class; the boys who made up the rest of the class were students who most mainstream teachers dread having in their class. They are energetic and, whether because of lack of interest or because of years of systematic failure, they seem to resist schoolwork at all costs and, like Filad, are incredibly skillful at avoiding academic work.

The teacher, a kind motherly woman, began by telling me that normally they do serious writing, but because today was Valentine's Day they were going to have some fun. This fun involved reading some Valentine's Day quotations and creating posters that visually represented the sayings. Immediately all nine boys moaned and complained, and immediately I wondered who this "fun" was designed for, as the topic of love was obviously the last thing these boys cared about at the moment. Eventually, after the class read the quotations together and the teacher talked briefly about what the words meant, the boys agreed to begin working on the project; although they only agreed after a large imposing-looking boy in the back of the room, with obvious artistic talent, agreed that this assignment was "OK" and began working.

As other students selected their quotations and began working, I noticed a switch in Filad's behavior. At the beginning of class he was happy and loud, joking with the other boys. As everyone began working he became very quiet and just stared at his paper. It wasn't until the teacher came over and pushed him to pick a quotation 5 minutes later that he made any move to work on the assignment. Even after he selected a quotation, for the majority of the class period he seemed to struggle over what to draw and over his apparent lack of drawing skills.

I watched the same thing happen to Filad in here as happened in his Read-Right room when he started making mistakes; he stopped sitting up straight, slid lower in his chair, and his smile faded. He made several attempts to draw things and each time crumpled up the paper and asked for a new one. At one point he asked another boy to do the drawing for him but was told that this wasn't allowed. This continued until the last 10 minutes of class, when the teacher stopped the students to have them write their 100 words for the day.

Throughout the class, I watched as Filad performed the same routine he often does in my class. As soon as the class started, he began asking the teacher questions about the specifics of the writing, then switched to asking questions about school in general and then questions about the teacher. By the end of the class period, Filad had written a total of three words and drawn a heart on a piece of paper. I found myself wondering once again: How are we as a school serving someone who is struggling but trying to be present as a student?

Filad's final class of the day was his ELL language arts class. The period began with two quotations about love, and the students were asked to write 200 words in response as an entry task. Filad immediately said, "I have to do this again? I already wrote this in my last class, Can I just turn that in?" In the 15 minutes that followed, as most of the class was writing, I was amazed at Filad's ability to stay incredibly busy while actually doing nothing at all.

In the time that followed I recorded his actions and will recount them here simply because I am amazed at how well he stays under the radar of the teacher and never manages to complete any of his work. In that 15-minute period of time, he spent several minutes organizing the papers on his desk, asked to go to the bathroom three times and was told no each time, asked a series of questions (e.g., "How many minutes do we have?" "How many words do we need to write?"), opened and closed his notebook several times, put the date on his paper, stared out the window, stared at the clock, spoke in Somali to another student, stared at the overhead and copied the quotations, asked again, "We have to write 200 words?," flipped through his notebook and read previous entries, put dates on future papers, looked at his watch, talked to the student next to him, asked a few more questions, and then with 3 minutes remaining wrote a few words and remarked, "Halfway is good enough for me!"

I watched as Filad continued this system to avoid work for the entire rest of the class period, and I became more and more perplexed. Was he simply not interested in the writing topics of today's class? Was he unable to access the information because of his low reading level? I noticed that all of Filad's teachers, including myself, are constantly telling Filad to focus and although he always seems agreeable, he does this only for a few minutes at a time.

After Filad left school and I reflected back on the day, I tried to think of one single thing that he had learned or accomplished in his classes. If this was a typical school day for him, how frustrating it must be to waste so much time at something that people consistently say is so important.

Home and Family

Filad's family lives in a duplex down the street from the local elementary school that Filad's younger sister attends. A family who moved from Mexico to the United States 3 years ago lives in the other half of the duplex, which is old and in need of repair. Other houses and small apartment complexes that look similar in age and quality surround the duplex. There is a small porch where both families store various items like coolers and toys. Although there was no one outside when I drove through the neighborhood in the late afternoon, it was obvious that many families with children lived in the area.

The home shared by Filad and his family consists of a living room, a kitchen, two bedrooms, one bathroom, and a basement. I talked to Filad's family while sitting with them in the living room, which had a beautiful thick carpet over the floor and dark carpets hanging on all walls. The windows were covered with deep purple curtains. The room was dim due to all the coverings but had a very warm feel. There were two small couches, a chair, a coffee table, and a VCR and small TV in the room. The kitchen, which was attached to the living room, was all white with a white table and chairs, and nothing else visible. Filad's two sisters share one of the bedrooms, his parents sleep in the second bedroom, and Filad sleeps in the basement. When I first walked into the house, Filad's younger sister walked into the living room but then quickly turned around and ran back into the bedroom followed by shouts from her father because she was wearing jeans, a t-shirt, and no head scarf. Her casual clothing was obviously not appropriate when there were guests. She joined her sister and mother in one of the bedrooms and returned with them a few minutes later, each dressed in a headscarf and long skirt.

From the beginning of our conversation it was evident that Filad's family is very close. His younger sister sat next to me during our entire conversation, sometimes helping Filad translate while I spoke with his parents and sometimes working on her homework. Every so often she would ask me questions about the assignment she was working on. Both Filad and his parents emphasized several times during our conversation that spending time with family was their highest priority. This family has done an amazing job of staying close despite the path they have traveled over the last 10 years.

Filad's parents did not readily talk about the time period when the war began and leading up to their departure from Somalia. They obviously have painful memories from the start of the war and have kept these memories from Filad and his younger sister, who were too young to remember most of what happened. Filad's father was the first to leave Somalia because the men in the family were the first ones who would be taken and killed. He made his way to a refugee camp in Kenya. At some point later, Filad's mother left with Filad, one of his brothers, and two of his sisters. Leaving six children behind, they made their way to a refugee camp in Ethiopia. Filad's father had no contact with the rest of his family during this time.

Filad's father had a brother who lived in Connecticut and eventually brought Filad's father from Kenya to the United States, where he was finally able to reestablish contact with his wife in Ethiopia. He managed to bring his family to Connecticut a year or two later. Soon after Filad, his siblings, and his mother arrived in Connecticut and were reunited with their father, they all moved to the West Coast on the assumption that more jobs were available there. They have lived in their current home ever since.

For a while both of Filad's parents worked several jobs. His father was a referee for local children's basketball and baseball games, worked as a custodian, and worked packing boxes. Filad's mother also worked packing boxes, helped with children a local day care, and cleaned homes. All of these things were very different from the lives they had lived in Somalia.

Before the war Filad's parents had a store where they sold everything from household goods to food they grew in their backyard. They owned their own home and had their own land. One of Filad's few memories from childhood is having a pet tiger and lion cubs in their backyard, which they kept until they grew too big and had to be released into the wild.

When I visited, neither one of Filad's parents had a job. Filad's mother has diabetes, and her health has deteriorated to the point that she can no longer work. Filad's father was working a night job up until recently, when he hurt his back. He is not able to return to work until it heals. Both of Filad's parents expressed concerns about their lives in the United States. They do not understand why this society is so centered on money. Filad's father commented, "You must have money to do anything in this country.

You cannot have a store unless you have the money to buy one and to pay every month. You cannot have electricity or water unless you have money. You cannot just sell things to people to make a living. No one will buy them from you; you must first have money." This was a big adjustment for the family when struggling to establish their lives in the United States.

They expressed surprise at how disconnected people in this country are from one another. They noticed this especially with the large homeless population in their city. "Where are these people's families?" commented Filad's mother. "Why do their families not take care of them? In Somalia no one would let their family stand on the street and beg from strangers. They would help them work; they would help them eat." Family is the number-one priority in their lives, and I find it amazing how strong this family has managed to stay despite the things they have been through for the last 10 years and are still going through.

Filad's family attributes their strength to their religion, Islam. Although I did not see any religious artifacts in the house, their religion was evident from their clothes and from their words. Religion has taught them that family is more important than anything. It keeps them from picking up bad habits such as alcohol, drugs, and greed that they feel are some of the many things that tear people apart. They told me that it teaches them generosity and honesty.

Another thing that struck me throughout my entire interaction with Filad's family is their dedication to having fun. Recreation is very important to them. Every member of the family mentioned that some of their favorite activities included going to Family Fun Center together and going out to a Somali restaurant together, which they try to do once a month. Perhaps this commitment to relaxation and enjoying one another's company is part of what has allowed them to stay so strong because it eases some of the strain from all of their experiences. Filad told me, "If I want to go to the park and shoot hoops, I never go by myself, we all go. My family wouldn't let me play alone. We do everything together. We play together."

Filad's education is very important to the family. They have dreams of Filad becoming a doctor or an engineer someday. They say that he talks about school often and is excited about his teachers and the things he is learning. They are aware that he has some trouble with reading and writing, but think that his high level of math skill can make up for it. Filad's mother went to a religious school as a child, but otherwise had no formal education. She cannot read or write. Filad's father had some formal education in Somalia, and when he compares his schooling to Filad's he does not believe there is much difference. He laments the lack of contact he and his wife have with his children's schools in the United States. He feels that

U.S. schools are too easy on children. In Somalia, schools and parents work together to make sure a child succeeds. Children cannot fall through the cracks like they do here; parents and teachers won't let it happen. Both parents want their children to be successful, but it was obvious from talking to them that they did not realize what Filad's education is like in this country. They talked to the teachers and administrators at Filad's middle school fairly frequently because Filad struggled with school, and they fought to keep him out of special education. They think that now all of his problems have been solved.

They believe that Filad's only struggle with school is that he does not try hard enough, and they do not seem to understand that although Filad is not classified as needing special education he still struggles significantly with school and is not in classes that will put him on track to graduate from high school on time. I think Filad understands that he is not performing in school as well as his parents think and hope. He understands that he is not in mainstream classes. I also get the impression that he does not want to let his parents down and therefore is intentionally positive but vague about his school experiences.

Conclusions

I believe that Filad's experiences as a high school immigrant child are representative of experiences being had by many of his peers, particularly those coming from similar backgrounds. He is trying to navigate his way through a school system that was not designed with him in mind. He is a struggling learner. He is struggling because he can't stay focused and because he cannot read or write even close to a high school level. He is struggling because he spent the first half of his life in a refugee camp and then arrived in the United States and began school in the second half of sixth grade. He is struggling because he is proficient enough in English by 10th grade to be in mainstream classes, but after only 4 years of school he cannot handle the work. He is struggling because no one has explained to him why he is learning the things he is learning or why he has been placed in the classes he is taking. The entire process of shadowing Filad through both his school and his home life was incredibly enlightening for me as a teacher and as someone who cares about learning and motivation. The idea that a child, particularly a child who is in classes that are designed to provide extra help, can learn nothing in an entire school day is very troubling.

The education of children who immigrate to the United States at the high school level is a ticking clock. Students who are new to the United States have a large amount of life experiences behind them that are significantly different than the lives most of their teachers know. They often enter schools at the high school level with, at best, spotty educational backgrounds. Unlike immigrant children entering at the elementary or even middle school level, they have only 6 years at most, and often more like 2 to 4 years, to catch up with their non-immigrant peers. Once this time passes they are adults and society is much less forgiving of the knowledge and experiences they are lacking, particularly if they stay in the United States. It is simply not okay to ignore the backgrounds these students are coming from and expect them to have the same skill to navigate their way through U.S. high schools as teenagers who were born in the United States.

Students like Filad are getting lost. The education they are receiving is not working for them. Like Filad, many students are placed in classes designed to catch them up to grade level as quickly as possible. Rather than participating in education that helps them learn, they end up receiving education that is confusing, disjointed, and primarily a combination of basic skills instruction. It has never been more apparent to me than it is now how essential it is to provide students with meaningful education experiences that draw on their backgrounds and are relevant to their lives.

Discussion Outlines for a Case Study

The Filad case can be used as one of two kinds of case study methods: analytical or problem-oriented. Generally, an analytical approach involves examining the case study to try to understand what has happened and why. Problems and solutions do not need to be part of the process. A problem-oriented method is just as it sounds: Students identify major problems and investigate solutions to the problems.

The directions listed before the Filad case study suggest that this case has elements for both methods because students can identify relevant connections to their lives and create discussion questions for the class that could include problem formation. You could approach the discussion of the case by making a three-column chart to fill in as a student speaks. The left column is labeled "Issues," the middle column "Questions," and the right column "Resources" for investigating questions. Of course, the approach you use will vary according to the purposes of using a particular case. Examples of questions you might ask to stimulate discussion with a case study follow:

1. Which issues in the case stand out for you? Why?

2. Were any of the issues familiar to you because of your own experience?

3. What issues are most important to resolve? Why?

4. What might make you apprehensive about trying to resolve an issue you think is important? Why? What could be done to change this?

5. If you were going to research a particular problem in the case, how would you turn it into one or more researchable questions? What steps would you follow for a thoughtful study? What resources would you use? Why those?

6. How does the case connect to other topics you have been studying in school? What are those connections?

7. What would you say to _____ if she or he asked you _____?

When time permits, it can be clarifying to role-play aspects of the case. For example, with the Filad case, students might role-play a response to the question: "What would be your remarks to a teacher who asked to shadow you? Let's hear them, and one of us can react as she might." Other times, it is beneficial to record key information on the board or a chart, whether with the aid of the previously mentioned three-column approach or with a graphic organizer or set of bullets. Direct quotes from a case are another way to focus the group, as are main ideas written as newspaper headlines and posted on a wall for easy viewing. Headlines can be an interesting way for students to summarize the significance of a case study or role-play.

If you use an action research approach, after students read the case, the pattern of learning moves through a cycle of reflection and analysis to the surfacing of concepts and principles, to the development of possible solutions, to theories that support those solutions, and to the application of action strategies to individuals' own purposes. An effective analysis guides students to answers based on the facts of the case rather than pure speculation. An action research cycle that requires students to develop, implement, and assess a possible solution typically involves helping students think through timing, strategies, barriers, and consequences, intended or otherwise (Marsick, 2004). For this process, you could adapt the project-planning form in Exhibit 5.2 for students to consider the range of details that a solution may require.

Closing a Case Study

How you close the case discussion is very important. Most cases do not end with "the answer" or in a confident resolution of the problem. Nevertheless, there should be an opportunity for learners to reflect on what they have learned, to privately or publicly identify new understandings, to air unresolved conflicts or questions, and to make plans for making changes or taking action. Here are some approaches to closing a case study activity:

- Ask students to describe specific issues or concepts they understand at a deeper level and possibly why as well.
- Ask students to write answers to questions such as these: What new insights did you gain from this case study and its discussion? What are your lingering questions? What new ideas do you want to continue to think about?
- Ask learners to brainstorm insights, personal changes in thinking or action, or new areas to explore as a result of their work.
- Go around the entire class and ask each student to provide one insight or question that emerged as a result of the process.

The next section provides additional ways to help students formulate questions that stimulate critical thinking. It begins with a brief discussion of the significance of critical thinking.

THOUGHT-PROVOKING QUESTIONS TO FACILITATE STUDENT ENGAGEMENT AND LEARNING THROUGH CRITICAL THINKING

Philosopher and educator John Dewey (1933) believed that thinking is questioning. If teachers and students are to realistically engage in the construction of knowledge, they must be capable of thinking about information in ways that transform that material into new knowledge. In many instances this transformation occurs when thought-provoking questions prompt critical thinking about contradictions between what is known and new information. This critical questioning stimulates students and teachers to use their own information, perspectives, and experience to become involved, deepen learning, and transform ideas and concepts into new meanings. Most definitions of critical thinking involve analyzing, inferring, synthesizing, applying, evaluating, comparing, contrasting, verifying, substantiating, explaining, and hypothesizing (Beyer, 1988).

Critical thinking also tends to foster discussions that are exploratory, unpredictable, risky, and exciting (Brookfield & Preskill, 2005). In fact, scholar and adult educator Stephen Brookfield (2012) argues that

if you can't think critically your survival is in peril because you risk living a life that—without your being aware of it—hurts you and serves the interests of those who wish you harm. If you can't think critically you have no chance of recognizing, let alone pushing back on, those times you are being manipulated. And if you can't think critically you will behave in ways that have less chance of achieving the results you want. So critical thinking is not just an academic process that leads to good scores on SAT's, elegantly argued essays, or experimental hypotheses that can stand the toughest scrutiny. It is a way of living that helps you stay intact when any number of organizations (corporate, political, educational, and cultural) are trying to get you to think and act in ways that serve their purposes. (p. 1)

Many theorists believe that critical thinking is as much a philosophy as a skill. They distinguish between a make-sense orientation and a critical orientation to determining whether an idea holds together. A make-sense orientation is when something is considered valid or holds together based on information that is judged to be self-evident or that connects with personal beliefs. A critical orientation examines problems, data and reasoning for inconsistencies, alternative perspectives, and counterarguments. This approach to teaching correlates positively with high levels of academic achievement across the curriculum (Newmann, Bryk, & Nagaoka, 2001). In addition, it enhances motivation to learn (Meece, 2003). Just as important, it is essential to active and informed engagement in matters of social, economic, and political justice.

However, research suggests that less than 5% of teacher questions ask students to think critically. In fact, one of the biggest differences between Japanese and U.S. math classes has to do with the kind of questions teachers ask, *how or why* versus *name and identify* (Stigler & Hiebert, 2004). The frequency of student-generated questions (most of which are factual) is also low in the United States, averaging 0.11 per hour per student in classrooms (Dillon, 1988). As educators, we need procedures that challenge ourselves and students to pose and examine relevant thought-provoking questions. In Activity 5.3, the thinking strategy developed by Alison King (1994) helps students hone their ability to ask questions that require critical thinking. Activities 5.4 and 5.5 provide additional strategies that you can adapt to a topic for higher levels of intellectual challenge among students.

ACTIVITY 5.3

Thought-Provoking Questions

Purpose: To encourage students to think critically and to promote connections between ideas in a lesson to another context

Time: Varies

Format: Partners

Process

Give students a written set of question starters such as *What would happen if . . . ?* and *How does . . . apply to everyday life?* Students use these generic questions to guide them in formulating their own specific questions pertaining to a passage of material or class discussion on any given topic. Exhibit 5.1 contains a list of question stems that can be adapted for use by filling in the blanks with information relevant to the subject at hand. It also specifies the critical thinking skills these questions elicit (King, 1994).

When you provide question stems to students for use in their conversations, you encourage students to bridge academic language with their own everyday language. For example, a student might transform the question "What evidence is there to support your idea?" to "How do you know for sure?" The goal is for students to learn to question their own thinking and the thinking of others.

To the list in Exhibit 5.1 you might add Socratic questions (Paul & Binker, 1990). Socratic questions, such as those in the following list, help learners probe their assumptions and understandings related to a topic.

1. Clarification: "What do you mean by . . . ? Could you give me an example?"

2. Probing for assumptions: "What are you assuming when you say . . . ?"

3. Probing for reasons and evidence: "How do you know that . . . ? What are your reasons for saying . . . ?"

4. Other perspectives: "What might someone say who believed that . . . ? What is an alternative viewpoint for . . . ?"

5. Probing for consequences: "Because of . . . what might happen?"

One of several helpful resources on Socratic questioning is *The Thinker's Guide to the Art of Socratic Questioning* (Paul & Elder, 2006).

The next two exercises are ways to teach and use thought-provoking questions to deepen students' understanding of an issue or topic.

ACTIVITY 5.4

Fish Bowl Questioning Procedure

Purpose: To examine and strengthen students' understanding of an issue using thought-provoking questions and to practice using thought-provoking questions to realize their value for in-depth understanding and different perspectives on relevant issues

Time: 30 minutes

Format: Small and large group simultaneously

Process

One-third of the group sits in a circle and discusses with the facilitator a relevant topic using the list of questions in Exhibit 5.1 to stimulate dialogue. Each member of this "fish bowl" group is asked to choose an appropriate time to extend or deepen the dialogue by using at least one

Exhibit 5.1 Guiding Thought-Provoking Questioning

Generic Questions	Specific Thinking Skills Induced
What is another example of . . . ?	Application
How could . . . be used to . . . ?	Application
What would happen if . . . ?	Prediction/hypothesizing
What are the strengths and weaknesses of . . . ?	Analysis/inference
What is . . . analogous (or similar) to?	Creating analogies/metaphors
What do we already know about . . . ?	Activating prior knowledge
How does . . . affect . . . ?	Analysis of relationship
How does . . . relate to what we learned before?	Activating prior knowledge
Explain why . . . or explain how . . .	Analysis
What is the meaning of . . . ?	Analysis
Why is . . . important?	Analysis of significance
What is the difference between . . . and . . . ?	Compare-contrast
How are . . . and . . . similar?	Compare-contrast
How does . . . apply to everyday life?	Application to real world
What is a possible argument against . . . ?	Rebuttal argument
What is the best . . . , and why?	Evaluation and evidence
What are some possible solutions to the problem of . . . ?	Synthesis of ideas
How do you think . . . would see the issue of . . . ?	Taking other perspectives
What do you think causes . . . ? Why?	Analysis of relationship
Do you agree or disagree with . . . ? Support your answer.	Evaluation and evidence

higher-order question. The topics of cultural diversity and racism are used to exemplify the process: "How do we show respect for cultural diversity in our school?" or "How can we help ourselves and other students confront and work together to overcome racism?" The rest of the group (the remaining two-thirds) sits in a circle around the others. They listen and take notes, recording their own ideas for thought-provoking questions that extend or deepen the discussion. In addition, two scribes create group memory on newsprint. One scribe records higher-order questions that are asked. The other is content focused, noting ideas for further consideration. After the smaller group has had approximately 15 minutes to discuss the topic, there is a dialogue among the whole group, with questions and comments initially coming from the larger group.

Debrief: Ask students, "What are some of the ways we are learning to think deeply while listening well to others? What are some important ideas related to content, in this case respecting cultural diversity and confronting racism, that were discussed? What are some specific questions we may want to investigate further?"

ACTIVITY 5.5
Guided Reciprocal Questioning

Purpose: To examine and strengthen students' understanding of an issue using thought-provoking questions and to practice using thought-provoking questions to realize their value for in-depth understanding and different perspectives on relevant issues

Time: 30 minutes

Format: Pairs or small groups

Process

The examples that follow are intended to demonstrate two different ways to use guided reciprocal questioning. This process is easily adapted to other content and disciplines.

Example 1: Explain that *guided reciprocal questioning* (King, 1994) is a way for students to use thought-provoking questions in pairs and small groups. After an activity such as observing a project presentation, listening to a short lecture, or reading an article or a book, students use generic question stems and work independently to generate two or three questions based on the material. Next, in pairs or small groups, they engage in peer questioning, taking turns to ask their questions with a partner or group and to answer each other's questions in a reciprocal manner. This approach encourages a deeper dialogue and helps students check their understanding as well as learn from other students' perspectives.

For example, students who read Alice Walker's *The Color Purple* have developed two questions, each based on the list in Exhibit 5.1, regarding any aspect of the book that they found applicable to their own lives. In pairs, each student places two questions before his or her partner. In one pair the questions read: How does the novel's representation of conflicts stemming from the human need for equality apply to our everyday lives? How is the portrayal of family life in the novel strikingly similar to or different from family life today? The book has many strengths, but from your perspective what were some of its weaknesses? Will this book remain a classic? Why or why not? With these questions, students have an opportunity to relate ideas from their own thinking. This process provides an opportunity to infer, compare, evaluate, and explain, all of which can lead to a fuller awareness and better understanding of ideas and topics.

Example 2: To reflect on an article, provide the URL or distribute a print copy of a brief article that applies to an issue or topic students are studying. For example, to explore the topic of resilience in middle and high school, you might ask students to read Amy Azzam's (2013) interview with Maya Angelou. As students reflect on the article, which speaks to the topic of resilience, they select or generate two to three question stems. Next, in pairs or small groups, students engage in peer questioning, taking turns asking their questions to their partner or group and answering each other's questions in a reciprocal manner. To debrief, teachers at Greece Central School District in New York have posted a thoughtful reflection sheet online to help students think deeply about what they have learned (www.greece.k12.ny.us/district.cfm?subpage=49).

For a brief whole-class reflection on the process, you might ask students what kind of questions tend to generate the most thoughtful responses and why. If you teach at the primary level, you might ask students to draw a large square and a large circle on a piece of paper, perhaps in a journal. Within the square, students respond to the question: What squared with your thinking and why? Within the circle, students respond to the question: What is something that is going around in your mind that you will continue to think about? If time permits, students share their responses with one another.

Beyond the activities that help students probe their own and other people's thinking, there are numerous learning activities that stimulate thinking by their very nature. The following list can assist you in developing learning-focused assessment practices that go beyond simply auditing what students may have learned (see Chapter 6).

Discern a pattern	Infer a relationship
Teach someone	Create a model
Pursue an alternative answer	Disprove a notion
Reveal the limits of a theory	Exhibit findings creatively
Design an experiment	Evaluate a performance
Judge the accuracy of a superficially appealing idea	Explore and report fairly on an appealing controversy
Complete a cost-benefit analysis	Assess the quality of something
Display and illuminate a complex idea graphically	Find common elements in diverse and complex idea items or ideas
Rate proposals or candidates	Develop (and implement) a plan

To illustrate how this list can assist you and students in designing in-depth tasks, imagine a science teacher who works with students to design an experiment to *assess the quality* of their school's water supply and *present the results* to the student council. Or imagine a history teacher who works with students to *design an experiment* in which members of different student groups collaborate on a mural that features historical figures from their communities. After painting the mural on surfaces that are frequently targeted for graffiti, a psychology class collects and *graphically displays data* related to increased or decreased indicators of care for the artistic renditions on walls and walkways and in restrooms.

As with most well-designed, open-ended learning experiences, there are unanticipated rewards for students (and teachers) when outcomes are imaginative as well as academically substantive. The following section builds on this idea through a discussion of using relevant problems as the foundation of learning. It provides strategies for problem-based and project-based learning and shows how to use the Motivational Framework for Culturally Responsive Teaching as a guide.

USING RELEVANT PROBLEMS TO FACILITATE LEARNING

A relevant problem can be broadly characterized as any situation in which a person wants to achieve a goal for which an obstacle exists (Voss, 1989). Relevant problems go hand in glove with problem-based learning, inquiry-focused learning, and project-based learning, all of which provide students with the opportunity to learn about a topic or issue by exploring authentic problems.

Although the terms *problem-based learning* and *project-based learning* are often used synonymously, there are historical distinctions. Generally, problem-based learning is discipline-specific and emerges from vicarious sources such as case studies, fictional scenarios, and imaginative math or science problems. Generally, project-based learning is interdisciplinary, involves "real-world" tasks or settings, and includes a concrete product or demonstration. However, these distinctions are somewhat arbitrary and there may be more similarities than differences. For example, in both problem-based and project-based learning, teachers typically encourage self-direction, peer collaboration, inquiry, and creativity. Further, both approaches tend to require more time, intellectual engagement, and support than discrete classroom learning tasks.

When relevant and within the range of a student's capacity, problems are by definition engaging and challenging. To a certain extent, they are also culture-bound (Hofstede & Hofstede, 2005). Differences in perspective and social codes influence how people conceive and approach a problem. Whether solving a dispute or exploring the ecological implications of climate change, the variety in how a problem is perceived and resolved is limitless. Education has enjoyed a long history using problems as a procedure for learning. The use of ill-structured problems—those not solvable with certainty—and problem posing dates back to ancient times. In the 1970s and 1980s, the English translation of *Pedagogy of the Oppressed* (Freire, 1970), the publication of *The Politics of Education* (Freire, 1985), and the emergence of multicultural education contributed to a growing interest in problem solving for social justice. Today, ideas about student agency, deep learning, problem-based learning, and social justice continue to be fundamental characteristics of multicultural pedagogy (Nieto & Bode, 2011).

With problem-based learning at the center of many project-based learning initiatives, innovative schools such as New Tech High School, The Met, and Mission Hill; networks such as Expeditionary Learning and League of Innovative Schools; professional and philanthropic organizations such as the Buck Institute for Education and the Annenberg Foundation; and student empowerment networks such as Vermont-based Youth and Adults Transforming Schools Together and Seattle-based AIM Center provide valuable theories and resources for student engagement in problem- and project-based learning.

As previously mentioned, problem-based learning is characterized by the use of real-world problems as a means for students to learn critical thinking, problem-solving skills, and the essential concepts of a particular discipline. In most instances, questioning methods or brainstorming helps to draw forth a relevant problem based on student concerns and interests. Students then immerse themselves in research to learn concepts and develop skills that lead to insights and ideas for problem resolution. For example, students may question a popular historical viewpoint and need to become historians themselves, reading primary material and writing their own historical accounts. Or students may distrust the media's presentation of a "social problem" and investigate the issue themselves, through interviews, literature reviews, statistical analysis, and so forth. The following activity is one of several ways to identify relevant problems to study with students.

ACTIVITY 5.6

Identifying Relevant Problems With Students

This activity is adapted from the work of Paulo Freire (1970). For additional information on critical pedagogy and problem posing, see the Freire Institute's website (www.freire.org/paulo-freire) and *Freire for the Classroom: A Sourcebook for Liberatory Teaching* (Shor, 1987, p. 35).

Purpose: To identify issues and problems for special interest groups to study

Time: Varies

Format: Individual, small group, and large group

Process

Either on a board in front of the class or on the door into the classroom, post a large "problem tree" that has been designed with many branches. Using sticky notes for leaves of the tree, invite students to write problems or questions related to a particular topic the class will study. Provide two to three examples of your own to show the range of possibility. For example, if the topic is gun violence, you could post sticky notes such as the following: "What factors contribute to gun violence throughout our city?" "What organizations or programs have had the biggest influence on reducing urban gun violence and what is their approach?" "Who are some local experts on gun violence?"

Explain to students that they will form special interest groups (SIGs) to collaborate on research and present what they discover to relevant audiences based on their findings. Explain that SIGs will be determined according to the categories that emerge when students' "leaves" (sticky notes) cluster together with questions that share a similar focus. For example, if the topic is gun violence, imagine that students have posted leaves with the following questions: "What is the influence of county mandates increasing law enforcement in high incidence areas?" "What is the influence of incarceration on gun violence?" "What is the impact of mandatory drug sentences on gang warfare?" Students might cluster these leaves under a category that could be labeled "Legal Issues." There might also be leaves with questions such as these: "What is the influence of secure housing, strong schools, and access to mental and physical healthcare on gun violence?" "What nonprofit organizations have been most effective as stewards of peace?" Students might cluster these under a category labeled "Positive Community Influences."

To provide a glimpse of what it might look like to research one of these categories, teach a mini-lesson that demonstrates the assignment. Show how each group will agree on a research question and something that they want to learn about by doing inquiry (see Exhibit 5.2). Tell students that they will break out into smaller teams of two to three to research the question in different ways. Depending on the specific categories students have identified related to gun violence, and the questions students seek to explore, research practices will vary. For example, if a group has six students, two students might interview local housing, education, and healthcare experts; two students might review literature on community-based programs and visit influential community-based organizations to learn about their work; and two students might visit with families whose lives have been impacted by gun violence. All three teams would contribute perspectives that pertain to the research question they've selected to investigate in a particular category related to the topic of gun violence.

The project-planning matrix in Exhibit 5.2 illustrates one way to help students think through their research approach. It can be easily adapted to other problems and projects. Note that the primary motivational conditions for each category are identified along the left column in parentheses.

Another way to identify relevant problems is to place students *in* a relevant problem. For example, for courses in math or accounting, a problem might state: "You are the treasurer of a community organization and you are losing this amount of money per month. With these assets, liabilities, dues, and so forth, what do you do?" For a course in government, social issues, economics, or math the posed problem might state: "You are a 17-year-old student who is African American. You have your first automobile accident, for which you are not at fault. Although you have no previous driving violations, your insurance is canceled. Review your options using, as a part of your investigation, actuarial records and predictive statistics."

Exhibit 5.2 Planning Form

Names of team members:
Contact information for all members:
Team leader(s):
Date:

Planning Form for (Topic)		
Basic considerations and connections *(Motivational condition: Developing a positive attitude through choice and relevance)*	Name of project (or problem)	e.g., the role of organizations in reducing urban gun violence
	Pseudonyms for people with whom I/ we plan to interact	To be determined
	Connections to other learning experiences and priorities in this class and other classes	e.g., the forensics unit (science), statistics related to gun violence (math), examining the lyrics in urban hip hop (music)
	Times and places for project work (draft schedule)	e. g., dates, times, and meeting rooms
	Helpful literature	e. g., *Journal of Criminal Law and Criminology,* Bureau of Justice Statistics publications, etc.
	Key points to include in a statement of purpose/consent form to be signed by people whom we interview	(Note: Typically teachers provide a sample statement of purpose and consent form if students are conducting research as part of their project.)
Research question(s) *(Motivational conditions: Developing a positive attitude through choice and relevance; enhancing meaning through challenge and engagement)*	The general question for all students	e.g., What do communities need to know and be able to do to eliminate gun violence?
	The focus question for your student interest group (SIG)	e.g., What do local social service providers believe about the origins of gun violence? What do they do to create safer and healthier communities?
	Questions related to the inquiry process	e.g., What makes a good interview? How do researchers analyze interview data? How can we minimize bias?

Demonstration of understanding (*Motivational condition: Engendering competence through effectively learning something we value in a way that is authentic to our world*)	Major product(s)	*For our final project, we will* share our approach and summarize our findings in a report that includes a graphic organizer of social service agencies that work with the issue of gun violence and two to three important discoveries we made based on what we learned from interviews with representatives from a sample of agencies. In addition, we will develop a set of recommendations based on our analysis of interview data. Recommendations will respond directly to our SIG's focus question(s).
	A trusted friend or family member with whom I'll share what I am learning as I work on the project	To be determined
	Possible extension activities	e.g., work with a visual or graphic artist to enrich our presentation
Approach to an excellent final product (*Motivational condition: Engendering competence through effectively learning something we value in a way that is authentic to our world*)	Rubric(s), assignment notes, and media my group will use to organize a culminating paper or product	(Note: Teachers provide rubrics and, if possible, exemplars.)
	A supportive friend to help me edit my contributions to the final paper or product.	To be determined
	Feedback tools to assess the experience from the perspective of the people we interview, as well as interpreters if they have been a resource.	We will follow up with the people we interviewed to share our results and learn from their perspectives about how to improve our research process and findings. We will include their ideas in a self-assessment of the process.

Continued

Exhibit 5.2 Continued

	Presentation audience(s)	In addition to a 15-minute presentation to our class, we will schedule a meeting that includes community members such as an alderman, our school social worker, and her supervisor from the mayor's office, two to three staff members from influential community organizations, and our families.
	Creative products/ artwork/photography	In addition to text we will use music, graphic design, and photography to communicate with others about our project.
Activities that support implementation of the entire process *(Motivational condition: All four motivational conditions working together)*	First	Set a time to meet with research partner(s).
	Second	Clarify the research questions, methods, timeline, and research roles, such as who will: • convene the group and manage the schedule, including regular team meetings with the teacher and regular times to share journal entries (as appropriate) • take notes during meetings and act as the team historian • coordinate the final report • coordinate the final presentation to the class • serve as the copyeditor for the final report • oversee visual aids, artwork, and other creative media Clarify how the research team will work together and solve problems that emerge.

	Third	Research the work of different community-based organizations, read and take notes on at least two well-respected articles on urban gun violence (each research partner will read two different articles and prepare summaries to share), read about interviewing people, and discuss summaries and insights with research partner(s).
	Fourth	Develop interview questions, get feedback on interview questions, and refine interview questions. Create or adapt a one-paragraph statement of purpose and a consent form to share with people who are invited to participate in the project.
	Fifth	Identify organizations to visit and people to interview. Set up visits. Clarify the approach to visiting organizations and interviewing people, including note-taking and use of cell phones to record interviews and take pictures when appropriate (e.g., pictures of bulletin boards and other displays).
	Sixth	Make sense of notes and recordings, using an agreed-upon approach to identifying patterns and themes. Share insights with research partner(s). Outline draft report.
	Seventh	Begin to write report, with each research partner taking a different section and keeping track of questions that come up while writing. Consider visual aids such as charts and photos for each section.
Resources	Human resources	A graphic artist to provide tips on graphic organizers and cover art
	Technical resources	Bus passes, pens and two-column tablets for interview notes, copy machine, printer
	Financial resources	Note: Funds will be raised as a class, and the class will create and manage a budget for research teams.

USING THE MOTIVATIONAL FRAMEWORK FOR PROBLEM-BASED AND PROJECT-BASED LEARNING

The Motivational Framework for Culturally Responsive Teaching can serve as a guide to effective problem- and project-based learning in which students find solutions to relevant problems in ways that involve risk-taking and collaboration.

The following scenario provides a primary-level example of a problem-based learning experience in the subject of math. In this example, Ms. Kennedy is a teacher who has used the four conditions of the motivational framework to compose a lesson in which students create and solve their own story problems, working individually and with partners. In the scenario, parentheses identify which of the four conditions of the motivational framework are addressed through various aspects of the learning experience. As you will notice, the activities carrying out the motivational conditions are mutually supportive and sometimes overlap. Yet when developing learning experiences for a project based on the conditions of the motivational framework, your primary consideration should be to use a motivational condition to generate or plan an activity and not concern yourself with the overlap that may occur quite normally with other conditions from the framework.

Hiu Wan Chan loves her fifth-grade math class even though her grades are just a little above average. One reason is that Ms. Kennedy always seems enthusiastic about teaching math. She also has interesting ways for students to learn things. Today she begins by telling students how much she enjoyed visiting their homes before school started (motivational condition: establishing inclusion through resect and connectedness). She describes some of the things she learned, including the different kinds of collections students wanted to show her, such as action figures, dolls, and souvenirs. She asks students to turn to their elbow partner and share something they either collect or would like to collect. Afterward she writes everyone's ideas on the board (motivational condition: developing a positive attitude through choice and relevance).

Next, Ms. Kennedy tells students that today they are going to review double-digit division. She poses this question: If someone asked you to explain why being able to divide by a double digit is important to a collector such as yourself, what would you tell that person? As students volunteer their ideas, Ms. Kennedy shows appreciation and probes when she isn't sure she understands. She also makes a colorful chart on the board so students can identify patterns in their ideas (motivational condition: developing a positive attitude through choice and relevance).

After students recall their knowledge about dividing numbers by double digits, Ms. Kennedy asks them to create a double-digit division story problem about their collection. When everyone is ready, she asks for a volunteer to share her or his problem and works with the volunteer to make the problem clear enough for the rest of the class to solve it. Ms. Kennedy tells the class that they are going to do the same thing in small groups and writes down the instructions that are on the board. The instructions encourage students to use whatever problem-solving approach makes the most sense to the group. First, one by one, each person in the group shares his or her problem. Second, other group members help make the problem clear to everyone in the group. Third, each group member solves the problem individually. Fourth, the group discusses their answers (motivational conditions: developing a positive attitude through choice and relevance, and enhancing meaning through challenge and engagement). Ms. Kennedy assures the students that there can be different ways to solve problems and everyone's ideas should be respected. She asks, "What are some ways to show respect to other members of your group?" (motivational condition: establishing inclusion through respect and connectedness).

Ms. Kennedy has organized the class so that each group has a mix of students with different skill levels. Nonetheless, she knows that some groups will finish earlier than others, so she has a challenge for them. She wants groups who finish early to create a fictional story problem about the class as a whole. Since there are 30 students in the class, the divisor will be 30. The only catch is that they can't use food in the story problem, and the problem has to involve at least one other operation in addition to division (motivational condition: enhancing meaning through challenge and engagement).

She shows an example: In a science and social studies class, 30 students developed a way to improve recycling in the city. They want to visit the director of the city's recycling program to discuss their ideas. The students think they need $125 for the trip. Will that be enough money if they want to ride the city bus both ways? When the group answers the question, someone needs to be the writer, someone needs to be the editor to make sure spelling and grammar are accurate, someone needs to illustrate the problem, and someone needs to post the problem to the online math blog so that others can answer it (motivational conditions: developing a positive attitude through choice and relevance, and engendering competence through effectively learning something students value in a way that is authentic to their world).

Before the math lesson concludes, Ms. Kennedy asks students to take out their math journal and write something they learned in math about double-digit division that they want to remember to tell their family or a friend about (motivational condition: engendering competence through effectively learning something students value in a way that is authentic to their world).

As Hiu Wan leaves the classroom at the end of the day, she smiles at Ms. Kennedy, who is standing by the door. Hiu Wan can't wait to go home and organize her collection of shells from a trip to the beach with her grandmother last summer.

Let's analyze this scenario from Hiu Wan's perspective. She loves math for a number of reasons. She is connected to her teacher and friends. Home visits, elbow partners, and group work contribute to this feeling (*motivational condition: establishing inclusion through respect and connectedness*). Hiu Wan also enjoys the way Ms. Kennedy uses relevant contexts to help students learn double-digit division. In addition, there are several ways for students to determine their own approach to learning (*motivational condition: developing a positive attitude through choice and relevance*). It is safe to assume that even though Hiu Wan may find math to be challenging, she is willing to engage because the problems are real and creative, because learning is well scaffolded by the way Ms. Kennedy thoughtfully demonstrates how to create and solve problems (*motivational condition: engendering competence through authenticity and effectiveness*), and because Ms. Kennedy carefully structures peer interaction (*motivational condition: developing inclusion through respect and connectedness*).

In an article in the *New York Times Magazine,* Elizabeth Green (2014) confronts the question: Why does everyone hate the new math? She suggests that the culprit is primarily a problem of how to help teachers escape the "I, We, You" approach to instruction. This approach works against student interest and engagement and, according to Green, goes something like this:

> "Today, I'm going to show you how to divide a three-digit number by a two-digit number" (I). Then they (teachers) lead the class in trying out a sample problem: "Let's try out the steps for 242 [divided by] 16" (We). Finally they let students work through similar problems on their own, usually by silently making their way through a worksheet: "Keep your eyes on your own paper!" (You). (p. 26)

> This approach to teaching turns school math into a sort of arbitrary process wholly divorced from the real world of numbers. Students learn not math but, in the words of one math educator, answer-getting. Instead of trying to convey, say, the essence of what it means to subtract fractions, teachers tell students to draw butterflies and multiply along the diagonal wings, add the antennas and finally reduce and simplify as needed. The answer-getting strategies may serve them well for a class period of practice problems, but after a week, they forget. (Green, 2014, p. 26)

Green's article raises a vital question: How could you teach math in school in a way that mirrors the way children learn it in the real world? On this topic, the work of Magdelene Lampert (2001) and Deborah Ball (2000) is especially informative. Their emphasis on constructing sequences of deep, relevant, and well-contextualized learning is compatible with the topic of the next section: project-based learning.

PROJECT-BASED LEARNING

From community service to dramatic presentations, intrinsically motivating and academically effective projects offer multiple ways to connect with others and make connections across subject areas, pursue relevant goals and interests, work through meaningful challenges, and create new knowledge and demonstrations of learning. These virtues make learning motivating and capable of embracing cultural diversity. They draw on a wide range of intelligences and elicit new concepts and skills in ways that authentically contribute to the lives and aspirations of learners. Of course, this requires motivational and academically rigorous planning on the part of teachers. It also requires ongoing attention to the unpredictable consequences of personalized learning.

According to Larmer and Mergendoller (2012), there are eight essentials that distinguish project-based learning from doing projects. I would add that these eight essentials also distinguish project-based learning from the ubiquitous label of "active learning." These essentials are significant content, need to know, a driving question, student voice and choice, in-depth inquiry, critique and revision, a public audience, and 21st century competencies such as curiosity, caring, confidence, and courage. In *21st Century Skills: Learning for Life in Our Times*, Bernie Trilling and Charles Fidal (2009) cluster the skills that students will need in an ever-changing 21st century into three primary categories: learning and innovation skills, digital literacy skills, and career and life skills. In most ways the conditions that Trilling and Fidal identify as necessary to make high performance powerful closely correspond to the four conditions of the motivational framework, in parenthesis as follows:

1. Very high levels of learning challenge (enhancing meaning: challenge and engagement), often coming from an internal personal passion (developing a positive attitude: choice and relevance)

2. Equally high levels of external caring and personal support—a demanding but loving teacher, a tough but caring coach, or an inspirational learning guide (establishing inclusion: respect and connectedness)

3. Full permission to fail—safely and with encouragement to apply the hard lessons learned from failure to continuing the struggle with the challenge at hand (engendering competence: authenticity and effectiveness). (pp. xxvi–xxvii)

In these approaches, who students are as cultural beings is an essential consideration. Take any of the 21st century skills or motivational conditions and imagine four students from different cultural back-grounds, one of whom is an English language learner, one of whom is identified for special education services, one of whom is from a middle-income Jewish American community, and one of whom is from a high-income African American community. Skillful teachers understand that teaching of any sort is culturally mediated, including what kind of sup-port students need for learning that involves passion, challenge, and authentic consequences.

Personalized, project-based support is a highly nuanced endeavor. For some students high support for high challenge may require crossing boundaries that busy teachers sometimes try to maintain. This may be particularly necessary in communities where trusting another person with personal challenges is reserved for family and close friends. In this case, to develop a trusting relationship, a teacher might offer to assist a student with transportation or discuss a student's project over lunch in the stu-dent's community.

For another student whose immediate help for her or his family is the highest priority, a teacher will need to understand that commitment to school and to completing homework may be a distant luxury. The teacher may have to help this student manage schoolwork so that it can take place during the school day or at times interspersed with the student's need to assist family.

And for a student with a strong sense of efficacy and a family that turns personal projects into family projects so that everyone can learn together, a teacher will need to respect and plan for family involvement. In the case of projects that have a cultural theme that is outside of some stu-dents' experience, a teacher might also consider developing a council of project mentors who not only support these students' work, but offer sup-port to the teacher as a learner as well.

Pragmatic Considerations for Projects

There are numerous online project templates and ideas to assist teach-ers with planning. These are freely available from websites such as Edutopia, the Buck Institute, state departments of education, school dis-tricts, and many schools. Typically, plans include a number of decision points, with the implicit question of whether a teacher can realistically engage with this approach to learning. In addition to being time-consuming, project-based learning doesn't conform to a lock-step sequence of activi-ties. Flexibility is essential. One of the most rewarding characteristics of projects, for teachers as well as students, is the very thing that many human beings seek to control: unpredictability.

Other considerations include the following:

- whether projects will be individual or collaborative
- the extent to which students will assist in the project's conception and initial planning
- how students will personalize and update their goals and approach as they learn
- the kind of project timeline that will help students schedule their learning activities in ways that coordinate with others and can be realistically completed
- with whom students will share/present their final products
- how students will receive feedback throughout the process
- whether the audiences for student presentations will offer feedback and, if so, what kind
- whether, in addition to what students learned in relation to research questions, the final evaluation will take into account the quality of project planning, execution, and presentation; challenge level; creativity and originality; use of resources; and evaluation of and from co-learners
- access to knowledge from people outside of the class, such as local experts

Adapted from the work of Beverly Daniel Tatum (1992), the following scenario provides a glimpse at a project in which the class shares an overarching goal, with opportunities to personalize the experience. The overarching goal is to provide students with an understanding of the psychological causes and emotional reality of racism as it appears in everyday life. Imagine that the class size is 30 students, most of whom are white European Americans from socioeconomic backgrounds ranging from low to high income.

American Studies With Josephine Butler

In her 11th-grade American Studies course, Josephine Butler and her students have been using literature, film, and music to explore the problem of racism. Today she will introduce a project that requires students to investigate firsthand everyday circumstances that people of color may encounter in their communities. She wants students to have a fuller range of understanding about this complex and virulent problem.

Although Ms. Butler will work with students to personalize their specific approaches to the project, the experiences will include visiting supermarkets in various neighborhoods to compare costs and quality of goods and services, interviewing racially different couples (e.g., a man who is white and a woman who is black) who have experienced looking for an apartment to rent in the broader community, and attending a service with another student at one of several churches, mosques, or temples that welcome all people but are primarily attended by a particular non-white ethnic group.

In addition to the questions that Ms. Butler wants students to consider, students will develop some of their own questions and some of their own activities as part of the learning experience. Ms. Butler explains to students that one of the reasons she will work with everyone to carefully structure their project is because she wants to ensure that students avoid slipping into default judgments about complex situations and people in communities other than their own. All students will keep journals to keep track of and critically reflect on their experiences in relation to research questions. Their journals provide an opportunity to examine their own underlying beliefs and assumptions after each experience. At this time, there will also be an opportunity to engage in dialogue with peers and with a team of community mentors to explore their interpretation of events and deepen their understanding. Volunteer mentors are selected because of their membership in the communities that students will visit, their experience discussing racism, and their respect for high school youth.

Through self-generated knowledge (generated by students based on literature, experience, and reflection), students will explore possibilities for change and ways to take effective action. Eventually, they will work in small groups to develop realistic action plans to further understand and confront racism. Groups will share their ideas with and receive feedback from project mentors.

Students will also have the opportunity to privately record an interview of themselves regarding their racial views at the beginning and end of the project. After reviewing these two recordings, students will write about their perceived changes in racial understanding.

Ms. Butler will accept the validity of students' experiences, thinking, and judgments, and, with context and meaning making as central considerations, construct learning in a way that has the potential to be transformative. For the purposes of this project, transformative means that there will be a shift in perspective, students will see the world differently, and students will be interested in other forms of action to confront racism (Pugh, Linnenbrink-Garcia, Koskey, Stewart, & Manzey, 2010). Ms. Butler will work with students to assess their transformation by teaching them how to code their journals, observation notes, and self-interviews using key words and phrases to identify themes. Students' grades will not be based on evidence of transformation but rather on their engaged participation in each of the experiences and the products their project requires.

In this scenario, Ms. Butler uses several strategies for students to reflect and receive feedback on their learning throughout the project. This includes frequent opportunities for sensemaking through journals, class discussion, peer collaboration, interactions with project mentors from the community, and engagement in authentic settings. In addition, Ms. Butler uses literature to help students explicitly anchor and illuminate the significance of their experiences.

While problem-based and project-based learning encourage deep, sustained learning, they are only two of many instructional strategies for the motivational condition of enhancing meaning through challenge and engagement. Case study method, which was examined earlier in this chapter, is a more vicarious and short-term approach and is also valuable as a catalyst for learning. The same can be said of role-playing and simulations.

ROLE-PLAYING AND SIMULATIONS TO ENHANCE MEANING IN A MORE REALISTIC CONTEXT

When students experience perspectives, ideas, skills, and situations approximating authentic instances of life, they have an opportunity to enhance the meaning of what they are learning. *Role-playing* is acting out a possible situation by personifying another individual, imagining another scene or set of circumstances, or both. Because role-playing has broad applicability across subject areas and provides a context for multiple perspectives to emerge, it is a highly useful strategy.

The main goal of role-playing is to create an experience that involves students' intellect, emotions, and physical senses so that their experience is as realistic as possible. Role-playing offers students the opportunity to think in the moment, question their perspectives, respond to novel or unexpected circumstances, and consider different ways of knowing. It can be used to practice a specific skill such as critical questioning, a collaborative skill such as collective bargaining, a problem-solving skill such as a computerized simulation of the procedure for a biochemistry experiment, or a synthesizing skill such as how to organize a project plan using procedures from throughout this book.

Role-playing can also help students develop empathy and validation, especially when they imagine the viewpoints and rationales of people from different backgrounds, as in the case of a European American border guard in southern Texas or an immigrant from Central America offering opinions on the conditions that influence immigration. When there is a chance to reverse roles and act out roles from opposing or different perspectives, or from an unfamiliar or conflicting perspective, students have a chance to consider a position they may never have engaged before. This process can be quite powerful.

Simulation is an umbrella term for learning procedures that include role-playing and simulation exercises and games that allow students to practice and apply their learning in inauthentic yet sufficiently realistic contexts (Meyers & Jones, 1993). Simulation exercises and games are situations in which a whole group is involved, with students assuming different roles as they act out a prescribed scenario. These scenarios allow students to acquire or put into practice particular concepts or skills. Often in a more structured manner, simulations immerse students in another social reality, providing the opportunity to experience what might remain abstract in text materials—for example, power, conflict, or discrimination.

In recent years, simulations have become popular for school-to-career preparation, and rapidly evolving technology makes them more creative and accessible for classroom and online learning. A well-designed simulation elicits a variety of feelings in learners, allows for practice of new learning among unpredictable events, replicates potential roles in work and the community, offers feedback from a variety of sources, supports collaboration, and stimulates decision making with cause-and-effect consequences (Vaughan, 2006).

The elements in Exhibit 5.3, adapted from an outline by Michael Vaughan (2006), are for a simulation to teach leadership skills but are relevant for a range of topics. The elements in this outline are also instructive for a simpler simulation you could construct for a particular course or learning experience.

Exhibit 5.4 provides an overview of a large-scale simulation taught by a team of three teachers at a fictional high school.

Following are some additional guidelines for simulations and role-plays:

Make sure the simulation or role-play is a good fit. Role-plays that feel contrived or trivialize an important issue undermine learning.

Plan ahead. Students should be familiar and moderately proficient with the concepts or skills that will be practiced during the activity. Do students have a fair knowledge of the cultural or personal roles they may assume? If they are uncomfortable, can they excuse themselves or observe until they are more comfortable with playing a role?

Be relatively sure students understand the role and scenario before you begin. Often it is helpful to write a script with a description of the role's attitudes, experiences, and beliefs. The students use the script to deepen their familiarity with the role. For example, "I'm a new student in the school. I come from a much poorer neighborhood than most of my new classmates. Although I am usually self-reliant, I feel intimidated by the way others talk and dress."

Set aside enough time for the simulation and the discussion that follows. The discussion and analysis are as important as the simulation itself. What are some different perspectives, reactions, and insights? What has not been dealt with that still needs attention? Have the goals for learning been accomplished? How is this known?

When role-playing seems potentially embarrassing or threatening, it is often helpful to model the first role-play and discuss it with students. This may alleviate some initial hesitation and allow students to see how potential imperfections and mistakes can be used to learn.

Exhibit 5.3   Elements of a Simulation

Learning to filter information. The simulation should require a student to discriminate between relevant and irrelevant information in order to make decisions.

Learning to deal with interruptions. The simulation should entail situations in which a student has to adapt to impositions and prioritize responsibilities within time constraints.

Implementing clearly defined goals. The simulation should challenge students to reach a particular goal that is well defined and that can be tracked during the simulation.

Evaluating and responding to feedback. The simulation should provide several feedback elements that relate to performance and goal achievement.

Exploring options. Trying out different ideas is often not possible in real life because it's too risky. But a simulation should allow "what if" questions to be played out to realize the consequences of decisions and develop critical thinking.

Practicing collaboration. The simulation should provide opportunities for cooperation, discussion, developing common goals, and responding with mutual support.

Adapting to tension. Things do not always go smoothly in real life. There are mistakes, conflicts, stress, unmet goals, and so forth. The simulation should offer some demanding and challenging situations in which reasonable tension occurs and the learners can accommodate or resolve problems as they progress toward their goal.

Dealing with competition. The simulation should provide competitive situations. If desirable, these can be made into gaming elements with score keeping and comparisons. When appropriate to a situation, it can add fun to the simulation.

Benefiting from acceleration. In real life, learners can't accelerate time to see how their decisions work out. A simulation affords this opportunity. The simulation should manipulate time so that the learners can have insights about the consequences of their decisions.

Receiving coaching. The role of the coach is not to give advice but to stimulate reflection and deeper thinking on the part of the learners. Whether it is the teacher, the peers, or the simulation itself, there should be processes that stimulate the learners to evaluate their ideas and decisions.

Using a predetermined guide. The simulation should have a way to guide learner actions. Usually there is an evaluation component or engine in the simulation that electronically or through a teacher assesses a student's responses and indicates progress and flow. A simple example is a game board through which players advance to reach an ultimate goal. Each player's turn determines a variety of possible moves and consequences as she or he traverses the board.

Source: Adapted from Vaughan (2006, pp. 179–182).

Exhibit 5.4 Description of a High School Simulation for Organizational Leadership

In this fictional account, there are 40 students enrolled in the Academy for Organizational Leadership, a popular career-to-college course for high school students. A team of three teachers teaches the course, with three different and complementary areas of expertise: math/finance, language arts, and civics. Students can participate face-to-face and online.

After interviewing several nonprofit leaders in the community, the teacher team created an experiential challenge—to offer students the opportunity to actually lead an organizational enterprise rather than learn *about* how it can be done. To achieve this the three teachers created a functional model of a national organization to help students who dropped out of high school receive credit for learning they may have gained through work experiences, tutoring, the arts, athletics, caregiving, and so forth. This organization's goal is to help students accrue high school credit that can jumpstart their interest in high school graduation and college entry.

In their roles within the organization, students have a real-life environment with responsibilities to make decisions about strategic issues based on organizational vision, developing their capacity as "educational plan managers" and fiscally responsible employees.

As in the real world, there are news articles and other media that provide valuable as well as distracting information. For example, students might receive an article about new technology to inexpensively produce brochures. Because this information would affect their production and costs, they would have to study and analyze reports, conduct market analyses, and update their knowledge about current marketing practices.

In order to arrive at an effective business strategy, they would also have to be aware of educational policies, financial resources for employees and students, and ethical practices.

The context and complexity involved in students' decision making is realistic and substantial. Students receive feedback based on their progress in relation to clearly identified standards and rubrics. In addition, they have an advisory team comprising organizational leaders, two business education instructors from a local college, and their three teachers, which provides coaching that pushes their thinking and facilitates further learning. At appropriate intervals, teachers provide guidance for students to move forward with plans and strategies. With performance ratings and "employee evaluations" as part of the assessment process, students receive further relevant information about their progress toward professional goals.

While this kind of simulation requires ongoing revision to make it as authentic and motivating as possible, it provides a multidimensional experience for students to reach high academic standards through realistic and challenging circumstances. Their experience in this simulation gives them direct contact with work-related skills.

Freeze the action during a role-play when you need to. This can serve various purposes:

- to critique a perspective
- to explore students' reactions to a poignant comment
- to allow students to make beneficial suggestions to the actors
- to relieve tension

Plan follow-up activities for simulations and role-plays. This is extremely important. For example, a compelling next step after a role-play could be to create action plans to use what has been practiced and discussed.

For many students and teachers, simulations may be the only way to enter worlds that seem too distant or to try out actions that are initially too uncomfortable. In some instances, this procedure may not only enhance meaning but also nurture courage and the ability to act with new understanding.

Concluding Role-Plays and Simulations

Depending on factors such as the focus of the role-play or simulation and the experience, trust, and sense of community among the learners, small groups or a single larger group needs a chance to reflect on what they have learned. Here are some ways to start:

- Ask students to free-write for a couple of minutes after the experience so they have something to offer based on reflection.
- Ask students to speak with a partner for a few minutes about key issues that emerged for them in the role-play or simulation before requesting individual responses.
- Ask a couple of students to summarize the role-play or simulation before asking others to join in.
- Ask each learner to remark about one element she or he felt was important in the simulation, and record these comments publicly. This lets everyone know there is a range of interpretations before discussion begins.

During the discussion, the kinds of questions you ask can serve different purposes, for example, furthering analysis, challenging an idea, mediating between conflicting views, and compelling students to generate principles and concepts. Your role is one of a facilitator who provides opportunities for everyone to contribute but who also has the responsibility to challenge and inform, cautiously avoiding the temptation to impose your own perspectives.

Teachers often find it important to have students write responses to questions such as these: What new insights did you gain from this role-play (or simulation) and our discussion? What are your lingering questions? What are some new ideas with which you would like to experiment? What resources would be useful to you?

Here are some additional ways to conclude:

- In small groups or as a large group, brainstorm insights, personal changes in thinking or action, or new areas to explore as a result of the learning experience.
- Go around the group, and ask each student to provide one insight, question, lesson, change, or idea that has emerged as a result of the process.

Using role-plays or simulations in technical fields such as chemistry may require a more structured approach, but the challenge remains to employ this format in a manner that does not suppress the free flow of ideas and perspectives. Also, for generative, topical, and academic themes, students, individually and collaboratively, are a rich resource for constructing role-plays and simulations for an area of study.

Foreshadowing How a Role-Play or Simulation Works

Because of the complexity of these procedures and because of some students' unfamiliarity with them, students often need an opportunity to learn these approaches before they apply them more independently. Beyer (1988) offers the following set of guidelines, which can be easily adapted:

1. Introduce the procedure by describing and demonstrating the steps of the process with a vivid relevant example, clearly outlined on paper or on PowerPoint slides (even better when the example comes as a suggestion from the learners).

2. Have students work in guided practice with a short and relevant process that captures the form of the procedure.

3. Have students take notes on their reflections while they are involved in guided practice and discuss them collaboratively afterward (reflection-in-action).

4. As a result of reflection-in-action, students may want to suggest changes in the procedure to align with their cultural perspectives and intellectual strengths.

When students are not familiar with a learning activity for enhancing meaning, whether it be a case study, role-play, or simulation, and have had no chance for guided practice, you will need to coach them more closely through the process.

Games

Games can be similar to simulations but they are usually very structured and have a competitive win-lose quality. Video and computer games are popular across the lifespan, and in recent years they have evolved into multiplayer online games that range from Free Rice, which is published by the United Nations World Food Program, to Peacemaker, which was created by Carnegie Mellon students seeking to explore and solve the conflict in the Middle East with a two-state solution. In Peacemaker, players take the roles of leader of Israel or leader of the Palestinian Authority, and the events they deal with are presented using compelling and authentic media. The recently released Migrant Trail is another example of a social impact game. It puts students in the roles of border patrol agents and people who cross the U.S.-Mexico border without legal documents. These games bring certain realities to life, including issues with which players can identify and the conditions with which people struggle in serious ways. These are examples of games created for educational and humanitarian impact, and there are more than a hundred interactive "Games for Change" (www.gamesforchange.org) that teachers and students can find for a broad range of academic disciplines, topics, and developmental levels. For more information on ethical gaming, see Helmore (2014).

USE IMAGINATION AND ARTISTRY TO EVOKE MEANING AND EMOTION IN LEARNING

Imagination and artistry promote creativity and intellectual depth as well as an enjoyable and meaningful life. As part of an educational process, they invite self-expression, a variety of interests, reactions to experiences, and the creation of connections between the known and the unknown. In addition, the arts mediate language and connect people throughout the world.

In education, artistry is an embedding of art in learning rather than as a separate and frequently disenfranchised experience ("Now we are going to do art!"). As Jamake Highwater (1994) has said, "Knowledge is barren without the capacity for feeling and imagination." One of the reasons that school lacks meaning for so many students is that learning is too often separate from imagination and artistry. These are fundamental parts of life and learning across cultures. Imagination and artistry should be part of the curriculum for every subject area. Both processes are open-ended and serve as kindling for creative and academic goals. For example, in helping a class of students prepare for service-learning, a teacher approached students with the question: "What are the things we most deeply want to contribute to and accomplish in our communities?" After reflecting, writing, and sketching their responses to this question, students decided to paint a mural depicting the theme of community, contribution, and learning. Using poster paints and a large roll of paper, the students created a mural that covered the entire bottom half of the circumference of the classroom. During creation of the mural, two of the students took photographs of the process and created a collage for the class. Each student wrote a reflective paper discussing the ideas represented in the mural and delineating issues to explore. At the concluding class session, the students, encircled by the mural they created, summarized their responses to the process and content of their mural and made connections between their experience creating art and the work they intend to do in their communities. Then they set personal goals that included their ideas for how to creatively represent or demonstrate their accomplishments.

To further exemplify the role of imagination in learning, we recall a science teacher who was struggling to teach her students systems theory and who decided to work with them to invent games that could be used to teach students in other classes the fundamental concepts and principles of this theory. She told her students that, at a minimum, they would need to physically represent the planets and provide a way for participants to imagine, predict, coordinate, and simulate the movement of planets, either along a large cloth version of a solar system or through the use of computer technology. The games were so popular that, annually, the science teacher—in concert with students—developed an interactive solar system gallery for families and community members to explore.

Typically, students welcome the invitation to integrate academic work with imagination and artistry. Along with the visual arts, this includes music and musical composition, movement and dance, fiction, playwriting, performance art, and video. There are myriad possibilities, several of which are listed in Chapter 6, in the section, "Assessment Options Based on Gardner's Multiple Intelligences." The following activity helps students creatively prepare for a visit to an ecological center.

ACTIVITY 5.7

Visitation Maps

Purpose: To provide students with an opportunity to imagine and visually represent a visit to a community center

Time: 45–60 minutes

Format: Small groups of four students

Materials: Sheets of newsprint (one for each group), colorful markers, masking tape, a sample agenda

Process

Distribute a sheet of newsprint and several colorful markers to each group. Explain that the purpose of this exercise is to think through the way a sample visit to the ecological center might look, from the moment students wake up in the morning until they return home at the end of the day. Explain that their visual representations ought to be as creative as possible and may even verge on the outrageous, as long as they ultimately represent what their team might actually wish to do once they reach the center. For example, one group of students imagined that upon their arrival, the guides would be waiting with outstretched arms and as they greet students, representatives of the class would share a small gift of herbal tea and a signed photograph with all of the members of their class. As exaggerated as this visitation map may be, it allows students to imagine the potential of interactions that forge new relationships and inspire relevant learning experiences.

You may want to provide students with a sample agenda to initially stimulate their thinking, even though their conceptualization of the visit may vary significantly from the actual experience. A sample agenda might include the following:

- an interactive welcome between visitors and hosts from the environmental center
- a way to understand who everyone is and why they are excited to be at the center
- a way to learn about the history of the center
- an activity that teaches about mangroves and the shrimp or fish farms
- a dialogue about what students might wish to know that they may not be able to observe (e.g., What are some controversial issues the center has to grapple with? What are the opportunities for service learning?)
- choices about what parts of the center to visit
- interviews with or questions students might want to ask people who work at the center
- an "exit meeting" to share what has been learned, discuss emerging interests/ideas, and consider opportunities for ongoing communication
- a closure activity (e.g., everyone might mention one thing they intend to further investigate or do when they leave)

Debrief: Ask the groups to post their maps, gallery style, around the room. A docent from each group stands by the map to point out highlights or answer questions that viewers (other participants) may have as they quietly wander around. When students are called back together as a large group, they consider these questions: What have you learned from each other's ideas? What do you wonder about? What should we do to prepare?

ACTIVITY 5.8

Spotlight Presentations

Purpose: To review topics and issues from students' perspectives and to creatively develop well-organized presentations on relevant topics

Time: 7 minutes per student group

Format: Small groups of four participants

Materials: Literature such as newspaper articles, biographies, stories from different cultures, portions of textbooks, and so forth

Process

Explain to students that the first (or last) 7–10 minutes of selected class periods will be reserved for students, in small groups, to do a creative presentation about something they have learned from class that they have found to be particularly interesting. Explain that students will have adequate time to prepare and will be able to sign up in advance for specific times and dates. Explain that each group will identify two to three trusted peers to give them feedback on what worked and why and suggestions for making their work stronger in the future.

Work with the class to develop criteria for effective Spotlight Presentations, and model the criteria with an initial presentation. Criteria might include (1) an intriguing introduction to team members, the topic, and what viewers will learn; (2) creative methods to convey key points; (3) a strong ending; and (4) active participation of all team members. *Note:* Teachers often invite volunteers to collate presentation resources for future reference.

ACTION RESEARCH WITH STUDENTS

Action research is a form of disciplined inquiry in which there is no satisfactory present answer to a problem in a particular context. An important quality is that this approach to research is conducted by people in their own contexts, rather than by professional or academic scholars. For example, a group of fourth-grade students are concerned about people in wheelchairs after the grandmother of a student was nearly struck by a car while crossing an intersection near the school. They work together to pose a question that teams of students investigate using different sources of information. Their question has two parts: What do communities consider when they develop crosswalks that are safe and accessible to everyone? What can community members do when a particular location seems unsafe? One team of researchers participates in a local webinar on transportation equity; one team reviews a best practices design guide posted online by the Federal Highway Administration; and another team searches the Internet for news items about when, where, and why people in mobile chairs have been hurt at a crosswalk. Next, the teams pool their data and theorize what needs to be done now and what needs to be done as part of a long-term process. They use data to support their ideas. After deciding on a course of action, they implement their plan and learn from evaluation data about its effectiveness. They build on this knowledge with new questions to investigate further and renew the process until their goals have been satisfactorily accomplished.

As this example shows, action research is a cyclical process that has five primary components—clarifying a problem, planning, acting, observing, and reflecting—with subsequent cycles based on revised plans (Stringer, 2014). Although this approach to research can lead to valuable insights that can be helpful to others, results are rarely generalizable. This is because the research focuses on a problem that exists in a particular context and the context is usually limited in size.

Other important qualities of action research are that it teaches students to think critically and understand from experience that their knowledge and perspectives matter. Students come to realize that empowerment isn't something that comes from another person, as in "I empower my students." Empowerment is the result of one's own beliefs and actions, often in collaboration with others. This is one of the major reasons why action research is often regarded as emancipatory. In schools and society there are many ideas, concerns, and events that have an emerging quality or debatable interpretation for which action research can make important distinctions leading to student (and teacher) learning and action of social consequence. The systematic process of learning to (1) identify a concern, (2) pose a question related to it, (3) reflect on the question, (4) plan a thoughtful course of action which includes the collection and analysis of data, and (5) make evidence-based claims for new action-oriented decisions is a formidable motivational force.

> **ACTIVITY 5.9**
> **Dot Graphing**

Purpose: To generate ideas for action research based on student perceptions of a relevant issue

Time: 45 minutes

Format: Individuals and large group

Materials: Newsprint, markers, circular sticky dots (the kind used to code files)

Process

On separate sheets of newsprint, one for each question, write a question related to a relevant topic. Begin each question with "To what extent. . . ." For example, if students are concerned about bullying on the playground, you might work with them to create dot-graphing questions such as these:

1. To what extent is school a safe place, physically and emotionally, for all students?

2. To what extent is there helpful assistance for someone who is being put down or bullied?

3. To what extent do you feel prepared to stand up for someone who is being put down or bullied?

4. To what extent do you think other students feel prepared to stand up for someone who is being put down or bullied?

On the bottom of each sheet of newsprint, create a Likert scale that spans from 1 to 10 (1 = *low*, 10 = *high*). Include a mark on the horizontal lines for each point along the scale. A sample appears below.

To what extent do you think other students feel prepared to stand up for someone who is being put down or bullied?

| 1 | 2 | 3 | 4 | 5 | 6 | 7 | 8 | 9 | 10 |

Distribute to students as many dots as there are questions. Tell students that in a moment they will post their dots along the Likert scale in response to the question on the sheet of paper. To prepare, they should make a note about where they want their dot to go. That way, they will be ready to place their dot on each Likert scale without deliberating in front of the class or feeling swayed by where other students put their dots. Students can also, if they prefer, give the paper and their dots to you to discretely post. Remind students that their dots need to be carefully placed in order to create a graph that is easy to understand.

Next, post two sheets of newsprint. At the top of one sheet write "Observations." On the second sheet write "Questions." If appropriate, ask for two volunteers to scribe the observations and questions that students offer. Explain that questions include those related to an observation, and show them what this means by modeling what you might say yourself. Next, ask students to carefully review the graphs and note their observations and questions. In this process, they should consider two things: what a specific graph might indicate and what graphs might mean in relation to each other. For example, if there is a cluster of dots around the midpoint for the question "To what extent do students feel prepared to stand up for someone who is being put down or bullied?" students might make an observation about that particular graph, for example: "There are 22 of 27 dots grouped between the numbers 4 and 6." Then they might ask the question: "Is it good enough to feel somewhat prepared, or should all of us feel very prepared?" Finally, students examine the observations and questions and rephrase them as researchable questions. Given the previous example, a researchable question might be "What do students in other classrooms think about being able to assist someone who is being picked on or bullied?" or "What would we need to learn and do to become expert at creating a school where every student feels safe and included?" After further discussion, work with students to prioritize which question(s) to pursue. Then discuss an approach to collecting information. If there is not enough time to conclude the range of important considerations for a class research project, ask for small group of volunteers to work with you on one or two possible ways to explore the class's primary concerns. (Exhibit 5.2 provides a planning template that can be adapted for action research.)

Note: Action research teams need adequate time and support for their designs. Productive teams meet on a regular basis with an experienced coach or the teacher. In addition, they negotiate clear agreements and a timeline for tasks to perform. Due to the rigor and duration of such a project, some teachers schedule regular intervals for students to share their accomplishments and challenges along the way.

SUMMARY

This chapter described practices that can challenge and engage learners in meaningful learning. Of course, repertoires of teaching strategies, no matter how promising, are only part of the equation. Nuanced interactions with students, routines and rituals, connections, and patterns influence student motivation. When it comes to enhancing meaning with children and youth, it is important to continuously estimate the motivational quality of teaching and learning, and adjust accordingly.

It's also important to remember that motivation will naturally ebb and flow. When students are tired or their energy seems diminished, it is easy to overreact. Skillful educators have high expectations, but they are also realistic about the fact that there is not one-to-one correspondence between time and motivation. Downtime can be a catalyst for intense periods of productivity.

Further, how teachers assess engagement is culturally mediated. A student who is silent and calm may be as motivated as, or more than, a student who is highly demonstrative. As with all things, teachers' assumptions and perceptions of a situation are culturally mediated. Nurturing optimal learning is like blowing on the embers of a fire to boost a flame. Personal conversations with students fuel optimal learning environments. The challenge of helping students find value in an opportunity is the challenge of student and teacher voices in constant dialogue with each other. Teachers who are fully present and keenly aware are more apt to increase students' motivation as they are learning, mutually creating great momentum for learning. This reciprocity is a primary topic of the next chapter, which focuses on engendering competence through authentic ways to support student success.

The following list can serve as a guide to teachers, providing considerations for creating the conditions in which challenge and engagement enhance meaning. The subsequent list includes the activities in this chapter.

Enhancing Meaning

How does this learning experience engage participants in challenging learning?

The teacher encourages all students to learn, apply, create, and communicate knowledge:

_____ Students build on prior knowledge and interests to guide deep learning.

_____ Teacher, in concert with students, creates opportunities for inquiry, investigation, and projects.

_____ Students actively participate in challenging ways, including regular reflection on learning.

_____ Teacher asks probing questions of all students throughout a learning experience.

_____ Teacher elicits high-quality responses from all students.

_____ Teacher uses multiple "safety nets" to ensure student success (e.g., peer support, cooperative learning).

Evidence

ACTIVITIES FOR ENHANCING MEANING

Where I'm From (Activity 5.1)

Case Study (Activity 5.2)

Thought-Provoking Questions (Activity 5.3)

Fish Bowl Questioning Procedure (Activity 5.4)

Guided Reciprocal Questioning (Activity 5.5)

Identifying Relevant Problems With Students (Activity 5.6)

Visitation Maps (Activity 5.7)

Spotlight Presentations (Activity 5.8)

Dot Graphing (Activity 5.9)

6 Engendering Competence

So much of childhood socialization in school is aimed at intellectual competence ... at helping children to compete successfully against their peers, gain public recognition for solo work, and demonstrate mastery by rapid response rates, quick articulation of ideas, and high scores on standardized tests. But these often turn out to be the very competencies that interfere with successful aging and learning, ... where collaboration, relationship building, slowness and deliberateness, risk taking, and irreverence are the coin of the realm; where work and play, restraint and expressivity, discipline and improvisation are joined.

—Sara Lawrence-Lightfoot (2009, p. 238)

It is 8:00 on Thursday morning and Ignacio Webb sits beside Mr. Middle, his seventh-grade teacher, to review his progress on a world geography and language arts assignment about chocolate. He and his team of three other students have been researching four related topics: production, marketing, consumption, and the origin of fair trade chocolate. Because there is too much information for each student to read, Mr. Middle expects the team to self-select topics and distribute tasks among themselves. There will be a final product in the form of a report and a final presentation in the form of a simulation. The simulation will include two volunteers from the community who will pretend to be investors who are interested in helping Ignacio's team launch a small import business. Based on Mr. Middle's presentation rubric, the students will introduce their research to the investors in the form of a stimulating 5-minute presentation with a brief question-and-answer period. It is up to the team to ensure that everyone participates in a meaningful way.

While Ignacio thought the project might be interesting, a number of things have gone awry for his team. They have struggled to find time to meet outside of class because one of the members takes care of his young cousins so his aunt can work the night shift at a local restaurant. Another teammate has been sick and unable to complete her work. Ignacio, who agreed to be the team leader, now finds himself doing most of the work and realizes the presentation won't be ready in time. He is worried about any delay or poorly prepared work because he can't afford to get a bad grade. Tryouts for junior varsity basketball are next week and he needs a B average in all of his courses. He wants to share his concerns with Mr. Middle, but he doesn't want to make his team look bad. In addition, Mr. Middle's "no excuses" policy means that Ignacio is responsible for solving his own problems. He worries that being honest about his experiences with the chocolate assignment might cast blame on himself and his peers.

Wanting to be competent—having the desire to be effective at what we value—extends across all cultural groups. This powerful human need connects with hopes and dreams, our sense of what makes life worth living. The quest for competence starts with something as simple as a baby searching for a toy behind a pillow and ends in later life with what Erik Erikson called *generativity*, our desire to leave an enduring and beneficent legacy. Across cultures, this human need for competence is not acquired, but rather already exists and can be strengthened or weakened through learning experiences.

As the scenario suggests, engendering competence among students is wrought with challenges, even when teachers devise creative ways for students to learn and demonstrate their knowledge. One can assume that Mr. Middle wants to avoid the perils of assignments that require students to learn in isolation from one another. However, by default, Ignacio is isolated from his peers. One might also assume that Mr. Middle understands the limits of paper-and-pencil tests and is sensitive to the fact that the very act of grading is problematic. We can assume that in the past he has passed back exams hearing "What did you get?" much more frequently than "What did you learn?" Nonetheless, even with project-based learning, grades are a prevailing force. As much as Ignacio may want to be an effective learner, he also wants to be a good friend to his peers and a junior varsity athlete.

This chapter explores these and other issues, anchored in a commitment to learning outcomes that benefit students as whole human beings. This means that in addition to being prepared to earn a living wage for their families, *all* students learn in ways that support fulfilling lives and advocate for opportunities and empowerment for others. Although the practices in this chapter exist within a broader policy environment that maintains an orientation toward competition and selectivity, and rewards and punishments, substantial research suggests that classroom assessment systems can be highly influential catalysts for serving students as learners with individual potential and a social conscience (Wehlage, Newmann, & Secada, 1996).

As is true for the three previously discussed motivational conditions—establishing inclusion (criteria: respect and connectedness), developing a positive attitude (criteria: choice and relevance), and enhancing meaning (criteria: challenge and engagement)—the name of the motivational condition is the essential motivational condition or goal. The two criteria that accompany the motivational condition are themes that research suggests as most influential to accomplish that goal. For the motivational condition of engendering competence, the two themes that emerge from interdisciplinary research are effectiveness and authenticity.

EFFECTIVENESS AND AUTHENTICITY AS LEVERS FOR MOTIVATION AND LEARNING

As mentioned, assessment that engenders competence meets two primary criteria: effectiveness and authenticity. This section begins with an examination of the meaning and relevance of the term *effectiveness*. It includes considerations for intrinsically motivating feedback, followed by grading practices that promote effectiveness.

In some ways, academic effectiveness is best understood through the problem of academic ineffectiveness, a chronic condition in schools. For students, ineffectiveness is not only the failure to produce intended results. It is feeling *incapable* of doing so. This is not only an issue that plagues students who have records of low performance. It can affect all students, even those who have become skillful takers of quizzes, tests, and examinations and survivors of the disempowering quest for a good grade. Research by Claude Steele and Joshua Aronson (1995) suggests that when historically underserved students believe that a test is a measure of their intellectual ability, they underperform. Carol Dweck (2006) found that students who believe intelligence is a fixed characteristic that is outside of their control tend to avoid challenges that can make them look unintelligent. Looking smart becomes more important than being smart. Bottom line—students need to believe in their capacity to be academically effective. This isn't everything, but it's a lot.

Unfortunately tests have become a prevailing measure of academic effectiveness. While tests can be informative—depending on their quality, the context, and the extent to which students value them—one of their consequences is that students direct their attention to what gets tested and graded and, in doing so, suppress their curiosity. Of equal concern is tests' tight association with grades. As a single reductive measure, grades rarely represent the full range of what a student knows and can do. Nonetheless, in much of the United States tests and grades have become sacrosanct as indicators of knowledge and future success (Schneider & Hutt, 2013).

Interestingly, grades first appeared in education in the late 1700s as an alternative to time-consuming interactions with individuals (Swanson & Elwood, 2005). It appears that a Cambridge tutor devised a grading system to increase his class size and avoid time-consuming interactions with individual students. Grades arrived in the United States around the turn of the 19th century, when assembly-line classrooms provided a way to sort, categorize, and group students. In essence, education had found a way to override the very thing that assessment needs to be: a rich conversation about learning.

From a motivational perspective, effectiveness means that students not only feel capable; they are aware of *and value* new knowledge. By design, learning experiences encourage students to consider, in relation to valued goals: How well am I doing? How well is this turning out? How might I improve? Valuing a learning experience intensifies awareness of and concern for quality. Through practices such as reflective journaling, purposeful conversations, interpretive arts, and action research, students become deeply aware of how to strive toward their desired goals. Not only do they have evidence that they are becoming effective in ways that they value, they develop a metacognitive infrastructure for meaning making in other areas of life.

Knowing we are becoming effective in ways that we value connects to intrinsic motivation because when we know we are competently performing an activity that leads to a highly regarded goal, it naturally elicits motivation. If someone wants to learn how to use a new digital program because it is a valued skill and increases his or her range of occupational opportunities, that awareness will evoke motivation. The progress and competence gained while learning will influence the motivational value of the original goal. In other words, becoming more effective often increases the value of the goal. With increased competence, skill with technology and related occupational opportunities acquire even greater value for students. For many students, knowing they can effectively learn values concepts and skills provides a vital connection to a hopeful future. Addressed earlier, this is pivotal to the success of large numbers of youth for whom the promise of valued credentials, well-paying jobs, and a satisfying life seem remote.

Although educators have made great strides in the realm of assessment, this area of practice is complex and nuanced. What encourages motivation for one student might be very different for another student, as in the case of feedback. Because feedback is essential to student effectiveness, the following section precedes discussion of the second criteria for engendering competence, which is authenticity.

EFFECTIVE FEEDBACK

The interactions through which students assess their effectiveness can fundamentally affect their motivation. These interactions fall into two primary categories: informational or controlling (Deci & Ryan, 1991). Informational interactions communicate about effectiveness and support a sense of self-determination for learning. In contrast, controlling interactions reinforce a teacher's authority and the expectation of compliance. When this occurs, students are more likely to believe the reason for learning is some external condition, such as a reward or pressure. In addition, it can undermine mutual respect. When teachers exert undue control over students, it propagates conflict and blame. Blame cycles are difficult to interrupt and erode the effectiveness of students and teachers alike (see Chapter 2). The characteristics in Exhibit 6.1, offered in a bulleted format for easy reference, are associated with motivating and high-quality feedback.

A simple mnemonic device for feedback that educators find useful is the acronym AIRE (**a**ccomplishment, **i**nquiry, **r**esources, and **e**ncouragement). It reminds teachers to begin comments on student work with an accomplishment, provide questions for further inquiry or investigation, suggest resources that may be helpful, and conclude with encouragement. For example, a teacher might say, "I appreciate the way you developed your argument in this paper. You began with a story that made me, as a reader, care about the topic because I once had a similar experience. I can also see your growth as a writer because of the way you have been organizing your thinking so that each paragraph focuses on a particular point (accomplishment). Something I encourage you to further investigate is opposing perspectives on your central claim (inquiry). To support this endeavor, I would be happy to send you a couple of citations for two articles I have found helpful (resource). I hope you'll continue to explore this topic. You are becoming an expert on it as well as an excellent writer (encouragement)." This kind of feedback builds competence and self-direction, which go hand in hand. It relates to goals students understand, find relevant, and want to accomplish.

This section concludes with two additional feedback-related concerns: group feedback and personal restraint. When it comes to group feedback,

Exhibit 6.1   Characteristics of Effective Feedback

The following guidelines, adapted from *Diversity and Motivation: Culturally Responsive Teaching in College* (Ginsberg & Wlodkowski, 2009), encourage student motivation and learning in culturally diverse classrooms. Effective feedback is:

- *Feedback that is informational rather than controlling.* It emphasizes a student's increasing effectiveness, creativity, or capacity as a self-determined learner. When combined with examples from a student's work, informative feedback sounds like this: "In your paper you clearly identified three critical areas of concern, your writing was well organized and vivid, and you have supported your rationale with facts and anecdotes. Recently, I found an article that offered an entirely different perspective on your topic and I've been thinking about how I would respond. If you'd like, I'd be happy to share this with you. When a writer shows their awareness of other perspectives, it supports the credibility of their argument because it indicates they have considered and researched alternative viewpoints."

  On the other hand, controlling feedback sounds like this: "You met the basic standards for this assignment, although I was disappointed in your conclusion. You made a leap into unfamiliar territory and got confused about the purpose of this paper. I wasn't looking for personal opinions. If you want a satisfactory grade in this course, follow the outlines I provide."

- *Feedback that is based on agreed-upon standards, models, and criteria for success.* The closer standards and criteria come to students' own words, including those that are represented by rubrics, the better. In the case of models, students can compare their work against "excellent" and "not-yet-excellent" examples of work. They are then in a position to determine characteristics of excellence in comparison to not-yet-excellent work. When students determine standards and criteria for success and can judge how well they are performing in relation to a specific target, they can continuously self-assess and self-adjust. For example, in creating metaphorical picture books on social justice issues for younger students, middle school students look at models of excellent work and not-yet-excellent work to explicitly determine what counts as quality work and to articulate gradations of quality. As they draft their picture books, they use the criteria on a rubric as a guide to a satisfying product. If a student overlooks part of what is on the rubric, a gentle reminder and possibly a helpful suggestion encourages further self-scrutiny.

- *Feedback that is specific and constructive.* It is difficult to improve performance when we have only a general idea of how to proceed. Most people prefer specific information and realistic suggestions from teachers and peers. For example, "I found your insights on government spending compelling. In the second paragraph you express strong feelings. It might make your paper even stronger if you provide an example of a situation that prompted this kind of emotion. To emphasize your conclusion, you might consider restating your initial premise in your last paragraph. Let me know if I can be of further assistance. I very much enjoyed reading your work and am looking forward to the next draft!" When you are giving guidance with feedback, it's important to keep in mind how much a student *wants to* or *ought to* decide on a course of action relative to the feedback. In general, the more a student can self-assess and self-adjust, the more self-determined she will be. Sometimes the most constructive feedback is that which simply seeks clarification or suggests concrete examples, illustrations, or details.

- *Feedback that is quantitative.* In such areas as athletics, quantitative feedback has definite advantages. It is precise and it can provide evidence of small improvements. Small improvements can have long-range effects. One way to understand learning is by *rate,* which is to indicate how often something occurs over a fixed time. For example, students are told they completed 30 laps during a 1-hour swimming practice. Another way is to decide what percentage of learning performance is correct or appropriate. Percentages are calculated by dividing the number of times the learning performance occurs correctly by the total number of times the performance opportunity occurs, as in batting averages and field goal percentages.

  Another common form of quantitative feedback is *duration,* which is how long it takes a learning performance to be completed. For example, an environmental science student might receive feedback on how long it takes her to complete a practice analysis of a particular ecosystem, given that she will eventually perform the analysis under potentially adverse conditions. Whenever progress on learning a skill appears to be slow or difficult to ascertain, quantitative feedback may be an effective means to enhance learner motivation.

- *Feedback that is prompt.* Promptness characterizes feedback that is provided as the situation demands rather than immediately. Sometimes a moderate delay in feedback enhances learning because the student considers such a delay respectful. For example, some learners experience discomfort with direct mention of specific performance judgments shortly after the occasion. Also, a brief interval may allow learners to forget incorrect responses more easily and reduce their anxiety, as in the case of a public performance. In general, it is best to be quick with feedback but to respect the need for nuanced interactions with students.

- *Feedback that is frequent.* Frequent feedback is probably most helpful when new learning is first occurring. A good rule of thumb is to provide feedback when improvement is most possible. Once errors have accumulated, learners may see improvements as more difficult to accomplish. Also, once multiple errors become established, the new learning encouraged through feedback may seem overwhelming and confusing to learners, making further progress seem more remote.

- *Feedback that is positive.* Positive feedback places emphasis on improvements and progress rather than on deficiencies and mistakes. It is a particularly

Continued

Exhibit 6.1 (Continued)

important way to encourage intrinsic motivation. Feelings of well-being and a sense of competence help students form a positive attitude toward the source of the information. Emphasis on errors and deficiencies can be discouraging. Even when students are prone to making mistakes, simply pointing out a *decrease* in errors may be a form of positive feedback. Of course, positive feedback also needs to be constructive. For example, a teacher might say to a student, "You've been able to solve most of this problem. Let's take a look at what's left and see if we can understand why you are getting stuck."

- *Feedback that is related to impact criteria.* Impact criteria are the main reasons why a person is learning something, the heart of the individual's learning goal (Wiggins, 1998). Often these are unique or strongly related to a cultural perspective. One person may produce a speech or a piece of writing to inspire, arouse, or provoke. Another may wish to create a design or a performance to be a gift for family or friends. Assessment and feedback should support such goals and respectfully deal with what may be ineffable or accomplished in a realm beyond mechanistic objectivity. This may require feedback that is more akin to dialogue or what artists do when they respond to how another artist's work affects them.

- *Feedback that is personal and differential.* Differential feedback involves self-comparison and focuses on the increment of personal improvement that has occurred since the last iteration of learning. In skill or procedural learning, such as writing, operating a machine, or learning a particular sport, emphasizing small steps of progress can encourage motivation. Here again, the amount of time that elapses before we offer differential feedback can be quite important. For example, students may be able to see larger gains and feel a greater sense of accomplishment when improvement is based on a daily or weekly schedule, rather than after each performance.

- *Feedback that considers progress and readiness.* For example, graphing or charting encourages student motivation when it makes progress more concrete and shows a record of increasing improvement. Asking students what they would like feedback on can make a teacher's comments more relevant and motivating. Students' *readiness to receive feedback* is another factor. When we are resistant to feedback, we are not likely to learn or self-adjust. For teachers, this may mean waiting to give written feedback and arranging for a personal conference.

- *Feedback that is received as it was intended.* To be sure that the message received is what they intend, some teachers occasionally check in with students. They ask students to provide a written response to feedback they have received and reviewed. This can be as simple as asking: What aspects of the feedback were most helpful? Are there aspects of the feedback about which you have a different perspective? If so, please explain. How will you use the feedback?

everything that has been said thus far applies. Motivationally, whether the group is a team, a collaborative group, or an entire class, feedback on total performance can influence individuals. However, because feedback to a group consolidates members' mutual identification and sense of connection, it also has the potential to strengthen group cohesiveness and morale. As effective as this can be, at times restraint is necessary.

In some situations, the best form of feedback to groups and individuals is to encourage moving on to the next challenging learning opportunity. Too much comment by teachers can undermine student autonomy. Along this line of reasoning, in class discussions when we respond to students' each and every comment, it can imply that a perspective is incomplete if it does not include our own. In the absence of other student-generated comments, students appreciate a simple acknowledgment of participation in the form of a sincere "thank you." Although there are times when additional information from a teacher is necessary, we undermine our respect for student autonomy when we position ourselves as the ultimate authority on a topic. To promote student achievement, one of the most important skills a teacher can have is quiet and attentive listening.

GRADES

Grades are one of the mostly hotly contested issues in education. They can dampen intrinsic motivation, promote last-minute learning, enhance the fear of failure, reduce interest, decrease enjoyment in the classwork, increase anxiety, hamper performance on follow-up tasks, stimulate avoidance of challenging tasks, and heighten competitiveness (Schinske & Tanner, 2014). This renders educators as well as students vulnerable. In addition, it is possibly one of the most idiosyncratic things we do across our entire profession.

Among educators, there is little agreement on what should be included in a grade, whether the grade should be criteria- or norm-referenced, and whether grades should be used to motivate, communicate, or both. Some teachers grade according to a set of standards. Others consider effort and individual progress. Still others factor in classroom behavior. Further, grading policies vary widely among schools and teachers, and where policies exist, implementation is inconsistent.

Many educators respond to this conundrum by focusing on how they arrive at grades and what those practices do to support learning and motivation. No matter what the scale, grades should be clearly specified and based on reasonable standards that students can use to guide their learning. The most academically beneficial grading practices offer accurate, specific, timely feedback that improves student learning (Marzano, 2007).

Prior to offering specific suggestions for fair, equitable, and learning-focused grading practices, let's examine what to avoid. Douglas Reeves (2008) identifies three practices for grading that are so ineffective that they can be considered toxic. The first is to use a number system, such as 100 points, and to assign zero credit for a missing assignment. This is essentially a punitive practice that dramatically lowers a student's chance for a higher grade. In such a case, when the real thing that benefits learning is completing the assignment, this practice diminishes student motivation and does little to improve learning. Finding ways to coach or collaborate with learners to support completion is much more beneficial.

The second practice is averaging all scores throughout a semester or quarter to arrive at the final grade. This practice infers that all learning is equal and that performance early in the course is as important as performance later in the course. Because complex learning is developmental and the result of practice and revision, this approach to grading is typically reductive and unfair. Students' first papers, early tests, and beginning projects are the means by which they learn their errors and make improvements based on feedback and guidance. It is also the way the real world works: We construct and then refine a product to achieve quality, or learn and then practice a skill to become proficient. This is one of the reasons for the common belief that learning follows a curve and why editors, managers, and coaches do not evaluate on the basis of initial or even midlevel performance. In general, authentic performance at the end of a course is likely to be more accurate than throughout the course.

The third precarious practice is the single test, assignment, or project that is so high stakes that it determines nearly all of the student's grade but is based on significantly less material or length of the course's duration. An example of this is a project that determines 80% of a student's grade but takes only about 4 weeks out of a 16-week semester to complete, or a final paper-and-pencil test that determines 60% or more of a student's grade but is only an initial yet final assessment. In the project example, unless there have been successive opportunities for feedback, revision, and development over the semester, such a grading practice undermines the learning that preceded it. In the case of a test, an intrinsically motivating and valid representation of learning would include a series of formative and related assessments, covering similar content and with specific, relevant feedback that allows self-correction.

Another grading practice that deserves caution is to strictly ascertain grades through quantification. Understandably, because we have to "give grades," we want to be objective. Using numbers such as scores may seem to easily offer this possibility. However, when we assign a number as a value for a component of an assessment or a test, it influences the construction of that element and consequently what students will study and learn. A common example is the use of multiple-choice tests as formative assessments.

Because they are easy to score and average, many teachers are attracted to the format of multiple-choice, true-false, and short-answer tests. However, if these formats are to assess *and* encourage learning, they require very careful construction (Chappuis, Stiggins, Chappuis, & Arter, 2012). A common pitfall is to rely on factual recall at the expense of intricate thought.

Poorly constructed or overly simplified "objective" tests promote cramming because superficial information can be rapidly covered and retained for a short period of time. In a few days, the information is gone, but the grade has been documented. To avoid such complicity, many educators are moving toward grading practices that use authentic assessments (discussed later in the chapter). These are presented to students with graded exemplary models that include relevant specific criteria introduced early in the learning cycle. Contracts and rubrics strengthen this approach.

Contracts have a structure that allows mutual understanding and agreement as well as dialogue about the content, process, criteria, and outcomes. For historically underserved students, especially students who are learning English, the negotiation of a contract can be clarifying and reassuring. Contracts also have the benefit of targeting what is required for an excellent grade that represents excellent learning and removing some of the insecurity that tests can engender regarding which grade will be attained. Negotiating a contract ought to be a democratic process between teacher and student, but not a permissive one that sacrifices the integrity of the learning experience.

Exhibit 6.2 suggests practices and policies that are generally considered equitable, motivating, and informative. While not all of the suggestions will fit within the pragmatic limits of different contexts, these ideas can contribute to conversations about personal grading philosophies and approaches.

Exhibit 6.2 Grading Practices and Assessment Considerations

The following assessment and evaluation practices are aimed at helping students strive for and achieve excellence.

1. *Limit the attributes measured by grades to individual achievement.* Accurate grades represent what students know and can do. While effort, participation, and attitude are important, these qualities should be reported separately, if at all. This may require an extended report card format. Be careful to avoid the mistake of using your assessment policy for things that ought to be addressed by your behavior or discipline policy.

2. *Sample student performance.* Don't mark everything students do, and don't include all marks in the final grades. Provide feedback through formative assessments and include only summative assessments in grade calculations.

Continued

Exhibit 6.2 (Continued)

3. *Grade in pencil.* Emphasize the most recent information when grading progress. For example, it makes little sense to average the marks of a student in the first week and the last week of a world languages class; the most recent marks offer the best assessment of the student's language skill. When possible, offer opportunities to improve the grades. This doesn't mean teachers have to offer unlimited chances to pass a test or improve a paper. Some teachers require students who want to retake a test or to revise an assignment to demonstrate that they have done additional work that increases the chance that they'll do better the second time around. Those who offer repeated opportunities for revision sometimes require a well-written paragraph that explains why a third or fourth revision is worth both the student's and the teacher's time.

4. *Relate grading procedures to the intended learning goal.* The emphasis given to different topics or skills in a class should be reflected in the weight they have in determining the final grade. If you include "participation" in a grade, ensure that students can demonstrate this in different ways. For example a teacher might say, "At a minimum, every person in this class needs to be actively engaged and make strong contributions during each class session. However, there are different ways to do this, for example, by taking and posting notes for the class, helping to ensure that all voices are heard, and volunteering to facilitate a small group. Should an unusual situation prevent you from actively engaging, please speak with me in advance of the class session."

5. *Use care when "crunching" numbers.* One of the biggest quandaries is what to do when a student gets a zero on an assignment. If scores on all assignments are simply averaged, a single zero can yield a grade that doesn't reflect the student's performance. Teachers might consider using students' median score. If a student earns a zero or a very low score on a major assignment, the teacher might consider a way for the student to revise the work or demonstrate progress on an alternative assessment. If this is not possible, consider if a future assignment can demonstrate new learning and count for more credit.

6. *Use criterion-referenced standards to distribute grades.* In addition to other problems, grading on a curve does not allow all students to see how close they are coming to high standards of performance. If all students reach the standard, all students should receive the highest grade.

7. *Discuss assessment and grading with students at the beginning of a new class.* The criteria for high-quality work should not be a mystery to students. It is important for students to see the grading schemes and rubrics that will be used to judge performance and to be able to use these tools to guide superior performance. It is even better if grading schemes and rubrics are co-created with students to enhance their sense of agency and understanding of assessment criteria.

Additional Considerations

- For each new area of study, work with students to compose a letter to parents or family that outlines what is being studied and the performance standards parents/family/students can expect and how families can support their student's success. This process can be clarifying and can further connect families to the learning experiences of their children.

- Consider agreed-upon, common districtwide or schoolwide rubrics that help students, across content areas, master literacy and learning skills such as vocabulary, details, organizing ideas, skills, processes, and behaviors that contribute to personal and community success. Schoolwide rubrics in writing promote responsibility among all teachers for teaching reading, writing, speaking, and listening in their subject areas. Because vocabulary is a strong predictor of overall success on standardized tests and speaking well is foundational to representing oneself in public and in a workplace, teachers should share and implement ideas to develop these skills regardless as part of their instructional repertoire. *A word of caution:* Although rubrics can teach as well as evaluate, many rubrics have not been carefully evaluated for their reliability and validity. Further, rubrics for writing run the risk of factoring out student voice. There needs to be a clear developmental or learning theory that justifies criteria on a rubric (Humphry & Heldsinger, 2014).

- Be careful not to confuse standards with standardization. The cliché "all kids can learn" does not presume that all human beings can learn the same thing in the same way at the same time. We can avoid the trap of homogenizing curriculum, instruction, and assessment by teaching conceptually. For example, when the topic is the Civil War, the concept might be conflict within a nation and within the minds of human beings; when the topic is planets, the concept might be systems; when the topic is equations, the topic might be balance (Tomlinson, 2014). In the case of conflict and the Civil War, a teacher might encourage students to research how Lincoln's being "of two minds" on the issue of slavery connects to contemporary contradictions in the struggle for human rights. To accomplish this, students would select or design different but related topics, questions, and methods of inquiry.

- Bring in experts from the community to work with teachers and students to ensure that tasks and scoring systems are authentic. For example, an editor of a local paper might help create a scoring rubric based on what she or he looks for in a good article. Students might interview a panel of community experts to discuss assessment criteria that fit with a range of perspectives.

- Consider a dissertation or defense model for major assignments where students create inquiry-based projects with the support of a committee with a teacher, peer, family member, and community partner.

- For major projects, have students engage peers in dialogue about an aspect of their work. A roundtable format is especially suited for this interaction.

- Model for students and the community your own interest in personal growth through learning. Find ways to share things that you are learning and that matter to you.

Source: Center on Learning, Assessment, and School Structure.

WELL-CONSTRUCTED PAPER-AND-PENCIL OR COMPUTERIZED TESTS

Many teachers believe that there is a role for multiple-choice tests, especially because they are a part of most district and state assessment practices and they influence other people's assumptions about student learning and knowledge. The primary issue is how to construct tests so that they are worth taking. This section spotlights ideas to create substantively better assessments. An important goal is to help teachers critique and revise testing decisions within a culturally responsive and comprehensive framework of understanding. Here are some ways to accomplish this:

- *Design tests to resemble real-life learning tasks that have instructional value.* Although open-ended paper-and-pencil tests tend to accomplish this better than multiple-choice tests, many teachers aim for a blend of these two methods for understandable pragmatic reasons. An example of a real-life learning situation that can be represented on paper is an item on an introductory bilingual education midterm that asks students to outline a letter to the school board explaining the short-term and long-range benefits of bilingual education programs for students, families, and the broader community.
- *Aim for tests to include complex and challenging mental processes* (Donovan, Bransford, & Pellegrino, 1999). For example, in a social studies class, a test item might require learners to create and present their reasoning for five interview questions that would help to determine which individuals are best suited to working well in a culturally diverse setting.
- *Acknowledge more than one approach or right answer.* For example, in a science class, students might be asked to select and respond to one of the following two items: (1) Construct a schematic chart or another graphic illustration that illustrates three to five key influences on the health of people who live in agricultural communities, or (2) Which environmental safety precautions should fruit growers be concerned with when they employ migrant workers to pick summer berries? Which is the most important? Why? Which seems least important to you? Why? Please select at least two influences of most importance and at least two influences of least importance.
- And perhaps most important, *tests should be meaningful to students* (Eisner, 1999). This is likely to occur when students see tests as an opportunity for self-enhancement and relevant meaning.

Designing tests to fit a range of student interests and perceived needs supports the awareness that they have to understand and act in this world.

Furthermore, whenever students are able to make deliberate connections between what is new and what is known, they are more likely to see learning as a compelling opportunity. Tests that are meaningful usually foster a sense of high challenge with low threat. Sometimes referred to as *relaxed alertness*, this is the optimal state of mind for expanding knowledge. Research on language acquisition, for example, suggests that people learn language most easily when they are relaxed and the emphasis is on communication rather than error. Being calm and alert allows us to access what we know, think creatively, and more easily pay attention (Zull, 2002). When tests are meaningful, when the topics teachers choose matter to students and are even somewhat playful, students are less fearful and better able to engage their talents in even the most challenging processes.

There are more significant criticisms than easy answers to questions of fairness, accountability, and how to revise testing practices in ways that promote consistently accurate judgments of learning among diverse student groups (Stobart, 2005). Although uncomfortable at times, self-critique is essential. Pulitzer Prize winner John Patrick Shanley (2007) might as well have been talking about assessment when he wrote:

> Doubt requires more courage than conviction does, and more energy; because conviction is a resting place and doubt is infinite. . . . You may want to be sure. Look down on that feeling. . . . We've got to learn to live with a full measure of uncertainty. There is no last word. (p. 6)

Some of the challenges that educators face as we strive to create and administer worthwhile tests are the language we use, the values we reflect, the environments we create, and the quality of the tests we select or design. All of this demonstrates our fidelity to both equity and excellence.

AVOIDING CULTURAL BIAS

With respect to cultural diversity, discussion of the limitations of tests and rubrics must include cultural bias. As Ovando and Combs (2011) contend, it is virtually inevitable that any test that uses language as a means of assessment will have accompanying cultural content. The most common type of bias identified is item content that favors one cultural frame of reference over another (Kornhaber, 2004). These issues often relate to ethnicity and gender. For example, items about baseball averages tend to give males an edge, whereas an item of similar difficulty but focusing on childcare may favor females (Pearlman, 1987). An item such as "Bananas are (a) black, (b) yellow, (c) red, or (d) green" is clearly invalid to anyone who has traveled south of the United States and knows that all of the answers are correct depending on the kind of banana a person is referencing. Although these examples oversimplify the issue, they are a reminder to examine possible assumptions embedded in the items selected for classroom use. The following questions, which apply to curricular materials in general, can help teachers select or construct test items and rubrics:

- *Invisibility:* Is there a significant omission of women and minority groups in testing materials? (This implies that certain groups are of less value, importance, and significance in our society.)
- *Stereotyping:* When groups or members of groups are mentioned in tests, are they assigned traditional or rigid roles that deny diversity and complexity within different groups? (When stereotypes occur repeatedly in print and other media, it perpetuates stereotypes and myths about women and members of historically marginalized ethnic and linguistic communities.)
- *Selectivity:* Is bias perpetuated by offering only one interpretation— or allowing only one interpretation—of an issue, situation, or group of people? (This fails to tap the knowledge of learners regarding varied perspectives.)
- *Unreality:* Do your test items lack a historical context that acknowledges—when relevant—prejudice and discrimination? (Glossing over painful or controversial issues obstructs authenticity and creates a sense of unreality.)
- *Fragmentation:* Are issues about women or marginalized ethnic groups separate from the main body of the test material? (This implies that these issues are less important than issues about people with the most power in society.)
- *Linguistic bias:* Do materials reflect bias in language through the dominance of masculine terms and pronouns? (The implication of invisibility devalues the importance and significance of women.)

Even directions for tests can constitute a form of bias. This is especially true for language-minority students. Students who are learning English benefit from test instructions that are direct and that include short sentences. Whenever possible, it is best to avoid the passive voice and ambiguous comments.

The testing situation itself can manifest cultural bias. The discomfort that is familiar to many students can be especially devastating for students who have less experience in such situations or for whom such situations evoke feelings of alienation or inadequacy. Norms and ground rules for testing should be clear and explicit, with advance preparation to learn about the kind of responses that are expected for different types of questions. In addition, students who are learning English, as with all students, need adequate processing time to understand questions and directions. In some cases assessments should be available in audio or video, with allowances for responding, such as dictation or the assistance of an interpreter (Kornhaber, 2004).

AVOIDING THE IMPOSITION OF LIMITATIONS ON KNOWLEDGE

Paper-and-pencil tests can take the form of product assessments such as essays, stories, poems, and critiques. They can also be constructed-response or selected-response items. When many of us think of paper-and-pencil tests, we think of constructed-response items: filling in a blank, solving a mathematics problem, labeling a diagram or map, responding to short-answer questions, and so forth. Although these tests generally allow for application of a broader and deeper range of knowledge than selected-response tests (multiple-choice, true-false, and matching), constructed-response items can still have limitations:

- The content may be limited in its breadth and depth. The consequence is that imaginative and challenging problem solving is negotiated out of the test content domain (Shepard, 1989).
- The content may not cover the full range of important instructional objectives. The consequence is that instructors may end up teaching two curricula: one that promotes mastery of the content to be tested and the other that involves creative classroom pursuits that are often seen as tangential to measurable success and therefore less important (Popham, 1987).
- Tests may be limited in terms of format. For example, a short-answer question restricts the amount of knowledge students can convey. Therefore, students may not have an opportunity to demonstrate knowledge or, more important, how they might use that knowledge because the format does not allow it (Nitko & Brookhart, 2010).

Bear in mind these limitations as you consider ways to create tests that are fair and equitable and provide opportunities for the application of knowledge. Constructed-item responses are only one of many ways in which learning can be measured. Multiple forms of assessment yield more authentic and reliable information about learning experiences and ways of making meaning from those experiences: constructed-response tests, product assessments (essays, stories, research reports, writing portfolios, projects, etc.), performance assessments (music, dance, dramatic performance, exhibitions, science lab demonstrations, debate, experiments, action research, etc.), and process-focused assessments (oral questioning, interviews, learning logs, process folios, journals, observation, etc.). In addition, we know that learners are most likely to gain understanding when they construct their own cognitive maps of interconnections among concepts and facts. Relying only on decontextualized paper-and-pencil testing practices can cheapen teaching and undermine the authenticity of scores as measures of what learners really know.

AUTHENTIC ASSESSMENT

Authentic assessments in the form of "real-life" performance tasks are among the oldest forms of assessment. They have been extensively field-tested and are seen as powerful tools for focusing teacher attention on what constitutes good learning (Chappuis et al., 2012). Today we have a more sophisticated understanding of these procedures and their central idea: that assessment should resemble as closely as possible the ways students will apply in their real lives what they have learned. Thus, if students are learning math, teachers might assess their learning by asking students to solve or create math word problems that reflect compelling current challenges related to their families, community, or environment. For example, in the learning activity Spoonful of Sugar (available at www .nextlesson.org/performance-tasks) students use the sugar contained in different serving sizes of their favorite soda to practice finding and comparing rates. As "family nutritionists" they have to find how the amount of sugar compares to other sodas and the recommended daily amounts.

The closer that assessment procedures come to providing opportunities for students to demonstrate what they have learned in the areas where they will eventually use that learning, the greater will be their motivation to do well and the more they will understand their competence and feel the self-confidence that emerges from effective performance. Providing the opportunity for learners to complete an authentic task is one of the best ways to conclude a learning activity because it promotes transfer of learning, enhances motivation for related work, and clarifies learner competence.

According to Wiggins (1998), an assessment or performance task is authentic if it has the following characteristics:

- *Is realistic.* The task replicates how people's knowledge and capacities are "tested" in their real world.
- *Requires judgment and innovation.* Students have to use knowledge wisely to solve unstructured problems, as a director of a film or play must do more than follow a routine procedure.

- *Asks students to "do" the subject.* Rather than recite or demonstrate what they have been taught or what is already known, students explore and work within the discipline, as when they demonstrate their competence for a history course by writing history from the perspective of particular people, using original documents, in an actual historical situation.
- *Replicates or simulates the contexts that students find in their community, personal life, or—for older students—jobs.* These contexts involve specific situations and their demands. For example, students engage in a role-play in which, as union stewards and business owners, they apply conflict resolution skills, with consideration of the personalities and responsibilities involved.
- *Assesses students' current level of expertise, integrating knowledge and skill to negotiate a complex task effectively.* Students have to put their knowledge and skills together to meet real-life challenges. This is analogous to the difference between taking a few shots in a warm-up drill and taking shots in a real basketball game, or between writing a paper on a particular law and writing a real proposal to legislators to change the law.
- *Allows appropriate opportunities to rehearse, practice, consult resources, and get feedback on and refine performances and products.* Learning and, consequently, assessment are not one-shot enterprises. Almost all learning is formative, whether one is learning how to write a publishable article or bake a pie. We put out our first attempt and see how it reads or tastes. We repeatedly move through a cycle of perform, get feedback, revise, perform. That's how most high-quality products and performances are attained, especially in real life. We must use assessment procedures that contribute to the improvement of student performance and learning over time. Doing so means that some of the time assessment is separated from grading processes to assure learners that their mistakes are not counted against them but are a legitimate part of the learning process. In this regard, we may assign credit for completion of such tasks or make them part of the requirements for the course.

Authentic performance tasks avoid asking, "Do you know this material?" and instead ask, "What do you know?" Because students are invited to exhibit what they have internalized and learned through application, this process extends—rather than merely tests—learning. For example, one-sentence summaries ask students to reorganize a particular concept in a single grammatical sentence. This technique encourages learners to apply their understanding and analysis of information rather than regurgitate narrowly defined "correct answers."

COMPARING PERSONAL ASSESSMENT VALUES WITH ACTUAL ASSESSMENT PRACTICE

Exhibit 6.3 lists key qualities and characteristics of authentic assessment tasks. It provides an opportunity to compare assessment values to actual practices. With the insights provided by this exercise, teachers can consider possible changes and suggestions, several of which are in this chapter. Two of the most important items in the exercise are (1) using simulations or real-life challenges that require new academic knowledge or skill and (2) producing a high-quality product or performance.

An implicit goal of each item is, whenever possible, to use assessment as an opportunity to bridge the student's home community with the school context. Consider, for example, the enhanced meaning and intellectual value of a student-generated questionnaire on unemployment and immigration for a math lesson on statistics. Imagine the motivational and sociocultural significance of a student-designed workshop on cultural respect and communication patterns for a world language or social studies class.

SELF-ASSESSMENT

Self-assessment is a reflective process to develop perspective on how we understand ourselves as learners, knowers, and citizens in a complex world. It requires us to observe, analyze, and develop insight into how we might improve personal performance relative to a set of academic standards. Self-assessment also allows a person to validate her authenticity as a learner and cultural being. It can help weave important relationships and meanings between academic or technical information and, in doing so, discover important connections.

In addition to locating one's own perspectives relative to academic work, self-assessment can provide an opportunity for students in culturally diverse classrooms to reflect on and more clearly negotiate the tension between personal orientations and dominant norms. For example, a teacher asks students in a computer science course to visit two corporate settings to observe the ways in which technological skills are used and to develop insight into corporate norms and expectations. Prior to the field experience, students construct a brief set of semistructured interview questions through which to access the assumptions of three workers in each corporate setting about the meaning and nature of work. Subsequent to the visits, students share their interview findings and draft a brief essay on the potential value conflicts that they as individual workers might experience in one of the settings. From these essays, the teacher demonstrates how to identify inquiry questions for further study. Then the class explores

Exhibit 6.3 Considerations for Authentic Performance Tasks

Circle your own assessment, on a scale from 1 (*weak*) to 5 (*strong*), of your personal values and practices for engendering competence. Compare your values with your practices to determine areas in which to focus your attention for improvement.

Your Value Weak Strong	"Test" Components	Your Actual Practice Weak Strong
1 2 3 4 5	Convincing evidence that students can use their new knowledge and skills effectively and creatively	1 2 3 4 5
1 2 3 4 5	Simulations or real-life challenges that require new academic knowledge or skill	1 2 3 4 5
1 2 3 4 5	Tasks in which a multifaceted repertoire of knowledge and skill must be applied with good judgment; simple recall is insufficient for performing well	1 2 3 4 5
1 2 3 4 5	A chance to produce a quality product or performance	1 2 3 4 5
1 2 3 4 5	Demystified criteria and standards that allow students to thoroughly prepare, self-assess, and self-adjust with the resources that are available	1 2 3 4 5
1 2 3 4 5	Opportunities for students to learn from the experience itself and to improve before the course or class has ended	1 2 3 4 5
1 2 3 4 5	Reasonable chances to learn from mistakes without any penalty	1 2 3 4 5
1 2 3 4 5	Opportunities for students to justify their answers, choices, or plans	1 2 3 4 5
1 2 3 4 5	Evidence of the pattern and consistency of student work	1 2 3 4 5
1 2 3 4 5	Opportunities for teachers to learn new things with their students	1 2 3 4 5

Source: Adapted from materials provided by the Center on Learning, Assessment, and School Structure.

ways to access digital resources for continued learning. They conclude the learning experience with a self-assessment based on transformative learning theory (Pugh, 2011). The teacher asks students to consider (1) the extent to which their perspective may have shifted, (2) the extent to which they see things differently, in general, and (3) their motivation to engage in other activities and actions because of what they learned.

According to social scientists, the exploration of values is a complex process, and at times a lonely one (Tatum, 1992). Within and across social groups, there are diverse perspectives. Creating opportunities to make student frames of reference explicit is basic to intrinsic motivation. By exposing surprises, puzzlements, and hunches, structured self-reflection experiences can enhance student motivation to make sense of things they might otherwise not realize (Mezirow, 2000).

For each of the approaches in this section of the book, teachers may want to carefully structure opportunities for students to engage in personal reflection as a process of self-discovery and self-determination, even when self-assessment is primarily intended as a simple record of learning or a moment of accountability. In order to make this feasible, teachers should develop agreements for confidentiality, honesty, and speaking for oneself. This invites the expansion and deepening of knowledge and helps to avoid cliché or culturally biased "truths."

Some caveats: Too much ambiguity can overwhelm students who are unaccustomed to self-assessment. To the extent possible, try to clearly identify what students should consider in order to learn from the process as well as what you would like to learn as well. It is important for students to know how a teacher will respond to self-assessments. Not surprisingly, students appreciate and are encouraged by a teacher's personal interest and timely feedback to their self-assessments. Although not everything needs to be read and commented on, students are more likely to strengthen their reflective skills if they receive expected, sincere, specific, supportive, and timely feedback.

Self-assessment can be superficial when it is appended to a class as a single episode at the end of the term. To develop a habit or point of view about learning, a rule of thumb is to build self-assessment into a course as an ongoing process through such activities as portfolio development or classroom self-assessment strategies. Familiarity with shorter processes helps students develop ease and confidence with long-term forms of self-assessment.

There are several approaches that teachers and students find helpful across disciplines. Over time, these can be aggregated and summarized for a more long-range perspective. This includes student-invented dialogues, focused reflection, postwrites, journals, closure techniques, and summarizing questions.

CLOSURE ACTIVITIES

Closure activities are opportunities for students to synthesize what they have learned, to examine general or specific aspects of what they have learned, to identify emerging thoughts or feelings, to discern themes, to construct meaning, to relate learning to real-life experiences, and so forth. The activities can occur in the form of celebration, acknowledgment, or sharing. The basic idea is that something notable is reaching an end-point. At such times, positive closure enhances student motivation because it affirms the entire process, verifies the value of the experience, directly or indirectly acknowledges competence, increases cohesiveness within the group, and encourages the surfacing of inspiration and other beneficial emotions within the learners themselves. For example, at the end of a class, a teacher might ask students to formulate a plan to apply what they have learned. Closure, then, becomes a way of building coherence between learning that has occurred and personal experience beyond the class. But positive closure can also be simple statements, such as an opportunity for students to say "thank you" to one another for their contributions. It can also take the form of a social event, such as an awards ceremony where everyone is honored for being part of a vibrant learning community. Some ways to achieve positive closure are presented in the following activities.

ACTIVITY 6.1
Closure Note-Taking Pairs

Purpose: To cooperatively reflect on a lesson, review major concepts and pertinent information, and illuminate unresolved issues or concerns. This is especially beneficial when there is a lecture or video. It can be used intermittently or as a culminating activity (Johnson, Johnson, & Smith, 1991).

Time: 15–30 minutes

Format: Pairs

Materials: Notes from a lecture or another learning experience

Process

Explain to students that closure note-taking pairs are learners who pair with another person to cooperatively reflect on a lesson, review major concepts and pertinent information, and illuminate unresolved issues or concerns. They work together to review, add to, or modify their notes.

Many students, including but certainly not limited to students who are English language learners, benefit by summarizing their lecture notes with another person. You may request that students ask each other questions such as these: "What have you got in your notes about this particular topic?" "What are the most important points made by the person who gave the presentation?" "What is something that you are feeling uncertain about that we might clarify together?"

Debrief: Ask students how they might use closure note-taking pairs in other learning experiences.

ACTIVITY 6.2

Door Passes

Purpose: To reflect on experiences and feelings associated with a learning experience

Time: 5–10 minutes

Format: Individual and large group

Materials: 3 × 5 cards or sticky notes

Process

This process is easy to practice with students. Explain that door passes provide a quick way for you to check in with the students' perspectives. Ask students to respond to a question and to personally hand it to you as they leave the room for a break. While collecting students' door passes, explain that a goal is to connect with each student's opinion. They should try not to slip by!

Here are some sample questions:

- What is one thing that most surprised you in our work so far?
- What is one thing that you know you will tell someone else at home or in your community about today's work?
- When were you were most confused and what might have helped you at that time?
- What is one thing you know you will do differently because of our work together?
- What is one thing you know you will do the same because of our work together?
- What is a question you might have asked if we had more time?
- What is a piece of advice related to the topics we have been studying that you can offer others?

ACTIVITY 6.3
Seasonal Partners

Purpose: To reflect on experiences and feelings associated with a learning experience and to promote interaction among students who might not otherwise interact as learning partners

Time: 20 minutes

Format: Dyads that rotate

Materials: 3 × 5 cards (or notepaper)

Process

Distribute index cards to students and ask them to list each season vertically on the card: fall, winter, spring, and summer. Explain that students will rotate around the room four times, finding a new partner for each season. With each rotation, partners greet one another and introduce themselves (if needed) and then write the name of the new partner on the index card by the appropriate season. (This is important because it is easy to forget which partners coordinate with each season.) In addition, with each rotation, partners discuss their reactions or responses to one of the four questions on a chart, board, or slide that corresponds with the season. Questions may be of any sort, depending on the topic at hand. Some possible questions for each season follow:

Fall: Discuss with your fall partner something you have learned from a class, a piece of literature, or an experience that enhances your understanding of _____ (a concept).

Winter: Discuss with your winter partner something you would like to learn more about given some of the issues we have examined.

Spring: Discuss with your spring partner one recommendation to extend what you've learned.

Summer: Discuss with your summer partner something you learned today that you value and that you will definitely apply in your own school work or life.

Debrief: In a large-group debrief, ask students to share some of the ideas that emerged in their discussions. Also ask students how they might explain this activity to their families.

ACTIVITY 6.4
Head, Heart, Hand

Purpose: To make meaningful connections, especially at the end of a class period or day

Time: 5 minutes for personal reflection; 10 minutes for large-group sharing

Format Individual and large group

Materials: Questions written on flip chart paper or a slide

Process

Ask students to use these prompts to reflect on a learning experience:

HEAD (thought): One thing that I will continue to *think* about as a consequence of participating in this learning experience is . . .

HEART (feelings): One thing that I am *feeling* now is . . .

HAND (action): One thing that I will *do* as a consequence of participating in this learning experience is . . .

ACTIVITY 6.5
Reflection Logs

Purpose: To reflect on learning

Time: 15 minutes for individual writing; 5–15 minutes for large-group sharing

Format: Individual and large group

Materials: Handout 6.1 (p. 213)

Process

Ask participants to respond to the items in Handout 6.1.

HANDOUT 6.1

Reflection Log

Please complete each of the following in a sentence or two as you reflect on the learning experience in which you have just participated (Beyer, 1988):

I learned . . .

I wonder . . .

I am surprised . . .

I wish . . .

I think . . .

I suggest . . .

because . . .

ACTIVITY 6.6

Reflection Trees for Group Projects

Purpose: To reflect on group learning experiences

Time: 15 minutes for individual writing; 5–15 minutes for large-group sharing

Format: Individual and large group

Materials: Sticky notes on large, handmade trees (an art teacher or the students design the trees), Handout 6.2 (this page)

HANDOUT 6.2

Reflection Trees

Please write a response to each of the following questions and post it on the tree along the wall with which it is associated:

Linden Tree

What I liked best was . . .

Maple Tree

One thing I learned that I think is particularly important was . . .

Cottonwood

What surprised me most was . . .

Olive Tree

What I did best was . . .

Pine Tree

What the team did best was . . .

Flowering Plum

What I would like to happen as a consequence of our work is . . .

Fig Tree

What I am doing differently or more of now is . . .

Lotus Tree

The way I feel about what we accomplished is . . .

ASSESSMENT OPTIONS BASED ON GARDNER'S MULTIPLE INTELLIGENCES

In most classrooms, teachers give students the same assessment task. On the surface, this may seem fair and an orderly way to proceed. However, when students can use different intellectual strengths to learn and demonstrate new knowledge, they are more motivated to excel. This doesn't require multiple-choice surveys to pinpoint students' preferred orientation to achieving a specific goal. In fact, one could argue that multiple-choice surveys contradict the very idea of letting students communicate through their strengths. Rather, when they are offered a set of assessment options, students will likely select one that speaks to their strengths.

According to Howard Gardner (2006), there are eight categories of intellectual strengths and these are deeper and broader than the kind of intelligence that is associated with IQ tests. In fact, Gardner asserts that a question such as "Are students intelligent?" is based on highly flawed assumptions about intelligence. The better question is "How are students intelligent?" The following list by Thomas Armstrong (2009) provides a quick glance at the different intelligences:

- linguistic intelligence ("word smart")
- logical-mathematical intelligence ("number/reasoning smart")
- spatial intelligence ("picture smart")
- bodily-kinesthetic intelligence ("body smart")
- musical intelligence ("music smart")
- interpersonal intelligence ("people smart")
- intrapersonal intelligence ("self smart")
- naturalist intelligence ("nature smart")

In addition, searching the Internet with the key words "multiple intelligences list" reveals a remarkable assortment of creative charts, diagrams, and other images for teaching with the eight intelligences. Although rich learning experiences require more thought than lists and colorful wall art, these tools can help teachers consider whether a single learning experience, or a set of learning experiences, provides adequate flexibility for a range of students to work from their positions of strength. The list in Handout 6.3 by Campbell, Campbell, and Dickenson (2004), organized by each intelligence, serves this purpose as well. In addition, it can prompt teachers to consider *how* students might represent similar academic goals, including homework goals, through different learning modalities. When students have the opportunity to select an assessment process that reflects their intellectual strengths, it encourages their participation and enthusiasm for demonstrating their competence.

HANDOUT 6.3 Menu of Assessment Options Organized by Gardner's Eight Intelligences

Linguistic

- Tell or write a short story to explain . . .
- Keep a journal to illustrate . . .
- Write a poem, myth, play, or editorial about . . .
- Create a debate to discuss . . .
- Create an advertising campaign to depict . . .
- Create a talk show about . . .
- Write a culminating essay to review . . .

Logical-Mathematical

- Complete a cost-benefit analysis of . . .
- Write a computer program for . . .
- Design and conduct an experiment to . . .
- Create story problems for . . .
- Conduct a mock trial to . . .
- Induce or deduce a set of principles on . . .
- Create a time line for . . .
- Create a crossword puzzle for . . .

Spatial

- Create a piece of art that demonstrates . . .
- Create a poster to . . .
- Create a video, collage, or photo album of . . .
- Create a chart, concept map, or graph to illustrate . . .
- Design a flag or logo to express . . .
- Create a scale model of . . .
- Create a mobile to . . .

Bodily-Kinesthetic

- Perform a play on . . .
- Invent or revise a game to . . .
- Role-play or simulate . . .
- Use puppets to explore . . .
- Create a sequence of . . .
- Create a scavenger hunt to . . .
- Create movements to explain . . .
- Create a poster session or exhibition to . . .

Musical

- Create a song that explains or expresses . . .
- Revise lyrics of a known song to . . .
- Collect a collage of music and songs to . . .

- Create a dance to illustrate . . .
- Create a music video to illustrate . . .
- Create an advertisement to . . .

Interpersonal

- Participate in a service project that will . . .
- Offer multiple perspectives of . . .
- Collaborate to resolve a local problem by . . .
- Teach a group to . . .
- Use what you have learned to change or influence . . .
- Conduct an interview or a discussion to . . .

Intrapersonal

- Create a personal philosophy about . . .
- Discern what is essential in . . .
- Explain your intuitive hunches about . . .
- Explain your emotions about . . .
- Explain your assumptions in a critical incident based on a personal experience . . .
- Keep a reflective journal to . . .

Naturalist

- Discover and describe the patterns in . . .
- Create a typology for . . .
- Relate and describe the interdependence of . . .
- Observe and describe . . .
- Use a field trip to analyze . . .
- Based on observation and field notes, describe your learning about . . .

The assessment options in this menu will need criteria for students and teachers to judge the quality of their learning and performance. As an example, creating an advertisement, a poster, or an exhibition might require criteria such as knowledge of the topic, creativity of delivery, supporting evidence, and organization of the format. (For further consideration of criteria and how to construct them, see the section on rubrics later in this chapter.)

In addition to accommodating multiple intelligences, this assessment menu offers a range of learning and performance options that require deep understanding—*design, teach, discern, explain, analyze, write, create,* and the like. These can be paired for greater authenticity and a more robust demonstration of learning. In life, most applications of knowledge require several tasks. For example, a scientist might design an experiment to analyze the chemicals in the local water supply *and* write an editorial based on the results for the local paper.

Assessment options provide opportunities for imaginative experiences that create an opportunity for students to use their perspectives, preferences, and strengths, and to challenge themselves with intelligences about which they are less confident. In addition, these assessments can be used to encourage students to develop deeper relationships between new learning and significant personal or cultural values.

The following exercise offers a way to introduce multiple intelligences to students and to explore this concept from several different perspectives.

ACTIVITY 6.7

Using Different Intelligences to Learn

Purpose: To cooperatively explore a topic from the perspective of several intelligences

Time: 15–30 minutes

Format: Small groups

Materials: Handout 6.3 (p. 216)

Process

Create small groups or dyads and assign a different intelligence to each group. Try to limit groups to five students, while helping students select a group that they feel represents one of their strongest intelligences. Explain to the groups that you would like them to use the intelligence to which they have been assigned to explain a concept. (For this example, we'll pretend students have been investigating intrinsic motivation.) Write the directions on a piece of newsprint and read them aloud, asking each group to (1) share notes related to the concept of intrinsic motivation, (2) determine a subtopic they would like to explore, and (3) create a 5- to 7-minute teaching segment that demonstrates the intelligence with which they are working through reteaching something about intrinsic motivation. For example, the spatial group might draw a series of shapes and ask participants which shape best represents the characteristics of intrinsic motivation and why? The logical-mathematical group might outline a math lesson that teaches a particular skill in a way that is intrinsically motivating. And the linguistic group might develop other words for intrinsic motivation. For example, in reference to the Motivational Framework for Culturally Responsive Teaching, one group of Japanese learners created a new framework they call SOBA. S stands for *success* (engendering competence), O stands for *ownership* (developing a positive attitude), B stands for *belonging* (establishing inclusion), and A stands for *active learning* (enhancing meaning).

Before the groups begin, ask everyone to consider what success will look like. Ask what the groups' criteria for success ought to be (taking into consideration time constraints). Limit it to three criteria. For example, the class might decide that success means (1) everybody in the group assists in the presentation, (2) the presentation holds the attention of the audience, and (3) the presentation makes clear connections between the concept of intrinsic motivation and their use of a particular intelligence. Tell the class that at the end of each presentation, the "audience" will provide brief feedback. The feedback will not be detailed because time constraints don't provide an opportunity to distill the gradations of each of the criteria for success. The audience will be asked to raise three fingers if all three criteria were met or two fingers for two out of three criteria. Since it is unlikely that a group of capable students would meet only one of the criteria, we suggest that you explain this and forgo a rating of one.

Debrief: Ask students to discuss what they learned from this experience. Ask them how they currently build on their strengths when they learn something new. Finally, ask students to think through with a partner one or two goals for using their multiple intelligences in other learning experiences. Afterward, have students create a goal for themselves on a 3×5 card and post the cards on a "reading wall" to share with classmates.

ACTIVITY 6.8

Journals

Purpose: To co-create a journal process

Time: At least 30 minutes

Format: Individual and large group

Materials: Prepared questions, Handout 6.4 (p. 220)

Process

Ask students to read the following synopsis on journals and, as they do so, to underline what is most important to help them push their thinking. Next, facilitate a discussion with students about the potential benefit of journals and ask them to share what they noted as they read the synopsis on journals. Also ask students to offer their own ideas for journal entries and feedback. As they speak, keep a record of their comments.

HANDOUT 6.4

Synopsis on Journals

Journals can take a number of forms. For example, there are science journals that provide a space to synthesize lab notes, address the quality of one's work, examine the processes on which the work is based, and address emerging interests and concerns. They provide information that conventional forms of assessment might miss.

In most subjects, there are opportunities to use journals to encourage critical awareness through questions such as these: From whose viewpoint are we seeing or reading or listening? From what angle or perspective? How do we know what we know? What is the evidence and how reliable is it? Whose purposes are served by this information? (Meier, 1995).

Journals can be used to address interests, ideas, and issues related to course material, recurring problems, responses to teacher-generated questions, responses to student-generated questions, and connections between courses. In addition, journals can help students make connections between current and past work, present and future life experiences. Directions for your journals may include the following:

1. Your journal is your conversation with yourself. Trust your own voice.

2. If you cannot respond to a prompt, try to explain why not.

3. From time to time I will ask you to submit a summary of your journal. You will choose what you would like me to read from your journal or what you have written that you would like me to know about.

4. Toward the end of the course, we will create a class anthology with at least one submission, or summary, from each person's journal. I will ask you to submit, along with your contribution, a brief preface about why you selected your piece.

5. In the back of your journal, please keep a section for words you are learning—from menus, signs, books, newspapers, and other people—that can help to enrich your writing.

If we wish to promote this level of reflection, then we need to ensure that there is space for this to happen. Students need time in class to respond in their journals to readings, discussions, and significant questions that build community around the journal process and make the classroom a place to further develop the skills of writing, insight, and personal meaning. For example, you might say, "As your teacher, I will pay less attention to the mechanics and organization of your thoughts and whether or not your writing makes sense. What is most important is to try to get your thoughts and feelings down on paper and for you to learn from them. Your journal entries can be reorganized and summarized later."

ACTIVITY 6.9
Postwrites

Purpose: To reflect on learning in relation to a final product

Time: 30 minutes

Format: Individual and large group

Process

Explain to students that postwrites are reflections that encourage learners to analyze a particular piece of work, how they created it, and what it may mean to them (Allen & Roswell, 1989). For example, "Now that you have finished your essay, please answer the following questions. There are no right or wrong answers. I am interested in your analysis of your experience writing this essay."

1. What problems did you face in writing this essay?

2. What solutions did you find for these problems?

3. Imagine you had more time to write this essay. What would you do if you were to continue working on it?

4. Has your thinking changed in any way as a result of writing this essay? If so, briefly describe.

ACTIVITY 6.10

Summarizing Questions

Purpose: To make meaning of an entire course or program of study

Time: Varies, depending on the question(s)

Format: Individual, dyads, and large group

Materials: Prepared questions

Process

Point out that tools for self-assessment provide opportunities for students to clarify the process and significance of a recent learning experience. One approach to self-assessment is the use of summarizing questions at the end of a class, semester, or year. For younger students, this may occur at the end of a lesson or unit. Provide questions such as the following (Elbow, 1986):

1. How do you feel now at the end? Why?

2. What are you proud of?

3. Compare your accomplishments with what you had hoped for and expected at the start.

4. Which kinds of things were difficult or frustrating? Which were easy?

5. What is the most important thing you did in this course?

6. Think of some important moments from this course: your best moments, typical moments, crises, or turning points. Choose five or six of these, and write a sentence or two about each. What can or did you learn from each of these moments?

7. Who is the person you studied that you cared the most about? Be that person and write the person's letter to you, telling you whatever it is they have to tell you.

8. What did you learn throughout the course? What were the skills and ideas? What was the most important thing? What idea or skill was hard to really "get"? What crucial idea or skill came naturally?

9. Describe this period of time as a journey. Where did this journey take you? What was the terrain like? Was it a complete trip or part of a longer one?

10. You learned something crucial that you won't discover for a while. Guess what that is.

11. How could you have done a better job?

12. What advice would some friends in the class give you if they spoke with 100% honesty and caring?

13. What advice do you have for yourself?

Students select several questions that they find valuable to respond to in writing and discuss with a partner. They begin with a rationale for selecting those items. In pairs and then in the large group, they share some of their insights.

ACTIVITY 6.11

Student Self-Assessment Aligned With Principles of Motivation

---

Purpose: To reflect on personal accomplishments, challenges, and goals (Questions are aligned with the Motivational Framework for Culturally Responsive Teaching.)

Time: 20–30 minutes

Format: Individual reflection

Materials: Handout 6.5

Process

Distribute Handout 6.5 and ask students to respond to the questions.

RUBRICS

Rubrics have become commonplace in education, and many teachers create them independently or with colleagues. In addition, they are freely available on the Internet and are standard components of curricula from publishing houses and consultants. Essentially, a rubric is a set of guidelines to guide and evaluate a student's work. It strongly controls learning because, as Wiggins (1998, p. 154) points out, a rubric is used by many teachers to answer the following questions:

- By what criteria should performance be judged?
- Where and what should we look for to judge performance success?
- What does the range in quality of performance look like?

- How do we determine validly, reliably, and fairly what score should be given and what that score should mean?
- How should the different levels of quality be described and distinguished from one another?

This set of questions suggests that the challenge to creating and using rubrics it to ensure that they are fair, are valid, assess the essential features of performance, and are sufficiently clear so learners can accurately self-assess. However, another challenge is that, as helpful as rubrics can be when it comes to defining clear criteria for success and for making it easier for teachers to explain why a student received a particular grade, rubrics can have the unintended consequence of causing students to think less deeply, avoid taking risks, and lose interest in the learning itself (Kohn, 2006). For example, purpose, organizations, details, voice, and mechanics are common categories for what counts in a piece of writing. For each of the criteria, there are gradations of quality, from "excellent" to "not yet ready." Yet one might ask if this is really how writers think when they produce a compelling narrative.

Generally, rubrics are "where the rubber meets the road." This is because they often mean more than assessment; they mean evaluation. Assessment describes or compares, but evaluation makes a value judgment. In evaluation we fix passing scores or criteria, which determine how acceptable or unacceptable a given performance is. Grades or scores are often assigned and recorded according to the rubric. Combined, these distinctions determine a great deal about how students see themselves as learners and the choices they will have as their schooling progresses. Many teachers have been cautiously using rubrics for several years and have come to see that they are more deceptive than they appear at first glance. In some ways they are like a large wall from a distance. You see the cracks only when you get closer. According to Wlodkowski (2008) baseball averages are an example of the complexity and elusiveness of rubrics. Rubrics contain a scale of possible points along a continuum of quality. Batting average is a rubric in the sense that we evaluate how good batters are by their percentage of hits for times at bat. The higher the average, the better the player. But is a .300 hitter a good hitter? Well, that depends. How many times has the player been to bat? Does she get extra base hits? How does she hit when players are on base? At night? With two strikes? When the team is behind? Against left-handed pitching? As many managers know, you don't use batting average alone to evaluate a player—even to judge only hitting. And that's how it is with rubrics: They may seem concrete, specific, and telling, but life's contexts and complexity can make the simplest performance a defying puzzle.

HANDOUT 6.5

Student Self-Assessment

Name:

Date:

Class:

1. What have I done to demonstrate respect for other people in our class?

2. What kinds of decisions have I made throughout this period of time that have helped me to feel responsible for my own learning?

3. When have I felt so involved in learning that time seemed to fly?

4a. What are at least two things I can do to have this feeling more often?

4b. What are at least two things my teacher can do?

5a. What are some things I've been doing at school about which I feel academically successful?

5b. How are they important to other people (including my family or community) as well as to me?

6. What goals might I set for myself based on my responses to these questions?

Yet rubrics provide the answer to an important, if controversial question: What are you going to use to judge my work? If rubrics are fair, clear, reliable, and valid, and they address the essentials of performance and qualities that students care about, they can enhance motivation because they can provide a path to competence based on a set of shared expectations. Ideally, rubrics include models and indicators to make each level of quality concretely understandable. In addition, they are created or regularly revised with input from students to make them meaningful and culturally sensitive. For example, in a recent review of rubrics, I came upon one for public presentations that includes criteria, worded in children's language, such as "How did I look?" The gradations of this particular example range from "hair combed, "clean clothes," and "smiles" to "looks happy" to "looks lazy" to "just-got-out-of-bed look." Rubrics of this sort contain and perpetuate ideas about physical appearance that are *loaded* with cultural assumptions. The characteristics of the content matters. In this example, the rubric corroborates dominant narratives, perpetuated by popular media, about "alertness" and "enthusiasm." Further, it puts students in a position to either accept (at least in the short term) that such characteristics are desirable forms of public expression among the world's people or receive a bad grade.

Even culturally respectful and reasonably precise rubrics are flawed assistants in making judgments about learning. Let's look at one rubric to judge the clear expression of a main idea in an essay (Exhibit 6.4). The rubric, of course, would need to be extended to evaluate other dimensions of performance in the essay, such as critical thinking or writing mechanics. The purpose of this rubric is to help us better understand some of Wiggins's (1998) guidelines for effectiveness. The criteria are listed in the right-hand column of Exhibit 6.4.

Exhibit 6.4 A Rubric to Express an Idea Clearly

Rating	Descriptor With Indicators
Exemplary = 4	Clearly communicates the main idea or theme and provides support that contains rich, vivid, and powerful detail.
Competent = 3	Clearly communicates the main idea or theme and provides suitable support and detail.
Acceptable with flaws = 2	Clearly communicates the main idea or theme, but support is sketchy or vague.
Needs revision = 1	The main idea or theme is not discernible.

If we were using this rubric (and had a model for the descriptor of each level of performance) to evaluate 20 student essays *only for the main idea*, we should be able to do the following:

1. Use this rubric to accurately discriminate among the essays by assessing the essential features of performance. This makes the rubric valid.

2. Rely on the rubric's descriptive language (what the quality or its absence looks like). This is different than merely evaluative language such as "excellent product" to make the discrimination.

3. Use this rubric to consistently make fine discriminations across four levels of performance. When a rubric can be repeatedly used to make the same discriminations with the same sample of performances, it is reliable. To maintain reliability, rubrics seldom have more than six levels of performance. Make sure students can use this same rubric and its descriptors (and models) of each level of performance to accurately self-assess and self-correct their work.

4. Make sure this rubric is parallel. Each descriptor generally matches the others in terms of criteria language used.

5. Make sure this rubric is coherent. The rubric focuses on the same criteria throughout.

6. Make sure this rubric is continuous. The degree of difference between each descriptor (level of performance) tends to be equal.

Since this is a complex endeavor, in some schools teachers meet together to discuss their rubrics. In roundtable fashion, teachers share a sample of a rubric with which they have experienced the most success. Samples can be part of an "off the shelf" curriculum or "homegrown." With colleagues, they discuss questions such as these:

- Did you develop the rubric? If so, what was the process?
- In using the rubric, what do you do to clarify what each portion describes?
- How do you ascertain if all students understand the rubric before they begin a learning experience? Do you believe that all aspects of the rubric are equally important? If not, what do you do about that?
- In what ways do you find the number of performance levels to be sufficient?

- What do you do about student work that seems to fall between performance levels on the rubric?
- Are there any ways in which you would make your rubric more
  culturally respectful?

ACTIVITY 6.12
Class Evaluation From the Perspective of Students

Purpose: To provide feedback on instructional practice to a teacher

Time: 10 minutes

Format: Individual

Materials: Handout 6.6

Process

Distribute a handout similar to Handout 6.6 on page 229, and ask students to use it to provide feedback to you about their learning experiences
thus far. Let students know how you will use the feedback.

ACTIVITY 6.13
Critical Incidents From the Perspective of Students

Purpose: To reflect on significant learning experiences

Time: 10 minutes

Format: Individual

Materials: Handout 6.6

Process

This approach is adapted from the work of Stephen Brookfield (1995,
p. 115). It is a critical incident questionnaire with five questions, each of
which asks students to write details about important events that took place
while they were learning. For a course, it can be used at the end of each
week. For a class, it may have value at the end of each session. Type the
following questions on a form with space beneath each question for students to respond. Ask students to answer the questions anonymously.

1. At what moment in this class/course did you feel most engaged
   with what was happening?

HANDOUT 6.6

Students' Perspectives on the Motivational Conditions for Teaching and Learning

Please circle how you felt about the class today.

(4 is high and means *very true,* 1 is low and means *not true at all,* NA means *not applicable*)

1. What I learned is useful.	4 3 2 1 NA
2. What we did was interesting.	4 3 2 1 NA
3. I had some choices.	4 3 2 1 NA
4. What we did was challenging.	4 3 2 1 NA
5. What we did was involving.	4 3 2 1 NA
6. It made me really think.	4 3 2 1 NA
7. It was too hard.	4 3 2 1 NA
8. It was too easy.	4 3 2 1 NA
9. It was boring.	4 3 2 1 NA
10. I felt respected by my teacher.	4 3 2 1 NA
11. I didn't feel listened to by my teacher.	4 3 2 1 NA
12. As a class we tried to support each other.	4 3 2 1 NA
13. I sank or swam alone.	4 3 2 1 NA
14. I felt respected by my classmates.	4 3 2 1 NA
15. I did not feel respected by my classmates.	4 3 2 1 NA
16. I learned some things that are important to me.	4 3 2 1 NA
17. I learned some things that could be important to my community.	4 3 2 1 NA
18. I felt successful.	4 3 2 1 NA
19. I'm getting better at things I value.	4 3 2 1 NA
20. The work related to my life outside of the classroom.	4 3 2 1 NA
21. We had the opportunity to learn from our mistakes.	4 3 2 1 NA
22. I felt unsuccessful.	4 3 2 1 NA
23. I need more time to do well.	4 3 2 1 NA
24. The way we were graded was fair.	4 3 2 1 NA
25. I didn't have a chance to show what I learned.	4 3 2 1 NA

2. At what moment in this class/course did you feel most distanced from what was happening?

3. What action that anyone (teacher or student) took in this class/course did you find most affirming and helpful?

4. What action that anyone (teacher or student) took in this class/course did you find most puzzling or confusing?

5. What about this class/course surprised you the most? (This could be something about your own reactions to a topic or event, something that someone did, or anything else that occurs to you.)

After collecting responses, explore them for themes, patterns, and, in general, concerns that need adjustments or that warrant responses as well as aspects of teaching that have been affirmed. All of this contributes to suggestions for areas to elaborate on or strengthen.

ACTIVITY 6.14

Evaluating the Motivational Conditions of a Class

Purpose: To provide formative feedback on how well class is fulfilling the four conditions of the motivational framework with older students

Time: 5 minutes

Format: Individual

Materials: Create a handout as explained in the following "Process" section

Process

Distribute a handout with the following questions, asking students to respond using a four-point scale from *strongly disagree* to *strongly agree*.

1. The classroom environment is friendly and respectful. (establishing inclusion)

2. What we are learning is relevant to my life. (developing a positive attitude)

3. This class is challenging me to think. (enhancing meaning)

4. This class is helping me be effective at what I value. (engendering competence)

5. The teacher respects the opinions and ideas of students. (establishing inclusion)

6. In this class I can use my experiences and strengths to support my learning. (developing a positive attitude)

7. Most of the time during this class, I feel engaged in what's going on. (enhancing meaning)

8. I will use the information or skills I am learning in this class. (engendering competence)

DESIGNING LESSONS USING THE MOTIVATIONAL FRAMEWORK FOR CULTURALLY RESPONSIVE TEACHING

This topic differs from the previously outlined strategies for students. It provides tools to assist teachers with planning and implementing motivating learning experiences. The sample forms that follow can be modified to include content-specific instructional practices and/or to integrate the various instructional frameworks that teacher consider. For example, schools often use the motivational framework as an umbrella for specific instructional support for English language learners and students with physical and intellectual disabilities and to ensure that the school's instructional priorities are clearly identified. (See p. 39 for an example of how a high school incorporates project-based learning and annual instructional goals into the framework.) Handout 6.7 (p. 232. p. 247) is a spherical map for planning, and Handout 6.8 (p. 233) is a more sequential planning guide. Handout 6.9 (p. 234) is a tool to assess the implementation of plans. Some teachers use it as a self-assessment. Others ask a trusted colleague to serve the role of peer coach. Some people use motivational planning as an umbrella to plan content-specific instruction. Some use it to assess a lesson plan that they have outlined in another format. Others map an entire portion of a day to ensure that all four motivational conditions were adequately met over time. Teachers will notice that several strategies fit more than one condition. In such cases, it is a good idea to select the condition that seems most appropriate. Ultimately, the goal is to ensure that all four conditions have been addressed and that they cohesively support learning goals. What is *not* desirable is to use the framework in ways that make learning seem contrived or simply a set of activities scattered across a planning tool without much connection to serving motivational purposes.

HANDOUT 6.7

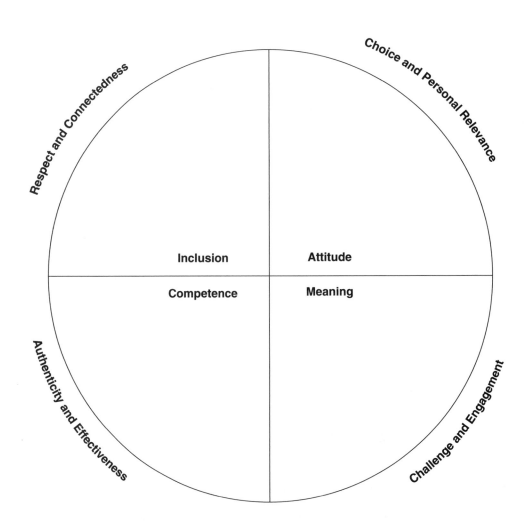

HANDOUT 6.8

Planning Guide

Based on the Motivational Framework for Culturally Responsive Teaching

Description of Lesson or Unit Including General Goals and Specific Learning Targets

Note: If your school is actively using content standards, please be sure to include the standards you are addressing in this lesson.

Establishing Inclusion

How does this learning experience contribute to developing as a community of learners who feel respected by and connected to one another and to the teacher?

Developing a Positive Attitude

How does this learning experience offer meaningful choices and promote personal relevance for all students in terms of what is learned and how it is learned?

Enhancing Meaning

How does this learning experience engage students in challenging learning that is so compelling that students may even lose their sense of time?

Engendering Competence

How does this learning experience include clear criteria for success and help all students see that they are becoming effective in learning that they value and perceive as authentic to their real-world experience and/or to the needs of their community or society?

HANDOUT 6.9

Guide for Personal Reflection or Peer Support to Continuously Improve Intrinsically Motivating Teaching and Learning

Description of Lesson/Unit/Learning Targets

Establishing Inclusion

How does the learning experience contribute to developing as a community of learners who feel respected by and connected to one another?

Routines and rituals are visible and understood by all:

_____ Rituals are in place that help everyone feel that they belong in the class.

_____ Students and teacher(s) have opportunities to learn about each other.

_____ Students and teacher(s) have opportunities to learn about each other's backgrounds.

_____ Classroom agreements and consequences for transgressions are negotiated.

_____ The system of discipline is understood by all students and applied with fairness.

Evidence

All students equitably and actively participate/interact:

_____ Teacher directs attention equitably.

_____ Teacher interacts respectfully with all students.

_____ Teacher demonstrates to all students that she or he cares about them.

_____ Students talk to/with a partner/small group.

_____ Students respond to a lesson by writing.

_____ Students know what to do, especially when making choices.

_____ Students help each other.

_____ Student work is displayed.

Evidence

Developing a Positive Attitude

How does this learning experience offer meaningful choices and promote personal relevance to contribute to a positive attitude?

Teacher works with students to personalize the relevance of course content:

_____ Students' experiences, concerns, and interests are used to develop course content.

_____ Students' experiences, concerns, and interests are addressed in responses to questions.

_____ Students' prior knowledge/learning experiences is/are explicitly linked to course content and questions.

_____ Teacher encourages students to understand, develop, and express different points of view.

_____ Teacher encourages students to clarify their interests and set goals.

_____ Teacher maintains flexibility in pursuit of teachable moments and emerging interests.

Evidence

Teacher encourages students to make real choices, such as

_____ how to learn (multiple intelligences)

_____ what to learn

Continued

HANDOUT 6.9 (Continued)

_____ where to learn

_____ when a learning experience will be considered to be complete

_____ how learning will be assessed

_____ with whom to learn

_____ how to solve emerging problems

Evidence

Enhancing Meaning

How does this learning experience engage participants in challenging learning?

Teacher encourages all students to learn, apply, create, and communicate knowledge:

_____ Teacher, in concert with students, creates opportunities for inquiry, investigation, and projects.

_____ Teacher provides opportunities for students to actively participate in challenging ways when not involved in sedentary activities such as reflecting, reading, and writing.

_____ Teacher asks higher-order questions of all students throughout a lesson.

_____ Teacher elicits high-quality responses from all students.

_____ Teacher uses multiple "safety nets" to ensure student success (e.g., not grading all assignments, working with a partner, cooperative learning).

Evidence

Engendering Competence

How does this learning experience create an understanding that participants are becoming more effective in learning that they value and perceive as authentic to real-world experience?

There is information, consequence, or product that supports students in valuing and identifying learning:

_____Teacher clearly communicates the purpose of the lesson.

_____Teacher clearly communicates criteria for excellent final products.

_____Teacher provides opportunities for a diversity of competencies to be demonstrated in a variety of ways.

_____Teacher helps all students concretely identify accomplishments.

_____Teacher assesses different students differently.

_____Teacher assesses progress continually to provide feedback on individual growth and progress.

_____Teacher creates opportunities for students to make explicit connections between new and prior learning.

_____Teacher creates opportunities for students to make explicit connections between their learning and the "real world."

_____Teacher provides opportunities for students to self-assess learning in order to reflect on their growth as learners.

_____Teacher provides opportunities for students to self-assess their personal responsibility for contributing to the classroom as a learning community.

Evidence

SUMMARY

This chapter provided a host of considerations and strategies to support intrinsically motivating and learning-focused assessment. Undergirding every strategy in this chapter is a belief that assessment ought to figuratively and sometimes literally include "sitting beside" students to understand what they value, how they learn, and how to create the conditions that will further inspire their intellectual, creative, social, and emotional growth. Returning to the introductory scenario, it is feasible that this will be Mr. Middle's approach to helping Ignacio and his team move forward. To accomplish this, he might begin his conversation with Ignacio by asking him to share his perspectives based on a question from Activity 6.10 such as "Think of some important moments from your work thus far: your best moments, typical moments, crises, or turning points." Perhaps afterward he and Ignacio will strategize and adapt the self-assessment survey (Activity 6.11) so that Ignacio and each of his team members has a way to regularly and explicitly take stock of their learning. It is possible that Mr. Middle will assure Ignacio that collaborating more effectively from a distance is possible, with a little creativity. It is also possible that Mr. Middle will extend the time period for Ignacio's team to complete their work or find a way to further personalize the assignment. Like most teachers, Mr. Middle has a lot on his plate and deadlines to meet. But he won't give up on students, and part of what he wants Ignacio to learn is that, with a little extra support, challenges can be opportunities.

In closing, I would like to address the process of making changes in instructional practice. Whether it's trying new approaches to engender competence or working hard to ensure that all four conditions of the motivational framework are always in play, none of us can ever know beforehand the exact consequences of our actions. As important as research and theory may be, imagination and experimentation are crucial to culturally responsive and highly motivating instruction. Risking cliché, there simply are no quick fixes to enhancing the significance of what and how we teach. This is why teacher research is important. When we continuously investigate our teaching, we find valuable patterns, some of which we want to further understand. To do this well, educators need time to learn with and from each other on a sustained basis. Yet as all teachers know, there will never be enough time, and there will be fears and hesitations, shifts in sentiment, and other human foibles—our own as well as those of others.

For the most part, teaching is an act of courage and conviction, with the occasional and momentary paradise of near-perfect interactions with every student. What great teachers do more than anything is use their example to reveal the potential of a just and caring world.

ACTIVITY GUIDE FOR ENGENDERING COMPETENCE

Closure Note-Taking Pairs (Activity 6.1)

Door Passes (Activity 6.2)

Seasonal Partners (Activity 6.3)

Head, Heart, Hand (Activity 6.4)

Reflection Logs (Activity 6.5)

Reflection Trees for Group Projects (Activity 6.6)

Using Different Intelligences to Learn (Activity 6.7)

Journals (Activity 6.8)

Postwrites (Activity 6.9)

Summarizing Questions (Activity 6.10)

Student Self-Assessment Aligned With Principles of Motivation (Activity 6.11)

Class Evaluation From the Perspective of Students (Activity 6.12)

Critical Incidents From the Perspective of Students (Activity 6.13)

Evaluating the Motivational Conditions of a Class (Activity 6.14)

Epilogue

This book began with a conversation about intrinsic motivation and the terrain within which teaching and learning occurs. Subsequent chapters, organized around each of the four conditions of the Motivational Framework for Culturally Responsive Teaching, provided strategies to support students' curiosity, engagement, and success as learners and community members. The central idea of this book is that an intrinsic theory of motivation more adequately represents and serves the interests of all people, within and across cultural groups, in educational settings and beyond. When people feel *respected* and *connected* in a learning environment, when people *endorse* or *determine* learning they find *relevant*, and when people *engage* in *challenging* and *authentic* experiences that enhance their *effectiveness* in what they value, people learn.

From research that cuts across academic disciplines, the motivational framework offers theoretical coherence to continuously improve teaching and learning. This model and its many related practices are easy to connect to and blend with other instructional or content frameworks. Any worthwhile instructional model needs to be specific enough to be useful and flexible enough to include and support local priorities. In essence, this means that any pragmatic instructional framework has two seemingly contradictory goals: to simplify instruction so that educators can apply new ideas and to encourage thinking about teaching and learning in increasingly complicated ways.

The motivational framework provides a macrocultural perspective on culturally responsive teaching. As a response to the question "How can teachers more consistently support intrinsic motivation to learn within and across cultural groups?" it avoids bracketing whole groups of people and prescribing learning strategies based on presumed cultural characteristics. Many educators are aware that there is as much in-group as across-group variation, even when groups are united by language, history, and a sense of peoplehood.

In order to maximize the potential of the framework, it is essential to know students well and be aware of students' lives and aspirations. Students and families have stories to tell, and many of these are about survival, love, creativity, and resourcefulness. Great teachers continuously discover and build on students' strengths.

Because it can be difficult for high school teachers with 130 students to know every single student with the depth they might like, one way to be mindful of diversity is to pay particular attention to three or four very different students who represent a spectrum of academic accomplishment and ethnic and linguistic diversity. This means selecting *focus students* who are current high, middle, and low performers and ensuring that at least one student speaks a language other than English at home and one student has been identified for special education services. Ideally, one or two students are from cultural backgrounds that are different than the teacher's. In the case of an African American academy with primarily African American teachers, diversity might be determined by religion, family income, the role of extended family, or geographical influences such as urban versus rural. As teachers plan, they keep the images of their focus students in mind and consider the significance of each motivational condition for different learners. Although they understand that four students cannot represent the entire range of diversity in a class, these students' strengths and needs can help teachers consider nuance when planning a motivating learning experience.

Concepts such as respect, choice, challenge, and success can mean different things to different students. For example, some students are taught early in their lives to be highly autonomous. Others learn to be deferent to authority. These two traits influence how students will respond to opportunities for choice. If two of my four focus students are different in this respect, I will keep this in mind as I plan a lesson. For example, if I am planning a collaborative project learning experience, as I consider the second condition of the motivational framework (developing a positive attitude toward learning through choice and relevance), I will build in time to conference with individual students, as well as collaborative teams, so that I can help all students set challenging goals without becoming overwhelmed or anxious.

Concentrating on students' strengths doesn't mean ignoring the number of students who struggle daily against the pernicious effects of racism, wealth disparity, and social alienation. This discord affects their relationships with other people, immediate priorities, and future aspirations. Although there are no easy answers to help students attend to academic learning when immediate needs are unmet, as the primary influence on student success, a teacher can refuse to rely on extrinsic rewards and the threat of putative sanctions that focus students on finishing a task—rather than learning (Shernoff, 2013). Not only would such contingent manipulation encourage superficial learning, it will ultimately erode students' potential as knowledgeable, skillful, and caring citizens who are immersed in learning as a way of life and as part of the struggle for justice. More than ever, students need teachers who are stewards of deep and respectful learning and who are hopeful and critically curious learners themselves.

Yet the challenge of becoming increasingly culturally responsive brings us face to face with long-held assumptions and points of view. Such potential disruption can lead to dissonance and emotions that range from fear to exhilaration. Very few of us are able to do this without some period of uneasiness. The following guidelines may be helpful to teachers who seek a more culturally responsive pedagogy:

- Proceed gradually and with care.
- Build on your strengths.
- Examine a single course.
- Create a safe environment in which to learn.
- Learn with others.
- Create action plans and recognize short-term and long-range success.
- Acknowledge doubt and anxiety as signs of change and potential for growth, rather than opportunities for retreat.
- Recognize the power of self-generated knowledge.
- Share your work with others.

Innovative pedagogies require collaboration, if for no other reason than people need support for the discomfort that new risks impose. There's an old saying that no one can avoid pain but that most people can escape suffering. One of the key aspects of this adage is "not going it alone," that is, sharing the burden or the challenge, whichever it may be. The literature on professional learning has been nearly unanimous in declaring that educators are most likely to effectively change teaching practices with support and feedback from other colleagues (Vescio, Ross, & Adams, 2008). When adults experience something that is relevant and somewhat unsettling, and have the time and the support of peers to gain insight into the experience, they are at the portal of a new perspective.

One thing in which we can take comfort is that, like the movement of the hour hand of a clock, pedagogical innovation may be imperceptible but quite dramatic over time. People do change: how we vote, how we confront injustice, how we educate our youth, how we alter our own teaching practices. Individual volition and professional learning matters. So do school, district, and local policies that seek to reverse the legacy of a system that has historically created winners and losers in public education. This inequality is a central concern of the forthcoming volume of this two-volume series.

BOOK STUDY TO INTRODUCE THE TEXT

Although the next volume provides in-depth information for sustained professional learning, an initial book study may be useful to teams of educators. There are many ways to approach a book study. This particular protocol is an introduction to this text and can be modified for the time frame within which faculty are working.

1. In a large group, review the layout of the book, using the Contents page and selected procedures to provide examples of how these motivational strategies and activities are organized in each of the four chapters related to the motivational conditions (Chapters 2–5).

2. In a large group, review the index, noting the range of topics (pair-share).

3. Divide into groups of four. Select a group facilitator and a timekeeper.

4. Each member of the group identifies a chapter to examine. Limit yourselves to Chapters 3–6 so that collectively your group has these four chapters covered.

5. Read Chapter 1, the introduction. (Everyone reads this chapter.)

6. Then read the designated chapter for which you have volunteered, and peruse the headings. Find a procedure that is relevant to you. Read this section twice: first for general understanding and second to apply an idea to your own work.

7. Develop a 10-minute presentation for your small group that
   - provides an introduction to your chapter,
   - lists some of the topics in the chapter that caught your attention,
   - involves your group in examining one procedure or topic that appears to be particularly relevant or interesting; reserve time for comment on the presentations.

THE NEXT CHAPTER

As this book concludes, a new one begins. The second book spotlights how leaders and teachers can (1) use adult learning theory to develop intrinsically motivating professional learning for teachers, (2) be creative with time to construct iterative forms of collaboration that allow teachers to regularly learn from each other's expertise, (3) develop policies and practices to connect relevant data to teacher practice so that there is a context for *how* to improve, not just *what* to improve, (4) develop instructional partnerships with community members and families, and (5) advance the purpose and identity of schools as centers of learning for educational leaders, teachers, families, and community members as well as students.

While governments, corporations, and political leaders debate the aggressions of globalization and local politics, teachers can be—and many are—agents of genuine educational empowerment. In classrooms, agency and consciousness are center stage, whether by intention or default. A sustained focus on motivation, culturally responsive teaching, and professional learning won't end the struggle for human rights. But it can help students engage willingly and productively in learning. The influence of a teacher who encourages motivation through word and deed may be difficult to quantify. At the same time, it's impossible to dispute.

Appendix

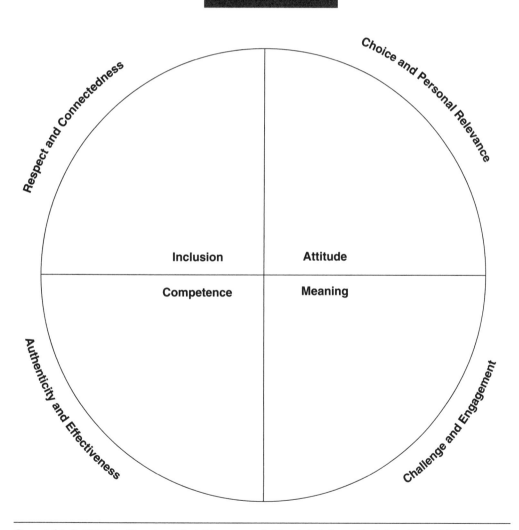

Instructor _____ **Goals:** _____

Inclusion

- Routines and rituals are established.
- Learning and interactions are respectful.
- Students are comfortable.
- Instructor treats all students respectfully and fairly.
- Students' lives, languages, and cultures are represented.

<u>Lesson Components:</u>

Attitude

- Classes are taught with students' experiences, concerns, or interests in mind.
- Students make learning-related choices that take into account their experiences, values, needs, and strengths.
- Students are able to voice their opinions.

<u>Lesson Components:</u>

Competence

- The criteria for success are clear.
- Grading policies are fair to all.
- Performances and demonstrations have "real world" connections.
- Students' perspectives are included in the assessment process.
- There are multiple ways to reach standards.

<u>Lesson Components:</u>

Meaning

- Students have opportunities for active participation in challenging formats, including projects, inquiry, and the arts.
- Activities integrate questions that go beyond facts and encourage different points of view.
- Teacher scaffolds new challenges.
- Teacher respectfully encourages high-quality responses.

<u>Lesson Components:</u>

Choice and Personal Relevance — ATTITUDE

MEANING — Challenge and Engagement

Respect and Connectedness — INCLUSION

COMPETENCE — Authenticity and Effectiveness

Source: Adapted from Ginsberg & Wlodkowski (2009).

Inclusion

(respect and connectedness)

	Yes/obvious	Yes, and	Not seen this visit	Ideas
Routines and rituals are present that contribute to respectful learning (e.g., ground rules, cooperative learning).				
Students comfortably and respectfully interact with each other.				
Students comfortably and respectfully interact with teacher (e.g., students share their perspectives).				
Teacher treats all students respectfully and fairly.				

General Information/Comments

Source: Copyright © 1999 by M. B. Ginsberg. All rights reserved.

Attitude

(choice and personal/cultural relevance)

	Yes/obvious	Yes, and	Not seen this visit	Ideas
Classes are taught with students' experiences, concerns, or interests in mind.				
Students make choices related to learning that include experiences, values, needs, and strengths.				
Students are able to voice their opinions.				
Teacher varies how students learn (discussion, music, film, personal interaction).				

General Information/Comments

Meaning
(challenge and engagement)

	Yes/obvious	Yes, and	Not seen this visit	Ideas
Students actively participate in challenging ways (e.g., investigations, projects, art, simulations, case study).				
Teacher asks questions that go beyond facts and encourages students to learn from different points of view.				
Teacher helps students recall what they know and build on it.				
Teacher respectfully encourages high-quality responses.				

General Information/Comments

Competence

(authenticity and effectiveness)

	Yes/obvious	Yes, and	Not seen this visit	Ideas
Teacher shares or develops with students clear criteria for success (e.g., rubrics, personal conferences).				
Grading policies are fair to all students (e.g., students can learn from mistakes, grades reflect what students know and can do).				
There are demonstrations or exhibitions of learning with real-world connections.				
Assessment includes student values (e.g., students self-assess, there are multiple ways to demonstrate learning).				

General Information/Comments

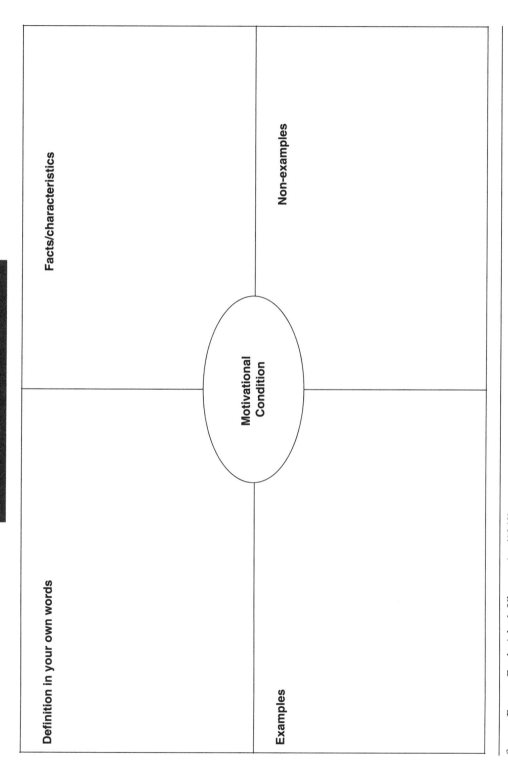

HANDOUT A.3 FRAYER MODEL

Definition in your own words

Facts/characteristics

Motivational Condition

Examples

Non-examples

Source: Frayer, Frederick, & Klausmeier (1969).

253

HANDOUT A.4 LOOKING FOR WOWS AND WONDERS

Wows

Team members comment on the *wows* of the lesson, using the motivational framework as a common tool from which to base comments. *Wows* are those observations that clearly demonstrate where conditions of the motivational framework are purposefully addressed in teaching and learning. Give specific instructional examples to illustrate important points. Chart comments made by members of the team.

Wonders

Team members comment on the *wonders* of the lesson. What could this teacher have done to produce deeper understanding? What might be included next time to deepen the quality of student work or responses? Chart comments made by members of the team.

Debrief

Colleagues reflect as a group on the *wows* and *wonders* for each of the four conditions of the motivational framework. They set individual goals and team goals intended to improve professional practice.

Relationships (Respect and Connectedness)	Relevance (Choice and Relevance)
Wows	Wows
Wonders	Wonders
Results (Authenticity and Effectiveness)	Rigor (Challenge and Engagement)
Wows	Wows
Wonders	Wonders

Source: Adapted from Ginsberg & Wlodkowski (2009, pp. 375–376).

References

Adams, M., Bell, L. A., & Griffin, P. (Eds.). (2007). *Teaching for diversity and social justice* (2nd ed.). New York, NY: Routledge.

Adichie, C. (2009). *The danger of a single story.* Retrieved from http://www.youtube.com/watch?v=D9Ihs241zeg

Ahissar, E., Vaadia, E., Ahissar, M., Bergman, H., Arieli, A, & Abeles, M. (1992). Dependence of cortical plasticity on correlated activity of single neurons and on behavioral context. *Science, 257*, 1412–1415.

Alber, R. (2013, August 30). Say what? Five ways to get students to listen. *Edutopia.* Retrieved from http://www.edutopia.org/blog-five-listening-strategies-rebecca-alber

Allen, M. S., & Roswell, B. S. (1989, March). *Self-evaluation as holistic assessment.* Paper presented at the annual meeting of the Conference on College Composition and Communication.

Andersen, P. A., & Wang, H. (2006). Unraveling cultural cues: Dimensions of nonverbal communication across cultures. In L. A. Samovar, R. E. Porter, & E. R. McDaniel (Eds.), *Intercultural communication* (11th ed., pp. 250–266). Belmont, CA: Thompson Wadsworth.

Anyon, J. (1980). Social class and the hidden curriculum of work. *Journal of Education, 162*(1), 67–92.

Anyon, J. (2005). *Radical possibilities: Public policy, urban education, and a new social movement.* New York, NY: Routledge.

Anzaldúa, G. (1987). *Borderlands/la frontera: The new Mestiza.* San Francisco, CA: Ante Lute Press.

Armstrong, T. (2009). *Multiple intelligences in the classroom* (3rd ed.). Alexandria, VA: Association of Supervision and Curriculum Development.

Artiles, A. J., Bal, A., & King-Thorius, K. (2010). Back to the future: A critique of response to intervention's social justice views. *Theory Into Practice, 49,* 250–257.

Au, W. (Ed.). (2009). *Rethinking multicultural education: Teaching for racial and cultural justice.* Milwaukee, WI: Rethinking Schools.

Azzam, A. M. (2013). Handle with care: A conversation with Maya Angelou. *Educational Leadership, 71*(1), 10–13. Retrieved from http://www.ascd.org/publications/educational-leadership.aspx

Baker, D., & LeTendre, G. (2005). *National differences, global similarities: World culture and the future of schooling.* Redwood, CA: Stanford University Press.

Baker, K. (2011). An alternative approach. *Definitions of normality.* Retrieved from http://normality.kimberlymbaker.com

Ball, D. L. (2000). Working on the inside: Using one's own practice as a site for studying mathematics teaching and learning. In A. Kelly & R. Lesh (Eds.), *Handbook of research design in mathematics and science education* (pp. 365–402). Dordrecht, Netherlands: Kluwer.

Ballasy, N. (2011, January 17). *U. S. secretary of education: Education is "the civil rights issue of our generation."* Retrieved from http://cnsnews.com/news/article/us-secretary-education-education-civil-rights-issue-our-generation

Banks, J. A. (2006). *Race, culture, and education: The selected works of James A. Banks.* New York, NY: Routledge.

Barnes, P. K. (2012). Motivation conditions experienced by diverse adult learners in cohort-based accelerated degree programs: Quantifying learner perceptions for assessment and enhancement of adult motivation to learn (Unpublished doctoral dissertation). Kansas State University, Manhattan, KS.

Barone, D., & Wright, T. (2008). Literacy instruction with digital and media technologies. *The Reading Teacher, 62,* 292–302.

Bean, J. C. (1996). *Engaging ideas: The professor's guide to integrating writing, critical thinking, and active learning in the classroom.* San Francisco, CA: Jossey-Bass.

Beyer, B. K. (1988). *Developing a thinking skills program.* Needham Heights, MA: Allyn & Bacon.

Blum, E. J. (2005). *Reforging the white republic: Race, religion, and American nationalism, 1865–1898.* Baton Rouge: Louisiana State University Press.

Brookfield, S. D. (1995). *Becoming a critically reflective teacher.* San Francisco, CA: Jossey-Bass.

Brookfield, S. D. (2012). *Teaching for critical thinking: Tools and techniques to help students question their assumptions.* San Francisco, CA: Jossey-Bass.

Brookfield, S. D., & Preskill, S. (2005). *Discussion as a way of teaching: Tools and techniques for democratic classrooms.* San Francisco, CA: Jossey-Bass.

Brophy, J. (2004). *Motivating students to learn* (2nd ed.). Mahwah, NJ: Lawrence Erlbaum.

Carnevale, A. P., Hanson, A. R., & Gulish, A. (2013). *Failure to launch: Structural shift and the new lost generation.* Washington DC: Georgetown University, Georgetown Public Policy Institute, Center on Education and the Workforce.

Campbell, L., Campbell, B., & Dickinson, D. (2004). *Teaching and learning through multiple intelligences* (3rd ed.). Boston, MA: Pearson.

Chappuis, J., Stiggins, R. Chappuis, S., & Arter, J. (2012). *Classroom assessment for student learning: Doing it right—using it well.* Upper Saddle River, NJ: Pearson.

Chopra, C. H. (2014). *New pathways for partnerships: An explanation of how partnering with students affects teachers and schooling* (Unpublished doctoral dissertation). University of Washington, Seattle, WA.

Christensen, L. (2000). *Reading, writing, and rising up: Teaching about social justice and the power of the written word.* Milwaukee, WI: Rethinking Schools.

Christensen, L. (2011–2012). The classroom to prison pipeline. *Rethinking Schools, 26*(2).

Christiansen, L. (n.d.). *The danger of a single story.* Retrieved from http://www.rethinkingschools.org/archive/26_04/26_04_christensen.shtml.

Cochran-Smith, M. (2004). *Walking the road: Race, diversity, and social justice in teacher education.* New York, NY: Teachers College Press.

Cochran-Smith, M., Davis, D., & Fries, K. (2004). Multicultural teacher education: Research, practice, and policy. In J. Banks & C. Banks (Eds.), *Handbook of research on multicultural education* (2nd ed., pp. 931–975). San Francisco, CA: Jossey-Bass.

Cole, B., Matheson, K., & Anisman, H. (2007). The moderating role of ethnic identity and social support on relations between well-being and academic performance. *Journal of Applied Social Psychology, 37,* 592–615.

Comer, J. (1993). *Creating learning communities: The Comer process.* Experimental session of the annual conference of the Association for the Supervision and Curriculum Development, Washington, DC.

Conrad, R., & Donaldson, J. A. (2004). *Engaging the online learner: Activities and resources for creative instruction.* San Francisco, CA: Jossey-Bass.

Crosnoe, R., & Turley, R. N. (2011). K–12 educational outcomes of immigrant youth. *Future of Children, 21*(1), 129–152.

Cruickshank, D. R., and associates. (1980). *Teaching is tough.* Upper Saddle River, NJ: Prentice Hall.

Csikszentmihalyi, M. (1997). *Finding flow: The psychology of engagement with everyday life.* New York, NY: Basic Books.

Csikszentmihalyi, M., & Csikszentmihalyi, I. S. (1988). *Optimal experience: Psychological studies of flow in consciousness.* New York, NY: Cambridge University Press.

Cummins, J. (2003). Challenging the construction of difference as deficit: Where are identity, intellect, imagination, and power in the new regime of truth? In P. Trifonas (Ed.), *Pedagogies of difference: Rethinking education for social change* (pp. 41–60). London, UK: Routledge.

Darling-Hammond, L., & Lieberman, A. (Eds.). (2012). *Teacher education around the world: Changing policies and practices.* New York, NY: Routledge.

Deci, E. L., & Ryan, R. M. (1991). A motivational approach to self: Integration in personality. In R. Dienstbier (Ed.), *Nebraska Symposium on Motivation* (Vol. 38, pp. 237–288). Lincoln: University of Nebraska Press.

Delle Fave, A., Bassi, M., Cavallo, M., & Stokart, Z. C. (2007, August). *The cross-cultural investigation of learning: Implications for individual development and educational policies.* Paper presented at ESCAP XIII International Conference, Firenze, Italy.

Delpit, L. D. (1988). The silenced dialogue: Power and pedagogy in educating other people's children. *Harvard Educational Review, 58,* 280–298.

Dewey, J. (1933). *How we think.* Boston, MA: D. C. Heath.

Dillon, J. T. (1988). *Questioning and teaching: A manual of practice.* New York, NY: Teachers College Press.

Donovan, M. S., Bransford, J. D., & Pellegrino, J. W. (1999). *How people learn: Bridging research and practice.* Washington, DC: National Academy Press.

Du Bois, W. E. B. (1949, May). Negro progress report. *Negro Digest.* Chicago: Johnson.

Dweck, C. S. (2006). *Mindset: The new psychology of success.* New York, NY: Ballantine Books.

Dweck, C. S., & Molden, D. C. (2005). Self-theories: Their impact on competence, motivation and acquisition. In A. J. Elliot & C. S. Dweck (Eds.), *Handbook of competence and motivation* (pp. 122–140). New York, NY: Guilford Press.

Echevarria, J., Vogt, M. E., & Short, D. (2004). *Making content comprehensible to English learners: The SIOP model.* Boston, MA: Allyn & Bacon.

Eisner, W. (1999). The uses and limits of performance assessments. *Phi Delta Kappan, 80,* 658–660.

Elbow, P. (1986). *Embracing contraries: Explorations in learning and teaching.* New York, NY: Oxford University Press.

Elliot, A. J., & Dweck, C. S. (Eds.). (2005). *Handbook of competence and motivation.* New York, NY: Guilford Press.

Enns, C. Z., & Sinacore, A. L. (Eds.). (2004). *Teaching and social justice: Integrating multicultural and feminist theories in the classroom.* Washington, DC: American Psychological Association.

EPE Research Center. (2007). *Annual state policy survey.* Retrieved from http://www.edweek.org

Erisman, W., & Looney, S. (2007). *Opening the door to the American dream: Increasing higher education access and success for immigrants.* Washington, DC: Institute for Higher Education Policy.

Farrington, C. A. (2014). *Failing at school: Lessons for redesigning urban high schools.* New York, NY: Teachers College Press.

Fink, S., & Markholt, A. (2011). *Leading for instructional improvement: How successful leaders develop teaching and learning expertise.* San Francisco, CA: Jossey-Bass.

Fischer, K. W. (2009). Mind, brain, and education: Building a scientific groundwork for learning and teaching. *Mind, Brain, and Education, 3*(1), 3–16. Retrieved from http://www.agcschool.org/filestore/MBEScientificGroundwork.pdf

Foner, N., & Frederickson, G. M. (Eds.). (2004). *Not just black and white.* New York, NY: Russell Sage Foundation.

Fordham, S., & Ogbu, J. A. (1986). Black students and school success: Coping with the burden of acting white. *Urban Review, 18,* 176–206.

Frayer, D., Frederick, W. C., & Klausmeier, H. J. (1969). *A schema for testing the level of cognitive mastery.* Madison, WI: Wisconsin Center for Education Research.

Frederick-Recascino, C. M. (2002). Self-determination theory and participation motivation research in the sport and exercise domain. In E. L. Deci & R. M. Ryan (Eds.), *Handbook of self-determination research* (pp. 277–294). Rochester, NY: University of Rochester Press.

Freire, P. (1970). *Pedagogy of the oppressed.* New York, NY: Seabury Press.

Freire, P. (1985). *The politics of education: Culture, power, and liberation.* South Hadley, MA: Bergin & Garvey.

Freire, F., & Macedo, D. P. (1987). *Literacy: Reading the word and the world.* Westport, CT: Greenwood.

Gardner, H. (2006). *Multiple intelligences: New horizons.* New York, NY: Basic Books.

Gardner, H., & Hatch, T. (1989). Multiple intelligences go to school. *Education Researcher, 1*(8), 4–10.

Gay, G. (2010). *Culturally responsive teaching: Theory, research, and practice* (2nd ed.). New York, NY: Teachers College Press.

Geertz, C. (1973). *The interpretation of cultures: Selected essays.* New York, NY: Basic Books.

Geertz, C. (1993). *Interpretation of cultures.* London, UK: Fontama Press.

Gere, A. R. (Ed.). (1985). *Roots in the sawdust: Writing to learn across disciplines.* Urbana, IL: National Council of Teachers of English.

Ginsberg, M. B. (2004). *Motivation matters: A workbook for school change.* San Francisco: Jossey-Bass.

Ginsberg, M. B. (2011). *Transformative professional learning: A system to enhance teacher and student motivation*. Thousand Oaks, CA: Corwin.

Ginsberg, M. B., & Wlodkowski, R. J. (2000). *Creating highly motivating classrooms for all students: A schoolwide approach to powerful teaching with diverse learners*. San Francisco, CA: Jossey-Bass.

Ginsberg, M. B., & Wlodkowski, R. J. (2009). *Diversity and motivation: Culturally responsive teaching in college*. San Francisco, CA: Jossey-Bass.

Giroux, H. A. (1992). *Border crossings: Cultural workers and the politics of education*. New York, NY: Routledge.

Glickman, C. D., Hayes, R., & Hensley, F. (1992). Site-based facilitation of empowered schools: Complexities and issues for staff developers. *Journal of Staff Development, 13*(2), 22–26.

Goldin-Meadow, S. (2003). *Hearing gestures*. Cambridge, MA: Belknap Press.

Gonzalez, N., Moll, L. C., & Amanti, C. (Eds.). (2005). *Funds of knowledge: Theorizing practices in households and classrooms*. Mahwah, NJ: Lawrence Erlbaum.

Gordon, L. M., & Graham, S. (2006). Attribution theory. *The encyclopedia of human development*. Thousand Oaks, CA: Sage.

Green, E. (2014, July 23). (New math) – (New teaching) = Failure. *New York Times Magazine*, pp. 22–27, 40–41.

Gudykunst, W. B., & Kim, Y. Y. (1992). *Communicating with strangers: An approach to intercultural communication*. New York, NY: Random House.

Haynes, M. (2014). *On the path to equity: Improving the effectiveness of beginning teachers*. Washington, DC: Alliance for Excellent Education. Retrieved from http://all4ed.org/wp-content/uploads/2014/07/PathToEquity.pdf

Heath, S. B. (1983). *Ways with words: Language, life, and work in communities and classrooms*. Cambridge, UK: Cambridge University Press.

Hebel, S. (2007, March 23). The graduation gap. *Chronicle of Higher Education*, pp. A20–A21.

Helmore, E. (2014, April 12). Ethical gaming: Can video games be a force for good? *The Guardian*. Retrieved from http://www.theguardian.com

Hernandez, D., Denton, N. A., & McCartney, S. E. (2007). *Children in immigrant families—The U.S. and 50 states: National origins, language, and early education*. Albany: Child Trends & State University of New York, Center for Social and Demographic Analysis.

Herreid, C. F., Schiller, N. A., & Herreid, K. F. (Eds.). (2012). *Science stories: Using case studies to teach critical thinking*. Arlington, VA: National Science Teachers Association.

Highwater, J. (1994, March). *Imagination as a political force*. General session address given at the annual conference of the Association for Supervision and Curriculum Development, Chicago, IL.

Hofstede, G., & Hofstede, G. J. (2005). *Cultures and organizations: Software of the mind* (2nd ed.). New York, NY: McGraw-Hill.

Humphry, S. M., & Heldsinger, S. A. (2014). Common structural design features of rubrics may represent a threat to validity. *Educational Researcher, 43*, 253–263.

Institute of Medicine. (2011). *The health of lesbian, gay, bisexual, and transgender people: Building a foundation for better understanding*. Washington, DC: National Academies Press. Retrieved from http://books.nap.edu/openbook.php?record_id=13128

Irvine, J. J. (1991). *Black student and school failure: Policies, practices, and prescriptions*. Westport, CT: Praeger.

Johnson, D. W. (2003). Social interdependence: The interrelationships among theory, research, and practice. *American Psychologist, 58,* 931–945.

Johnson, D. W., & Johnson, F. P. (2006). *Joining together: Group theory and group skills* (9th ed.). Boston, MA: Allyn & Bacon.

Johnson, D. W., Johnson, R., & Smith, K. A. (1991). *Active learning: Cooperation in the college classroom.* Edina, MN: Interaction.

Kanter, R. M. (1992). *The challenge of organizational change: How companies experience it and leaders guide it.* New York, NY: Free Press.

Katznelson, I. (2005). *When affirmative action was white: An untold story of racial inequality in the twentieth century.* New York, NY: Norton.

King, A. (1994). Inquiry as a tool in critical thinking. In D. F. Halpern & Associates (Eds.), *Changing college classrooms: New teaching and learning strategies for an increasingly complex world* (pp. 13–38). San Francisco, CA: Jossey-Bass.

Kitayama, S., & Markus, H. R. (Eds.). (1994). *Emotion and culture: Empirical studies of mutual influence.* Washington, DC: American Psychological Association.

Kohn, A. (2006). The trouble with rubrics. *English Journal, 95*(4), 12–15.

Kornhaber, M. L. (2004). Assessment standards and equity. In J. A. Banks & C. A. Banks (Eds.), *Handbook on research in multicultural education* (2nd ed.). San Francisco, CA: Jossey-Bass.

Kosciw, J. G., & Diaz, E. M. (2006). *The 2005 national school climate survey: The experiences of lesbian, gay, bisexual, and transgender youth in our nation's schools.* New York, NY: GLSEN.

Ladson-Billings, G. (1994). *The dreamkeepers: Successful teachers of African American children.* San Francisco, CA: Jossey-Bass.

Lampert, M. (2001).*Teaching problems and the problems in teaching.* New Haven, CT: Yale University Press.

Langer, S. K. (1942). *Philosophy in a new key: A study in the symbolism of reason, rite, and art.* Cambridge, MA: Harvard University Press.

Larmer, J., & Mergendoller, J. R. (2012). *8 essentials for project-based learning.* Retrieved from http://bie.org/object/document/8_essentials_for_project_based_learning

Lawrence-Lightfoot, S. (2009). *The third chapter: Passion, risk, and adventure in the 25 years after 50.* New York, NY: Sarah Crichton Books.

Lee, V. E., & Burkham, D. T. (2002). *Inequality at the starting gate.* Washington, DC: Economic Policy Institute.

Lightfoot, S. L. (1983). *The good high school: Portraits of character and culture.* New York, NY: Basic Books.

Lipsitz, G. (2006). *The possessive investment in whiteness: How white people profit from identity politics* (Rev. ed.). Philadelphia, PA: Temple University Press.

Locke, D. C. (1992). *Increasing multicultural understanding: A comprehensive model.* Thousand Oaks, CA: Sage.

Loden, M., & Rosener, J. B. (1991). *Workforce America! Managing employee diversity as a vital resource.* Homewood, IL: Business One Irwin.

Manzo, A. V., & Manzo, E. V. (1990). Note cue: A comprehension and participation training strategy. *Journal of Reading, 33,* 608–611.

Marabel, M. (2002). *The great wells of democracy: The meaning of race in American life.* New York, NY: Basic Books.

Marsick, V. J. (2004). Case study. In M. W. Galbraith (Ed.), *Adult learning methods: A guide for effective instruction* (3rd ed., pp. 383–404). Malabar, FL: Krieger.

Marzano, R. J. (2007). *The art and science of teaching: A comprehensive framework for effective instruction*. Alexandria, VA: Association for Supervision and Curriculum Development.

McIntosh, P. (1989). Curricular re-vision: The new knowledge for a new age. In C. S. Pearson, D. L. Shavlick, & J. G. Touchton (Eds.), *Educating the majority: Women challenge tradition in higher education*. New York, NY: American Council on Education/Macmillan.

Meece, J. L. (2003). Applying learner-centered principles to middle school education. *Theory Into Practice, 42*, 109–116.

Meier, D. (1995). *The power of their ideas: Lessons for America from a small school in Harlem*. Boston, MA: Beacon Press.

Merriam, S. B., Caffarella, R. S., & Baumgartner, L. M. (2007). *Learning in adulthood: A comprehensive guide* (3rd ed.). San Francisco, CA: Jossey-Bass.

Meyers, C., & Jones, T. B. (1993). *Promoting active learning: Strategies for the college classroom*. San Francisco, CA: Jossey-Bass.

Mezirow, J. (2000). Learning to think like an adult: Core concepts of transformation theory. In J. Mezirow and Associates, *Learning as transformation: Critical perspectives on a theory in progress* (pp. 3–33). San Francisco, CA: Jossey-Bass.

Molnar, A., & Lindquist, B. (1989). *Changing problem behavior in schools*. San Francisco, CA: Jossey-Bass.

Morrison, K. A., Robbins, H. H., & Rose, D. G. (2008). Operationalizing culturally relevant pedagogy: A synthesis of classroom-based research. *Equity & Excellence in Education, 41*, 433–452.

Mustoe, L. R., & Croft, A. C. (1999). Motivating engineering students by using modern case studies. *European Journal of Engineering Education, 15*, 469–476.

Nagaoka, J., Farrington, C. A., Roderick, M., Allensworth, E., Keys, T. S., . . . Beechum, N. O. (2012). *Readiness for college: The role of noncognitive factors and context*. Retrieved from http://vue.annenberginstitute.org/issues/99/readiness-college-role

Newmann, F. M., Bryk, A. S., & Nagaoka, J. (2001). *Authentic intellectual work and standardized tests: Conflict or coexistence?* Chicago, IL: Consortium on Chicago School Research.

Nieto, S. (2004). *Affirming diversity: The sociopolitical context of multicultural education* (4th ed.). White Plains, NY: Longman.

Nieto, S., & Bode, P. (2011). *Affirming diversity: The sociopolitical context of multicultural education* (6th ed.). Boston, MA: Pearson.

Nietzsche, F. W. (1920). *The antichrist*. New York, NY: Knopf.

Nitko, A. J., & Brookhart, S. M. (2010). *Educational assessment of students* (6th ed.). Cranbury, NJ: Pearson.

Ogle, D. M. (1986). K-W-L: A teaching model that develops active reading of expository text. *Reading Teacher, 39*, 564–570.

Olson, L. (2007, June 12). What does "ready" mean? *Education Week*. Retrieved from http://www.edweek.org

Ovando, C., Collier, V., & Combs, M. (2003). *Bilingual and ESL classrooms: Teaching multicultural contexts* (3rd ed.). Boston, MA: McGraw-Hill.

Ovando, C. J., & Combs, M. C. (2011). *Bilingual and ESL classrooms: Teaching in multicultural contexts* (5th ed.). New York, NY: McGraw-Hill.

Passel, J. S. (2011). *New patterns in U. S. immigration, 2011: Uncertainty for reform*. Retrieved from https://migrationfiles.ucdavis.edu/uploads/cf/files/2011-may/passel-new-patterns-in-us-immigration.pdf

Passel, J. S., & Taylor, P. (2010). *Unauthorized immigrants and their U.S.-born children.* Washington, DC: Pew Hispanic Center. Retrieved from http://pewhispanic.org/files/reports/125.pdf

Paul, R., & Binker, A. (1990). Socratic questioning. In R. Paul (Ed.), *Critical thinking: What every person needs to survive in a rapidly changing world* (pp. 269–298). Rohnert Park, CA: Sonoma State University, Center for Critical Thinking and Moral Critique.

Paul, R., & Elder, L. (2006). *The thinker's guide to the art of Socratic questioning.* Tomales, CA: Foundation for Critical Thinking. Retrieved from http://www.criticalthinking.org/TGS_files/SocraticQuestioning2006.pdf

Pearlman, M. (1987, April). *Trends in women's total score and item performance on verbal measures.* Paper presented at the annual meeting of the American Educational Research Association, Washington, DC.

Popham, W. J. (1987). The merits of measurement driven instruction. *Phi Delta Kappan, 68,* 679–682.

Priceman, M. (1994). *How to make an apple pie and see the world.* New York, NY: Dragonfly Books.

Pugh, K. J. (2011). Transformative experience: An integrative construct in the spirit of Deweyan pragmatism. *Educational Psychologist, 46,* 107–121.

Pugh, K. J., Linnenbrink-Garcia, L., Koskey, K. L. K., Stewart, V. C., & Manzey, C. (2010). Motivation, learning, and transformative experience: A study of deep engagement in science. *Science Education, 94,* 1–28.

Reeves, D. B. (2008). Effective grading practices. *Educational Leadership, 65(5),* 85–87.

Remland, M. S. (2000). *Nonverbal communication in everyday life.* Boston, MA: Houghton Mifflin.

Russell, S. T., & Joyner, K. (2001). Adolescent sexual orientation and suicide risk: Evidence from a national study. *American Journal of Public Health, 91,* 1276–1281.

Sarason, S. B. (1982). *The culture of school and the problem of change* (2nd ed.). Boston, MA: Allyn & Bacon.

Schein, E. H. (2004). *Organizational culture and leadership* (3rd ed.). San Francisco, CA: Jossey-Bass.

Schinske, J., & Tanner, K. (2014). Teaching more by grading less (or differently). *Cell Biology Education Life Sciences Education, 13*(Summer), 159–166.

Schneider, J., & Hutt, E. (2013). Making the grade: A history of the A–F marking scheme. *Journal of Curriculum Studies.* Retrieved from http://academics.holy-cross.edu/files/Education/schneider/Making_the_Grade.pdf

Shanley, J. P. (2007). Director's notes. In *Playbill for Doubt* (pp. 5–6).

Shepard, L. A. (1989). Why we need better assessments. *Educational Leadership, 46(7),* 4–9.

Shernoff, D. J. (2013). *Optimal learning environments to promote student engagement.* New York, NY: Springer.

Shneidewind, N., & Davidson, E. (2006). *Open minds to equality: A sourcebook of learning activities to affirm diversity and promote equity* (3rd ed.). Milwaukee, WI: Rethinking Schools.

Shor, I. (1987). *Freire for the classroom: A sourcebook for liberatory teaching.* Portsmouth, NH: Heinemann.

Shor, I. (1993). Education is politics: Paulo Freire's critical pedagogy. In P. McLaren & P. Leonard (Eds.), *Paulo Freire: A critical encounter* (pp. 25–35). New York, NY: Routledge.

Staples, B. A. (1986, December). Just walk on by: Black men and public spaces. *Harper's*, pp. 19–20.

Steele, C. M., & Aronson, J. (1995). Stereotype threat and the intellectual test performance of African-Americans. *Journal of Personality and Social Psychology, 69*, 797–811.

Stephens, N. M., Townsend, S. S. M., Markus, H. R., & Phillips, T. (2012). A cultural mismatch: Independent cultural norms produce greater increases in cortisol and more negative emotions among first-generation college students. *Journal of Experimental Social Psychology, 48*, 1389–1393.

Stigler, J. W., & Hiebert, J. (2004). Improving achievement in math and science. *Educational Leadership, 61*(5), 12–17.

Stobart, G. (2005). Fairness in multicultural assessment systems. *Assessment in Education: Principles, Policy, and Practice, 12*, 275–287.

Strickland, C. (2007). *Tools for high-quality differentiated instruction: An ASCD action tool.* Alexandria, VA: Association for Supervision and Curriculum Development.

Stringer, E. T. (2014. *Action research* (4th ed.). Thousand Oaks, CA: Sage.

Suárez-Orozco, M., Darbes, T., Dias, S. I., & Sutin, M. (2011). Migrations and schooling. *Annual Reviews of Anthropology, 40*, 311–328.

Swanson, R. A., & Elwood, H. F. (Ed.). (2005). *Research in organizations: Foundations and methods in inquiry.* San Francisco: Berrett-Koehler.

Tatum, B. D. (1992). Talking about race, learning about racism: The application of racial identity development theory in the classroom. *Harvard Educational Review, 62(1),* 1–24.

Tatum, B. D. (2003). *Why are all the black kids sitting together in the cafeteria? And other conversations about race.* New York, NY: Basic Books.

Thompson, C. M. (2010). *Problems and possibilities: On the ground professional learning in an urban high school.* Dissertation Abstracts No. 3421989.

Tienda, M., & Haskins, T. (2011). Immigrant children: Introducing the issue. *The Future of Children, 21*(1), 3–18.

Tomlinson, C. A. (2014). *The differentiated classroom: Responding to the needs of all learners.* (2nd ed.). Alexandria, VA: Association for Supervision and Curriculum Development.

Trilling, B., & Fidal, C. (2009). *21st century skills: Learning for life in our times.* San Francisco, CA: Jossey-Bass.

U.S. Census Bureau. (2007). Selected characteristics of the native and foreign-born populations. American Community Survey, 2007. Available from http://factfinder2.census.gov

Vansteenkiste, M., Lens, W., & Deci, E. L. (2006). Intrinsic versus extrinsic goal contents in self-determination theory: Another look at the quality of academic motivation. *Educational Psychologist, 41*(1), 19–31.

Vaughn, M. S. (2006). *The end of training: How simulations are reshaping business training.* Golden, CO: Keystone Business Press.

Vescio, V., Ross, D., & Adams, A. (2008). A review of the research on the impact of learning communities on teaching practice and student learning. *Teaching and Teacher Education, 24*, 80–91.

Voss, J. F. (1989). Problem solving and the educational process. In A. Lesgold & R. Glaser (Eds.), *Foundations for a psychology of education* (pp. 251–294). Hillsdale, NJ: Lawrence Erlbaum.

Vygotsky, L. S. (1978). *Mind in society: The development of higher psychological processes.* Cambridge, MA: Harvard University Press.

Wehlage, G., Newmann, F., & Secada W. (1996). Standards for authentic achievement and pedagogy. In F. M. Newman & Associates (Eds.), *Authentic achievement: Restructuring schools for intellectual quality* (pp. 21–48). San Francisco, CA: Jossey-Bass.

Weiner, B. (2000). Interpersonal and intrapersonal theories of motivation from an attributional perspective. *Educational Psychology Review, 12*, 1–14.

Wessler, S. F. (2011). *Shattered families: Perilous intersection of immigration policy and the child welfare system.* New York, NY: Applied Research Center. Retrieved from http://www.scribd.com/doc/75771961/Shattered-Families-Perilous-Intersection-of-Immigration-Policy-and-the-Child-Welfare-System

Whitehead, A. N. (1929). *The aims of education and other essays.* New York, NY: Free Press.

Wiggins, G. P. (1998). *Educative assessment: Designing assessments to inform and improve student performance.* San Francisco, CA: Jossey-Bass.

Williams, R. M., Jr. (1970). *American society: A sociological interpretation* (3rd ed.). New York, NY: Knopf.

Wilson, E. A. (1995). *Reading at the middle and high school levels: Building active readers across the curriculum.* Arlington, VA: Educational Research Service.

Wlodkowski, R. J. (2008). *Enhancing adult motivation to learn: A comprehensive guide for teaching all adults* (3rd ed.). San Francisco, CA: Jossey-Bass.

Wlodkowski, R. J., & Ginsberg, M. B. (1995). *Diversity and motivation: Culturally responsive teaching.* San Francisco, CA: Jossey-Bass.

Wlodkowski, R. J., Mauldin, J. E., & Gahn, S. W. (2001). *Learning in the fast lane: Adult learners' persistence and success in accelerated college programs.* Indianapolis, IN: Lumina Foundation for Education.

Yosso, T. J. (2005). Whose culture has capital? A critical race theory discussion of community cultural wealth. *Race, Ethnicity, and Education, 8*(1), 69–91.

Young, R. (1990). *White mythologies: Writing history and the west.* London, UK: Routledge.

Zakaria, E., Solfitri, T., Daud, Y., & Abidin, Z. (2013). Effect of cooperative learning on secondary school students' mathematics achievement. *Creative Education, 4,* 98–100.

Zigarelli, J., Nilsen, R., Moore, T., & Ginsberg, M. (2014). Home visits for relationships, relevance, and results. *ASCD Express.* Retrieved from http://www.ascd.org/ascd-express/home.aspx

Zull, J. E. (2002). *The art of changing the brain: Enriching the practice of teaching by exploring the biology of learning.* Sterling, VA: Stylus.

Index